Kimono IN THE BOARDROOM

Kimono

IN THE BOARDROOM

The Invisible Evolution of Japanese Women Managers

Jean R. Renshaw

New York   Oxford

Oxford University Press

1999

Oxford University Press

Oxford   New York

Athens   Auckland   Bangkok   Bogotá   Buenos Aires   Calcutta
Cape Town   Chennai   Dar es Salaam   Delhi   Florence   Hong Kong   Istanbul
Karachi   Kuala Lumpur   Madrid   Melbourne   Mexico City   Mumbai
Nairobi   Paris   São Paulo   Singapore   Taipei   Tokyo   Toronto   Warsaw

and associated companies in
Berlin   Ibadan

Copyright © 1999 by Oxford University Press, Inc.

Published by Oxford University Press, Inc.
198 Madison Avenue, New York, New York 10016

Oxford is a registered trademark of Oxford University Press

Library of Congress Cataloging-in-Publication Data
Renshaw, Jean R.
Kimono in the boardroom : the invisible evolution of Japanese
women managers / Jean R. Renshaw.
p.   cm.
Includes bibliographical references and index.
ISBN 0-19-511765-4
1. Women executives—Japan.   2. Businesswomen—Japan.
3. Women—Japan—Social conditions.   I. Title.
HD6054.4.J3R46   1999
331.4′816584′00952—DC21   98-3075

9 8 7 6 5 4 3 2 1

Printed in the United States of America
on acid-free paper

This book is dedicated to Ada Rehkop and
Anna Tieman Heins, my mother and grandmother,
whose strength guides me and to Mackenzie Mae and
Annabel Tru, who give me hope for our future world.

Preface

This is a book about Japanese women managers. Mention Japanese women managers, and the response is almost always the same, whether from Japanese, American, male, female, professional, or businessperson: "Are there any?" The misinformation or collective denial about this cadre of talent that fills 10 percent of Japanese management positions seems to be almost universal.

Yet the struggles and successes, dreams and disappointments of Japan's rising female managerial class have the potential to change in profound ways the male-defined culture of modern Japan. Furthermore, this invisible evolution that has seen the number of women managers double (from 140,000 to almost 300,000) in the past decade has lessons for American women as well.

Despite enormous barriers—cultural, organizational, and personal—Japanese women are finding paths to power. It's a curious phenomenon because female managers seem to exist outside the logic of Japanese men and often seem strange to Japanese women as well. Women managers are especially puzzling and incomprehensible to Japanese men in their forties and fifties, who seem to have no framework for the concept. Women are still seen as locked into serving positions or as wielding power indirectly. Japanese women are at the highest levels as cabinet ministers, Supreme Court justice, Speaker of the Diet, astronaut, and heads of companies, but they seem to exist outside logic and language.

Meeting, interviewing, and making friends with so many dynamic and competent women forced me to examine my own and popular stereotypes, resulting in this book. Caught in the crossfire between tradition and change, Japanese women are defining new identities. Long used as a reserve labor force, constituting 41 percent of the total workforce, they are transcending the subservient stereotypes, with the primary focus on "good wife, wise mother," and are assuming their rightful place as leaders and managers who also serve.

This book examines the confluence of individual women, organizational culture, and institutional values to show how women are surmounting barriers and succeeding in Japan using traditional paths and creating new ones. Women's paths to management are traced, and patterns in their lives and careers are described to distill lessons for other women, both Asian and Western. Suggestions emerge from the data for further ways to maximize women's resources by examining where and how they are succeeding, and why and how their successes and struggles remain invisible.

The title *Kimono in the Boardroom* demonstrates how women achieve success in spite of the odds and finds common factors in their success. Cultural and gender differences in definitions of success, equity, self-concept, visibility, and power are explored. This book asks what changes are needed in Japan's corporations, government, and families for women to contribute more fully to a creative and equitable society while also supporting the reforms Japanese people are demanding. It also supports the potential, indeed, the economic imperative, for further change if Japan is to reach its full potential. Japanese women managers can provide insights, questions, and potential role models for future generations of women in Japan and elsewhere.

Acknowledgments

This book owes its being to the many Japanese women managers who so warmly and openly shared their stories and their lives with me and who have become my friends. I am especially grateful to the early focus group, which still meets and welcomes me when I come to Japan. In addition, many people have contributed to the data, analysis, and learning. In Japan, Chiyo Fukushima is a delightful fairy godmother whose encouragement and quiet advice help me understand and love Japan, its art, music, and people. Irawati Kepper, whose support, encouragement, and wonderful Indonesian food kept me going over the rough spots, provided hospitality for deeper explorations.

Early supporters who launched my Japan adventures include Ryoko Akamatsu, Ginko Sato, Sen Nishiyama, Mitsu Kimata, Ryo Ochiai, Ryoko Dozono, Chikako Takahashi, Chieko Homma, Yuri Konno, Mitsuko Horiuchi, Naoe Wakita, and countless others. A Fulbright Senior Scholar Grant funded my initial year in Japan with Japanese Fulbright staff and alumnae(i) providing support. The Policy Study Group opened doors to top male executives, and the Overseas Women's Group gave encouragement and a forum. The International House of Japan and its competent staff provided a warm home away from home with answers to strange questions and directions to innumerable interviews.

Cliff and Nancy Forster provided introductions that proved invaluable in Japan. Haru Reischauer's patient response to questions started me on my way. Special thanks to Dr. LuAnn Darling, whose continuous support and encouragement brought me through the worst times, and whose insightful transcriptions of my interviews kept me going. My thanks to Hilda Ball and the Tadlocks, who kept my home fires burning.

The writing process would have terminated midcourse without the support of many people. Sheila and Chalmers Johnson inspired me to continue asking questions, while modeling the courage to put forth unconventional findings. Sumi Adachi contributed beautiful caligraphy and provided new perspectives and challenges. Kozy Amemiya put up with naive questions as she translated key words and collaborated unflinchingly in exploring Japanese culture. Syd and Dorothy Bearman critiqued the final versions. Aquababes kept my body healthy with admirable patience for my writing process. Carol Stark edited and encouraged on difficult passages.

Thanks to my family—Blair, Jeannine, Alan, Gina, and John—who keep me humble and whose perspectives stimulate me to ask new questions. To Blair Renshaw, whose loving guidance through the computer maze and haze was essential. To my mother and father, who provided my first experiences of the blending of masculine and feminine energy, as my mother taught me to accept challenges and my father gave me a notion of sensitive and strong masculine energy.

I am grateful to all the women—Japanese, American, and international—who help me understand the evolving world of women and encourage me to continue the exploration; to all who asked questions, argued, and otherwise stimulated my thinking, especially Women's Support Groups in Los Angeles, San Diego, and Hawaii. Mayumi Oda and her voluptuous Japanese goddesses first intrigued my curiosity about the many faces of Japanese women while at the University of Hawaii.

Herb Addison of Oxford University Press has been a model editor with excellent suggestions while insisting on my freedom and responsibility to write the book. My colleague and friend Jackie Young has provided essential support and challenge as we pursued parallel paths writing our books and encouraged each other to own our feminine power. I am grateful to all who contributed to what is an ongoing exploration and absolve them of all responsibility for errors and omissions which are mine alone.

Contents

Kimono IN THE BOARDROOM

Introduction

The Mystery of the Invisible Women Managers

> Japanese women managers—A contradiction in terms.
>
> Opinion asserted by my male colleagues

Contrary to popular opinion and despite enormous obstacles, Japanese women have become successful managers in business, government, and education. Often they are invisible, their presence and influence unrecognized or denied, but they are there. The research on which this book is based was undertaken as an attempt to understand how and why Japanese women become managers, the contradictions posed by their success, and why their presence is unrecognized. While women provide 40.6 percent of the workforce of Japan, less than 10 percent of managers are women, having increased from 6 percent a decade ago. Japanese women are among the best educated women in the world,[1] but their talents remain largely unused and underutilized. They have been exploited as a buffer for economic cycles, serving as temporary, and therefore less expensive labor, and then cast out at marriageable age for a new, younger crop of women college graduates. The role of "good wife, wise mother" is touted, while women's contributions in the public arena are denied and often denigrated. As noted Japan scholar Chalmers Johnson has said, "Japanese women are a flagrantly wasted national resource."[2] The head of the Japanese Economic Planning Agency lamented male-dominated hiring practices as "old-fashioned" and a "waste of Japan's capable women."[3]

At the current rate, Japanese women will achieve parity by the end of the twenty-first century. They're not holding their breath for the event. As this book indicates, some don't even want parity; they want more. Meanwhile, Japanese women are sailing the America's Cup race, circling Earth in a spaceship, starting companies at an increasing rate, joining the Self-Defense Forces, and generally shouldering essential elements of Japanese life.

The fabled foundations of Japanese management—lifetime employment, the seniority system, and the bureaucratic, tightly knit nature of industrial policy—have served as barriers to women's entry into management. Institutionalized discrimination against women, while not necessarily written policy, is widespread and accepted. Examples include help wanted ads that specify sex and age, and specific limits on the percentage of women college graduates who may be hired during the traditional hiring period in April (0 percent for many companies for the latest round). A 1994 Labor Ministry survey of fifty-four hundred companies found that 40 percent hired only male graduates.

Other practices such as restricting women to staff positions; not including women in informal meetings, or the routing of internal memos, or off-site training sessions; limiting transfer and travel, and requiring a choice at entry between career or noncareer track; all serve to restrict advancement for women. Attitudes assigning women decorative and service roles are not codified, but they are powerful institutional practices. In spite of these seemingly insurmountable obstacles, there are women in management, and they are effective managers. A sizable number of women (almost 300,000) have made it into management in spite of the barriers, but they are little known.

When the topic of Japanese women in management is broached, it evokes the automatic, almost predictable response, "Are there any?" It makes little difference if the questioner is Japanese, American, male, female, professional, dilettante, Japan specialist, or tourist. The belief that there are *no* women in management in Japan is widely held.

I lunched recently with three American male executives who had each worked and traveled in Japan for at least a decade and discovered that none had ever met a Japanese woman manager. Even young Japanese women ask me whether there are women managers and then are particularly concerned about whether they have families. Some American women ask me about the situation in Asia, saying they have heard of one or several successful woman managers. They want to know how this was accomplished in the face of such overt discrimination, perhaps to learn the techniques themselves.

As the world community struggles to find guidance and directions for the future, organizations that capture the energy of the "best and brightest," whether male or female, will unquestionably gain the competitive advantage. Nations and businesses need to marshal their best, most creative human resources to meet the growing challenges of our rapidly changing and turbulent world.

The 1993 United Nations Human Development Index found that "no country treats its women as well as it treats its men, a disappointing result after so many years of gender equality, so many struggles by women and so many changes in national laws."[4] The negative results apply to women of all nationalities, flavored by each culture's unique manifestations. To an American woman who is a manager, a business owner, and a professor of management, the findings are disturbing and create theoretical, as well as practical, challenges germane to management. The workforce in the United States, Japan, and Korea has become increasingly female, while the managerial role remains linked to traditional male models.

This book is a snapshot of Japanese women managers in a rapidly changing world. The camera angles provide an external, objective perspective of the system in which Japanese women live and work, as well as a view into their experiences within that system. The first perspective is achieved by reviewing the historical context in which today's women act and through an analysis of quantitative, cross-cultural data on labor and the economy. This is intended to set the scene. The second perspective was acquired through interviews with women managers, which provide subjective views of their experiences as economic actors and as family and community members.

My research for the book was carried out during the two years I lived in Japan and during frequent subsequent visits. In the course of my travels within Japan and Korea, I found successful Japanese women managers in every industrial category, and I interviewed over 160 of them. The interviews were conducted in English with a Japanese speaker at hand to clarify if necessary. While this approach introduced the danger of a biased sample, it also had advantages. Most Japanese women at management level understand English, and as an evaluator on scholarship committees in Japan, I observed that the same person spoke more freely in English than in Japanese, an observation corroborated by other Japanese.

My original intent was to use a triangular comparison of three countries, Japan, Korea, and the United States, to highlight differences and similarities. This plan had to be modified when the unexpected richness of the subject and the data spilled over my original boundaries. As a result, the current book focuses on the experiences of Japanese women leaders in a cultural, historical, and present context and compares them with their American counterparts. The Korean data and experiences that contributed significantly to understanding and defining the issues at each stage will be reported in a subsequent volume.

In the past decades, volumes have been written about the resurgence of Japanese industries, the "Japanese economic miracle," and the nature of Japanese management. The closed and enigmatic nature of Japanese business almost qualifies as folk wisdom. This book focuses on the exceptions, the women who, as outsiders to the "old-boy" management structure, have nevertheless succeeded and have become effective managers. How they succeeded and the factors contributing to their success are the primary interest of the book.

Japan's Equal Opportunity Act of 1986, combined with a rapidly expanding economy, now referred to as the "bubble" economy, provided increased opportunity for women who were ambitious and willing to work harder than men to become managers. Who are they? Where are they? How did they get there? and What are their lives like? were the questions to which I sought answers. The public perception is that women are managers in "feminine" industries. In actuality, whereas they are indeed owners and managers in fashion, food, cosmetics, and retail businesses, they are also represented in almost every industry, including finance, manufacturing, construction, and transportation.

My role as a professor of management and a management consultant is to help develop effective organizations and people. A successful organization blends the manager, the organization, and the environments. Each element in that equation is important—the person, with abilities, skills, experience, style, and potential; the organization, with its mission, product or service, personnel, resources, and culture; and the environments or circles of influence within which the action takes place. How these elements mesh determines whether individuals and organizations succeed or fail. This book explores each of these factors, beginning with women managers, then weaving among the person, organization, and environments, not necessarily in a straight line but trying to consider the complex interactions.

The field of management draws from many disciplines, with the primary concern being effective practice. The process is a continuous one of setting goals, planning, acting, executing, and measuring results within a constantly changing environment. The study of management has been less concerned with theoretical underpinnings and more concerned with what works.

Management studies have evolved from Taylor's scientific management,[5] with its focus on engineering and operations research, through the work of Frank Gilbreth[6] and Lillian Gilbreth,[7] the latter a pioneering woman management theorist who brought the study of the person more directly into the equation, to today's eclectic use of all the social disciplines to understand the behavior of people, organizations, and environments. Communication theory and information sciences are mobilized to collect, sort, and make sense of information. Psychology, sociology, social anthropology, political science, economics, and the strategy and tactics of war are tapped to help plan and strategize for the future, to control and measure performance, and to understand the manager as a person who engages in the practice of management. Important elements of a manager's repertoire are strategic thinking, communicating and managing with people.

Theories have fluctuated with changes in the economy, technology, and state of knowledge. Peter Drucker, the historian and self-proclaimed management philosopher, has remained an elder statesmen as various schools of management ebb and flow,[8] from Tom Peters,[9] McKinsey & Company, the Learning Organization,[10] Michael Porter,[11] Lester Thurow,[12] Kenichi Ohmae,[13] to the traditionalists advocating planning, organizing, and controlling, to systems analysis, chaos theory, and futurist trends.[14]

My research into women in management followed just such a pragmatic route, drawing on management theory, economics, psychology, sociology, and social and cultural anthropology to try to understand how Japanese women managers succeed within systems, environments, and societies that are unsupportive of their achievements.

Additionally, this book asks the question Why has the rise of women managers been invisible? Even though Japanese women are in management—in their own businesses, in corporations, in government, in education and the media—the idea of women in management seems to be outside the logic of most men, and strange to many women as well. When pressed, people interviewed in Japan usually know of at least one individual woman manager or have heard of others. But the very idea of women in management seems to be beyond the popular logic, that is, outside ordinary, everyday life and awareness. For most people, women in management do not exist. As a group, women managers are invisible, outside the boundaries of common knowledge. Younger Japanese women plied me with questions about successful women. They wanted models and clues to help answer their own life-choice questions.

Neither organizational structures nor prevailing definitions of management were designed with women in mind, the expectation being that if women became managers, they would adapt to the traditional model. For women to penetrate management ranks requires extraordinary effort and a lot of luck. The barriers to success for women in management are complex, varied, and often unacknowledged or denied. The accomplishments of the women who do succeed are noteworthy. Their paths to success in less-than-friendly environments provide clues to strategies and actions for other women and men.

Recent research on women in management internationally has affirmed the importance of national culture for all aspects of the management system. While working and living internationally, I have observed women's leadership roles in a variety of cultures.[15] In the majority, women are not encouraged to lead or manage, to use their competencies; nor are they supported to achieve success. A few women in each country do manage to achieve positions of leadership in spite of male-dominant cultures, but no one seems to know about them. It is often necessary to spend a great deal of time probing to find women managers. Conventionally their achievements are invisible, hidden, denied. Why?

One reason lies in the commonly held belief that management is not a proper role for women; that women managers are an aberration and therefore do not exist. This belief then renders such women invisible to those who accept it. In an interview with one Japanese male executive who was a graduate of my California university, I asked about women managers, and he said there were none. Knowing that his wife was president of one of their family companies and also an operating manager, I asked about her. He smiled sheepishly and said, "She's not exactly a manager. Well, I guess she's a kind of manager. She's my wife." Another prominent Asian male executive said bluntly, "Women can't boss men." And, of course, he didn't know any women managers, even though there were several in his own organization. This "blindness" has few cultural boundaries. When asked to describe men, women, and managers, American managers and students overwhelmingly find the characteristics of men similar to those of good managers and find women's characteristics different. The dynamics and consequences of keeping women leaders invisible are the subject of chapter 7, "Glass Ceilings and Shoji Screens."

In the agrarian society of feudal and preindustrial Japan, women played important roles in the economy and the life of the community, both by their own labor and through their children, especially sons, as they managed the households and families and determined the lineage. While the role of mother has always been held in high esteem in Japan, women's power was most often unseen, indirect, and puzzling to men.

Now that women are managing enterprises and are speaking out more directly, they are still puzzling and incomprehensible to men. This is particularly true for men in their forties and fifties who have had little experience with women in professional and leadership roles, who continue to maintain that there are no women in management. When questioned, they do realize that women are in the workplace, that a law recommends and advises equal treatment for women and men, that administrative guidelines exist to give equity to women. But there is a disconnection between this fact and thinking about management, with no framework to integrate the concept. Women's work is often unpublicized and invisible, and women as managers remain truly outside logic and language.

Having discovered so many exciting women doing work essential to the Japanese economy and daily life, I find it strange that the women managers themselves are not consistently factored into the thinking and planning of business, government, or the general population. Limiting women's contributions is a definite waste of resources. Some astute observers have said one of America's competitive advantages over Japan is its women managers.[16]

I interviewed, surveyed, worked, and socialized with Japanese women managers of all ages and career stages. Their stories reveal how individual women have become leaders and managers and contribute to Japan's success within the broader context of male-defined organizations and industries. Common patterns emerged from the lives and backgrounds of these successful women managers, which helped to set them apart from other women. Their life situation, a circumstance, an event, a person or influence, an accident of timing or world events allowed them to transcend the limits of gender role definitions and achieve success. The problems, as well as the potential for development and change, are illustrated by their stories. Who they are, their childhood and adult lives, their paths to management, with struggles and satisfactions, triumphs and disappointments, combine with their dreams for themselves and the world, and their struggles for competency and recognition to illuminate a shadow of the Japanese "economic miracle."

My quest for women managers led me to women who are transcending the established molds, as well as to others who are succeeding and contributing in more traditional ways. These women are making a difference in their own lives and in the lives of those around them. Sumiko Iwao's book describing the effect of tradition and change on Japanese women has termed what is happening to women in Japan, a "quiet revolution."[17] I am not convinced it is quiet, but it is ignored and virtually invisible.

This book was written to bring both the concept *and* the women managers into awareness, and to contribute to an increased understanding of changing gender roles and management requirements. It also provides an opportunity to reflect on the benefits and puzzles of women's changing lives. Gender roles and attitudes are in transition, as are relationships between women and men, between employers and employees, government and business, managers and workers in Japan and the United States. Understanding the impact of these transitions will aid in creating more effective organizations.

An example of the contradictions that abound in a period of change and the ambivalence women feel about the struggles necessary for success were illustrated by one particularly memorable interview over dinner at an exclusive Kyoto-style restaurant in Tokyo. Two top women executives, from the retail industry and the media, had invited me for dinner after a successful first interview. We were served a traditional seven courses, each artistic, elegant, and balanced with the others. During this extended dinner, the discussion covered the state of Japan's economy, their paths to success and their families, and the role of women in a male-dominant society. As they dropped me at home in a luxury car chauffeured by a man, I said, "Here are two powerful women being driven from a fantastic dinner by their employee, a man. That's change for Japan." Since we had talked at length over dinner about the barriers for women, they laughed, but they pointed out that what made the situation funny was its very rarity. They had suffered, as have many women, from discrimination and harassment, leaving scars as well as optimism. One hopes

that younger women will have fewer scars and less ambivalence as they become the global managers of the next century.

Part I begins with an overview of the situation of working women in
Japan. Chapter 2 focuses on the individuals at the center of the system, the
women managers and would-be managers, and seeks clues to success in their
early lives and socialization. Chapter 3 examines the historical roots of present-day gender roles, attitudes, and beliefs.

Part II moves to the drama of corporate life. Chapter 4 is about organizational culture and the nature of work in Japanese companies. The search for
successful women managers and definitions of success are the topic of chapter 5. Chapter 6 looks at paths to management taken by women, from traditional to unusual, and their view of and by the corporate world. Chapter 7
explores barriers and screens that have been erected to keep women out or
to shield them.

Part III looks at the interconnection of sex, power, and leadership, introducing a Japanese word adapted from English, *pawaa*, chosen by women
managers to distinguish a style of power with which they could be comfortable. Emerging redefinitions are examined as change poses dilemmas and issues for organizations. Elements of organizational culture, managerial beliefs,
attitudes, and practices that affect women's participation in management are
examined, as are the alternatives that women are choosing outside of traditional corporate life. Chapter 8 focuses on the relatively new phenomenon of
women-owned businesses established in growing numbers in Japan. Chapter
9 looks at what makes a company "woman-friendly" as company cultures
and women evolve. Beliefs and attitudes toward power and status in society
are explored, along with ways that women and men circumvent or confront
resistance, or simply, quietly change. Chapter 10 explores differing cultural
views of equity and the influence of culture on laws, strategies, and strategic
choices. Chapter 11 is about the men Japanese women live with at home and
in the office, and the dilemmas men face as women change and redefine their
roles and men seek rewards in uncharted roles. Chapter 12 summarizes visions women managers shared for themselves, their families, and society. Expanded horizons pose new choices for managers, for corporations, for men
and women at work, and for families, and they require flexibility and new approaches. Seemingly puzzling attitudes, behaviors, and practices are discussed
in light of historical roots and national culture.

Finally the epilogue asks about the future of Japanese women managers.
The possible futures seen by Japanese women managers varied widely, with
age a factor in whether the women were optimistic or pessimistic. Nor was
there unanimity on how to achieve a more effective and equitable world. The
women did agree that tapping the potential of the invisible women in Japan,
the United States, and the world is essential if we are to meet the challenges

of our times. Whether that will happen depends on decisions made by policy makers and managers, as well as the rising voices of women.

Japanese women have precedents in history and culture for speaking out, making their voices heard, and actively contributing to policy making and community. A poem written in 1911 by Raicho Hiratsuka to inaugurate a feminist journal issued a plea to Japanese women to remember their roots, and it serves as an appropriate challenge today.

> Women, please let your own sun, your concentrated energy,
> your own submerged authentic vital power shine out from you.
> We are no longer the moon.
> Today we are truly the sun.
> We will build shining golden cathedrals at the top of crystal mountains,
> East of the land of the rising sun.
> Women, when you paint your own portrait,
> do not forget to put the golden dome at the top of your head.
>
> Raicho Hiratsuka, Introduction to a new feminist magazine of
> SEITO, (Blue Stockings), Tokyo, Japan, 1911[18]

Part 1

JAPAN'S HIDDEN ASSETS

1

Today's Japanese Women

Workers, Managers, Wives, and Mothers

What is the situation of women in Japan today? Two views from women managers illustrate differing perceptions:

> Be ambitious. To dream is necessary for success. Be very sure of your possibilities. Women are on the way.
>
> Interview with Ryoko Akamatsu, minister
of education, ambassador to Uruguay, author of
Japan's equal employment opportunity legislation

> There is increasing consciousness in the society to promote women executives especially after the enactment of the equal employment law for men and women. There are women executives now and positions created in some companies. Unfortunately, compared to women in the States or any other nation, Japanese females have a lot of room to grow up. In other words, they are immature—dependent on others, especially men, and lack self-esteem for success or independent status.
>
> Interview with thirty-one-year-old
Japanese woman executive

To paraphrase Charles Dickens's view of the world in *A Tale of Two Cities,* "It is the best of times. It is the worst of times for women in Japan." Both observations are true, and together they reflect the contradictions and dilemmas faced by today's Japanese women. Depending on which side of the glass one peers, life is getting better or it's getting worse.

This chapter provides a brief overview of the situation of women in Japan in the last years of the twentieth century. Demographic data, labor force statistics, social trends, and national surveys provide a background for the stories of Japanese women managers.

Women who remember the war years and even the prewar years perceive that women's lot has improved enormously. They see that women are now accepted at national universities on an equal basis with men and hold faculty positions at those same universities, although not in large numbers. Women are found at all levels of government, including leadership positions. Women serve as elected officials at local and national levels. Young women have larger disposable incomes, live independently, and travel around the world.

But for the younger women who grew up in the 1960s and 1970s, like the one quoted at the beginning of the chapter, the progress is too slow. These women have traveled widely, have viewed life in other countries, and have observed different attitudes toward women's position in society, and they are not satisfied with what they find at home. Their generation believes Japanese females have a lot of room to grow up compared with women in the United States or any other nation, that they are immature, and that they lack the self-esteem necessary for success or independent status.

Reports of Japanese women since the invasion of Admiral Matthew Perry's ships in the nineteenth century have emphasized the exotic. Women were portrayed as doll-like figures—charming, beautiful, eager to please, enigmatic, and inscrutable. Lefcadio Hearn, a well-known early transplant to Japan in the early 1900s, wrote extensively about the country and married a Japanese woman. He said that the most wonderful aesthetic products of Japan are not its ivories, nor its bronzes, nor its porcelains, nor its swords, nor any of its marvels in metal or lacquer—but its women. His view of Japanese women as precious objects in the same category as other precious possessions, pleasing to behold, docile and manageable, was a popular perception. That perception is still popular among many men, both Western and Japanese.

Eighty years after the poet Raicho's call for empowerment for Japanese women, Juzo Itami, a prominent Japanese filmmaker, painted a grim picture of the possibilities for Japanese women. In an interview with a local business magazine, he described his view, as a social observer, of the difficult role of women in Japan.

For a woman [in Japan] to achieve real power, she has one of two choices. She can renounce men forever and launch herself on the rough road to corporate success, which means universal unpopularity for the rest of her life. Or she can become a geisha and get some powerful men to support her along the way. In terms of equal rights, this country still has a long way to go.[1]

Those who might like to be managers and leaders, according to Itami's observations, fly in the face of societal norms and should expect tremendous obstacles. His belief that women must choose either to serve men in a geisha-like fashion or to renounce men to achieve power is consistent with accepted stereotypes of Japanese women and supports the view that there are no women managers.

Other social observers bring forth different perspectives. Sumiko Iwao's *Japanese Woman*[2] emphasizes the advantages women retain over overworked and narrowly focused males who often have no life outside of work. At the other end of the continuum, Professor Hicks, whose book *The Comfort Women*[3] describes women forced into prostitution by the Japanese military before and during World War II, sees a systemic, pervasive discriminatory attitude, with historical roots continuing from ancient Asia and Europe, viewing women as chattel, servants and inferior beings, finding its extreme form in the brutal treatment of the wartime comfort women. With these stereotypes bombarding me, I chose to use a Fulbright research grant to experience the situation in Japan and Korea for myself and to look for women managers.

In Japan I found that, contrary to popular belief, there are Japanese women in management and their numbers are on the rise. Stories of Japanese women in management provide an opportunity to compare actuality with commonly held perceptions. Each story—women's views of their own roles, observations of the men in their lives, men's perceptions of women in management, and official perceptions of the proper role for women—brings a different perspective to the meaning, sources and distribution of power. Perceptions and socialization construct individual worldviews. Collectively, these views add up to the values and beliefs of society, beliefs about what is right and true and how to behave, which in turn become the stereotypes and myths embedded in social institutions. These embedded institutional rules often lag behind current thinking and actions.

Notwithstanding Itami's observations, some Japanese women do find alternate paths to power without renouncing men or becoming geisha-like. During the three years I lived in Japan, I found women managers who were successful, productive individuals, going to work every day, married and single, living with their families, contributing to the economy, active members of communities and knowledgeable about the world. Their stories illuminate women's struggles, triumphs, and dilemmas as they confront traditional rules and roles.

Japanese Labor Ministry statistics from 1996 identify 270,000 women as managers, not including those in government. Women hold 8.9 percent of all management positions in Japan. This compares with a decade ago, when there were 130,000 woman in management, or 6 percent of total managers. Women managers are in no way proportional to the number of women in the labor force, 40.6 percent, nor to women in the population, 51 percent, but there are women in management. Over 27 million Japanese women worked in paid employment in 1996, almost 41 percent of the total labor force. In the United States in the same year, 61 million women were in the paid workforce, 46 percent of the total. At least half of working-age women are in the paid workforce in both Japan (50 percent) and the United States (59.3 percent). This compares to the world as a whole, where approximately 40 percent of working-age women are in the paid labor force.[4]

One percent of Japanese women in the paid workforce are managers, while 6.6 percent of working males are managers. The percentage distribution for women in management has remained fairly constant since 1986, while men's has declined from 7.8 percent in 1975 to 6.6 percent in 1994. In addition, there are 2,500,000 self-employed women in official statistics. While the majority of these self-employed women are part-time piece workers, the figure also includes single-person small and medium-sized businesses, along with microbusinesses. The structure of Japanese business and women's participation will be discussed in greater detail in later chapters. Given the rate at which women are starting their own businesses and quietly entering management, offical statistics may lag, understating the actual number of women managers and business owners.[5]

Although Japanese women are not managers to an extent that is proportional to their representation in the workforce, they are there. The abundance of educated Japanese women, compared with their paucity in management, is an anomaly in a society noted for efficient use of its resources. In the United States, the percentage of women in management in 1996 had risen to 43 percent of the total number of managers from 30 percent a decade earlier. This compares with 8.9 percent in Japan. However, when top management is considered, the situations converge. In the United States, only one woman heads a Fortune 500 company, while one of Japan's three hundred largest companies is headed by a woman. A 1990 *Fortune* magazine[6] survey of the eight hundred largest United States companies found only 19 women among the 4,012 highest-paid officers, or about 0.47 percent. A later Catalyst study, in 1996, found that one in ten top officers in the Fortune 500 were women, but only 1.9 percent of the five top-earning officers of the same companies were women.[7] Certainly, formidable barriers stand in the way of women managers worldwide.

Each country manifests these barriers in forms that are unique to the society and culture. In Japan these barriers often seem more obvious and blatant than the United States, but they can also be subtle and masked. One young Japanese woman described the feeling of being tricked:

> We went through the best universities and were treated equally with the
> men. We competed with them and were sometimes better, sometimes not,

but always feeling on the same footing. We were told we could do anything we wanted to do, and then we left the university and went to work and we found that was not true. We were not treated fairly with the men and we couldn't do everything we wanted to do.

Her sentiments were echoed by other women describing their experiences. Dr. Takeo Sumioka, a psychiatrist in Tokyo, has written about the phenomenon the women were describing, calling it the "June Blues."[8] He said,

> Thousands of Japanese women hit the "glass ceiling" two months after starting work. Hired in April, many seek psychiatric help in June for depression caused by discrimination and the prospect of stultifying, dead-end assignments or the shame of quitting and looking for another job.

He strives to help his patients realize that they are not failures and that they do have other options, saying, "If their self-esteem is restored, they can cope with the male-dominated workplace even if they can't conquer it." Sumioka's objective is limited to helping women cope, seeing little possibility of changing the male-dominated workplace. His pessimistic view about the possibilities for women is shared by many observers.

The young women college graduates who took to the streets of Tokyo in the summer of 1994 to protest discrimination by major corporations did not hold such a pessimistic view of the inevitability of male dominance. They were willing to risk speaking out to change the workplace. The largest companies had publicly stated they were not hiring female college graduates because of the recession, but at the same time they continued to hire male college graduates. So, dressed in their new "recruit suits," the young women college graduates, carrying placards that read "We want to work, too," "Don't discriminate against women students," and "government and industry must guarantee our right to work," marched past the offices of major corporations to the Labor Ministry (see Figure 1.1).

Japanese people, even young men and women, were shocked by the women's protest demonstrations and feared their "un-Japanese" behavior had ruined their chances to be hired by any company. The young women were flying in the face of deeply held Japanese attitudes about preserving harmony and avoiding confrontation. "The nail that sticks out is knocked down" is a frequently quoted and deeply held metaphor in Japanese society. Women especially are expected to conform to cultural norms and avoid being knocked down. In a brilliant act symbolizing changes in corporate culture in Japan, the president of a major pharmaceuticals company saw the television coverage of the demonstration and instructed his human relations manager to find the women leading the demonstration and to hire them. "Anyone who can orga-

Figure 1.1 Young women college graduates protested discrimination in hiring practices by marching in their "recruit suits" past the Labor Ministry and corporate offices carrying placards saying "We want to work, too," "Don't discriminate against women students," and "Government and industry must guarantee our right to work." *Asahi Shimbun,* July 28, 1994.

nize a thousand women for such a dramatic and risky operation is a leader," he said, and the company hired two of the women.[9]

Women's prospects in Japanese corporations grew progressively bleaker after the bursting of the economic bubble, and their responses tended to become resigned. They again received subtle messages to conform and were urged to subordinate their individual wishes to the survival of the nation's economy. The phrase, *Shikata ga nai,* "There's no other way," was increasingly used to describe the situation.

Japanese women have made important advances in the last half century. The sample of dates in women's lives in the United States and Japan (see Table 1.1) illustrates milestones on the uneven paths toward human rights.

The pace of change and the force of resistance vary in each culture, corresponding to national prerogatives and beliefs about gender roles embedded in each society's values, institutions, and practices. While Japanese women lagged twenty-five years behind American women in obtaining the vote, and Japanese equal opportunity legislation was enacted twenty-one years after the United States law, Japanese women had a family leave law a year earlier than women in the United States. The parenting role of Japanese women has al-

Table 1.1 Milestones for Women

	Japan	United States
Right to vote First nation for women's vote: New Zealand (1893)	1945	1920
Right to enter state and national universities	1946	1776
Equal Employment Opportunity Law enacted	1985	1964
Family Leave Law	1992	1993
UN Convention on Elimination of Discrimination Against Women signed	1985	No
Glass ceiling officially recognized	No	1990
Legislation re violence against women	No	1994
Sexual harassment Official recognition	1993 Labor Ministry defines sexual harassment (sekahara)	1970s
Successful litigation	1992, using Labour Standards Law	1986, based on 1964 Civil Rights Act, 1991addendum

ways been emphasized. Japan passed a family leave law in 1992, while family leave law was not enacted in the United States until 1993.

In the arena of international recognition of women's rights, Japan signed the United Nations convention on the elimination of discrimination against women in 1985, while the United States has not yet signed. Cynics within Japan maintain that both the convention and the equal opportunity in employment law were passed solely to gain status in the international community. Even though this may reflect Japan's wishes to become a permanent member of the UN Security Council and its greater sensitivity to the power of international opinion, the failure to sign the convention does not speak well for the role of women in the United States.

Concerns about women's changing roles are not unique to the 1990s in Japan. In 1910 a writer was already worried about demographics, the position of women in Japan, and prevailing trends in gender roles:

Much has been written recently of alleged changes in the position occupied by woman in the mundane economy, and particularly, of a change in her relationship with man. From the economic point of view, it cannot be denied that the sex as a whole has made a substantial advance; but that, we venture to believe, is the economic consequence of its excess of numbers—a circumstance which will thus eventually remedy itself.[10]

A few years earlier, in 1899, a man on the other side of the Pacific, Edward P. O'Donnell, was warning Americans that the

> growing demand for female labor is an insidious assault upon the Home; it is the knife of the assassin aimed at the family circle. Employment of women . . . must gradually unsex them of that modest demeanor that lends charm to their kind.[11]

In spite of these dire warnings, women continued to work, and the issues remained. The problems did not remedy themselves, as the editor of the 1910 *Japan Mail* had seemed so confident they would when there were more men. Women continue to take their place in the "mundane economy," and the "excess of numbers of women" has shifted to women over 45, not the marriageable age that had so concerned the writer at the turn of the century. As we approach another turn of the century, the subject of women's place in the mundane economy remains at the forefront of social issues.

Women's place in Japan's economic life is complex and multifaceted. The percentage of women of working age in paid employment has increased steadily since 1970, reaching 50 percent by 1990, while the participation rate of men has decreased slightly. The term "labor force participation rate" denotes the proportion of working-age women or men in paid work, while "percent of workforce" is the male or female proportion of the total (see Table 1.2).

By 1997, the workforce in Japan was 40.6 percent female, comparable to the percentage in other industrialized nations. The United States labor force was 46.3 percent female. While 59 percent of women between the ages of fifteen and sixty-four work in the United States, 50.3 percent work in Japan, also relatively comparable (see Table 1.3).

There are more women than men in Japan today (61.6 million men and 64 million women). Worldwide, more baby boys are born than baby girls. In many countries, though, this ratio has been reversed by the time boys and

Table 1.2 Labor Force Participation Rates

	Male		Female	
	United States (%)	Japan (%)	United States (%)	Japan (%)
1970	80.6	81.4	43.4	45.7
1980	77.2	79.8	51.6	47.6
1990	75.4	77.2	57.7	50.1
1995	74.5	76.6	59.1	50.3

Table 1.3 Women as Percentage of Total Workforce

	United States	Japan
1981	43	34.1
1995	46	40.6

girls reach marriageable age, with more women than men aged twenty to twenty-nine. Not so in Japan today. The marrying age group still has more men than women. There are 8.5 million women aged twenty to twenty-nine and 8.8 million men of the same ages. The 300,000 excess men give women more choices and allow selectivity in picking mates for marriage. (see Table 1.4)

Continuing down the life path, Japanese women can expect to live 84 years, the longest life expectancy in the world, with the trend indicating continuing increases in longevity. The life expectancy of Japanese men is 77 years. Women today constitute a majority (60 percent) of the "over sixty-five" population in Japan, and that majority continues to grow. Of those aged one hundred and over, 82 percent are women. Interestingly, 79 percent of the "over 100" are female in the United States also (see Table 1.5).

The birth rate in Japan has declined steadily since the immediate postwar years and by 1998 reached 1.39. Projections suggest that in one hundred years the Japanese population will be half as large as it is today, that it will disappear in a thousand years with a continuation of the present conditions. For the population simply to maintain itself at its current level, the birth rate must be 2.08. The current birth rate is less than replacement rate. Demographers estimate that the total population of Japan will begin to decline by the year 2011 if current reproduction rates continue and immigration remains the same as it is today.

The declining birth rate has created concern and serious discussions in government and the media. In 1992 the Economic Planning Agency issued a

Table 1.4 Japan's Aging Population

Age	Total	Male	Female	% of total population
Total	126,166,000	61,805,000	64,361,000	
0–14	19,366,000			15.3500
15–64	87,042,000			68.9900
65 and over	19,758,000			16.6600
100 and over	8,491	1570 18%	6921 82%	.0007

Source: Management and Coordination Agency, 1998.

Table 1.5 Life Cycles of Women and Men in Japan and the United States

	Japan		United States	
	Male	Female	Male	Female
Life expectancy	77	84	73	79
Birth rate	1.39		1.5	
Population 65 and over	15.7%		12.8%	

Sources: Asahis Shimbun, *Japan Almanac* 1999; United States *The World Almanac* 1999.

white paper on people's livelihoods. One section was titled "Japan with a De-creasing Number of Children—Arrival of the *Shoshi Shakai,* its influence and measures to be taken." *Shoshi shakai* means "society with fewer children," and in the media has been coupled with the phrase *Korei shakai,* "aging soci-ety," to express concern about the future of Japan, given these demographic trends. In 1998 the Health and Welfare ministry's annual White Paper was de-voted entirely to the topic, "Thinking About a Low-Birthrate Society," indi-cating their continuing concern.

The populations of both Japan and the United States are getting older, but the rate of increase is dramatically higher in Japan than in the United States and most of the rest of the world for a number of interdependent reasons. One important reason is that both men and women live longer in Japan than in any other country; in addition, women live significantly longer than men.

Another factor lies on the birth side of the population equation. The so-called baby boom in Japan after World War II (1946) lasted only three years, compared with a longer period of high birth rate, a baby boom of ten to fif-teen years, in the United States and other Western countries. The birth rate fell 50 percent in Japan in the decade after the short postwar baby boomlet. The birth rate dropped from a high of four children per woman immediately after the war to two children per woman, so that there are proportionately fewer people in their late thirties and early forties in Japan now than in the United States. While the United States is concerned about the shift in popu-lation from young to old, the trend in Japan is more alarming because an even smaller group of young people balances the increased number of el-derly. The ratio of the population aged sixty-five and older to those aged zero to fourteen years rose from 13.1 in 1940 to 102 in 1997 indicating more people over sixty-five than fourteen and under. Japan calls this index the "aging index," and it is followed with great interest.

The majority of the aging population is female in both Japan and the United States because women live longer. Kin-san and Gin-san, one-hun-dred-year-old Japanese female twins, are popular national figures who appear on television and in the media, singing and expounding on a variety of subjects. Their advanced age allows them the un-Japanese privilege of saying exactly what they think. Their daily activites and sense of humor are reported and followed with great interest, providing a hopeful model of a happy old age. As more and more Japanese approach this age, the twins' activities foster the hope that all will be as energetic and active at one hundred.

The "graying" population in Japan is an important market, for which new products and marketing techniques are constantly being developed. Gerontology is a growing field, and there is heightened interest in recreation and sports for the healthy elders. The infrastructure of transportation and leisure systems will require a complete reevaluation in light of an aging but active population. In addition, concern for the ailing elder population and a scarcity of caregivers make the development of new methods of medical and long-term care a national priority.

The Japanese worry about who will care for this aging population, since fewer children are born each year and care of the elderly has traditionally been viewed as a family, rather than a public, responsibility. The proportion of the population that is over sixty-five currently is almost 15 percent. In 1990 Japan's over sixty-five population ratio overtook that of the United States, and it is close to those of Sweden and Germany, the only other countries with such a high proportion of individuals in this age group. If current trends continue, in 2020 more than 26 percent of the population will be over sixty-five, the highest proportion in the world. Traditionally, daughters-in-law have been caregivers for the husband's parents in Japan. Declining birth rates, urbanization, and changing values and lifestyles are eroding this support system.

Figure 1.2 presents changes in Japanese women's life cycle over the last decades.[12] It is a graphic representation of the shift in life patterns of women born in three different eras, 1905, 1927, and 1969. These trends in marriage, childbirth, and life expectancy have profound implications for the lives of Japanese women and men.

As shown by the Figure 1.2, Japanese women are choosing to marry later, with women's average age at marriage 26.3 years in 1995. Another factor that has implications for society but is not shown on the graph is the increasing number of women choosing not to get married at all. A recent *Asiaweek* cover story[13] highlighted the trend for women throughout Asia to remain single longer, sometimes all their lives, as a choice rather than a necessity. One said, "I like men, but they are the icing on the cake, not the cake." Husbands are decoration, not a necessity. Single women are creating new markets and lifestyles in Japan. Married women are also choosing to have fewer children or no children. An underground book written by a group of Japanese women justifying their position of a happy marriage without children had a surprisingly wide readership.

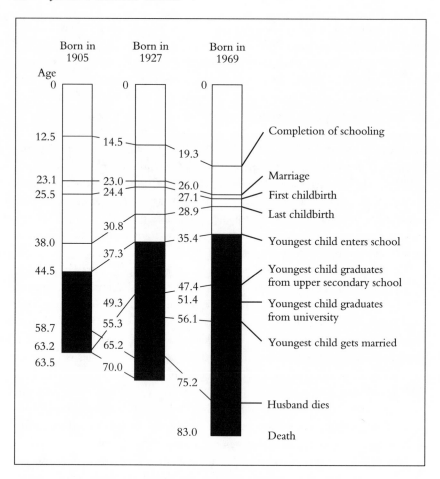

Figure 1.2. Changes in life patterns of Japanese women born in different eras—1905, 1927, and 1969. Ministry of Health and Welfare, *Vital Statistics and Abridged Life Tables,* Ministry of Education, *Basic Statistical Survey on Schools.*

Fewer children combined with increased life expectancy mean that young Japanese women who do marry and have children can expect to have more than 45 years of life after their youngest child enters school. Compare this with a woman born in 1905, who could have expected less than 20 years of life after her youngest child entered school. Even assuming that a mother devotes her life to her children during their entire school years, which younger women are less likely to do, a woman born in 1969 still has more than 30 years of life remaining after her youngest child graduates from the university. Such demographic trends have important implications for women and allow predictions about emerging challenges for education, communities, government, and business with a fair degree of certainty.

The divorce rate in Japan has increased in the last twenty years, from less than 1 per 1,000 to 1.66 per 1,000, still lower than the rate in the United States, at 4.6 per 1,000, or in Europe, at 2 per 1,000.[14] Twenty years ago, seven out of ten people in Japan felt that a couple should not get divorced even if they were not happy together. A similar survey taken in 1987 found that the majority, six out of ten, felt that a couple should divorce if they were not happy together. While the actual number of divorces seems low to out-siders, the rate of increase has been significant, and attitudes toward divorce have made a startling reversal. Such shifts in attitude are often a precursor to behavior change.

The greatest increase in divorce rates is found in couples married fifteen years or more. Older women who have created their own lives and developed outside interests while their husbands dedicated themselves to their compa-nies are becoming the initiators of divorce. The rate of divorce in this age group quadrupled in the last decade. The women in this age group have seen many changes, have developed satisfying lives while managing the house and budget, have reared and educated children, and have participated in commu-nity activities. They are not willing to spend their remaining years with a re-tired husband always around the house, one who expects to be served, has no outside interests, and with whom they have little in common.

In both Japan and the United States, many believe that women's economic role is consumption, spending the money that men earn. Women from other countries often learn with envy that Japanese men's salaries go directly to their wives and that husbands are given an allowance for expenses. Japanese men often quote this fact to demonstrate the power of Japanese women. Wives do manage the household budget, deciding on household purchases and entertainment.

Although it is commonly believed that decisions for major purchases and investments are made by men, albeit with a downward trend, manufacturers, retailers, and financial establishments are learning that this is not the case. One indicator of change finds the Japanese auto industry directing more of their advertisements to women, recognizing that women are fast becoming the primary decision makers in the purchase of cars. In recognition of this, manufacturers began hiring women in their design departments a decade ago to design cars more suitable to women's tastes and physiques. Shortly after-ward women were tentatively brought into the auto industry's marketing de-partments to consult on advertising and selling, instead of, or in addition to, adorning the cars as decoration for the advertisements.

Young single women are major consumers. They often live at home with their parents, allowing them a high proportion of disposable personal income for clothes and luxury items. Female consumption is a crucial economic force, helping to open a path for women in consumer affairs departments in major corporations to think of new ways to attract this important market. Women also make decisions about the percentage of savings and types of investment of the family income. In recognition of this, financial institutions are seeking ways to attract them, offering classes in investment specifically aimed at women and, following the lead of foreign firms, hiring more women for customer contacts.

In addition to their consumption roles, Japanese women also earn the incomes used for consumption and savings and contribute to production. Women have always been the managers of the family and home, the "care economy," assuming total responsibility for their families, freeing the husband, the "salarymen," to be devoted completely to economic production. Today women also constitute almost half of the paid workforce in Japan, with neither the care nor the income role fully acknowledged.

Japan has the highest per capita gross national product in the world and the highest savings rate. Its manufacturing industries are among the world's most productive, using techniques that have been emulated throughout Asia. All this has been accomplished in the half century since the end of World War II. Volumes have been written analyzing the reasons for this success, but one crucial conponent of Japan's economic success is missing in most analyses. In accounts of Japan's unprecedented economic growth, the role of women is rarely mentioned. In her book, *Women and the Economic Miracle,* Mary C. Brinton, a sociologist, put the two subjects, women and the economy, together with an incisive critique of the exploitation of women's work.[15]

Japan is not unique in this regard. Throughout the world, women's work and skills are necessary and yet are often ignored. Two-thirds of the total world's work is done by women. Sixty percent of the farming of the world is done by women.[16] Women's work is "often unrecorded, undervalued or not valued at all," not reflected in economic data, and not included in a nation's gross national product. Work in the home is not considered an economic product unless monetary payment is made. If someone outside the family, other than the wife or mother, does the work and receives money, it becomes part of the national product. Women's work in the home, in the community, and in their children's schools is almost always unpaid, so it is not considered in a nation's economic measures of productivity or noted in international statistics of resources, production, and work.

When a man marries his paid housekeeper, the gross national product declines, even though the same, or a greater, amount of work is accomplished. If unpaid house and family care work were counted as productive output in national income accounts, global output would increase by 20 to 30 percent, according to a 1990 United Nations survey. Ms. Sumiko Takahara, former head of Japan's Economic Planning Agency, hired a service to clean her bathroom when she became too busy to do it herself; she was billed a hundred dollars for two hours' work. She speculated that if men found they could earn that sum in such a short time at home, it might revolutionize the labor distribution of men and women.[17]

The Japanese Economic Planning Agency conducted a study of the value of unpaid "voluntary" work in Japan, including housework, nursing, and other voluntary activities, and found a value estimated between 66.7 and 98.8 trillion yen in 1991, which was 14.6 to 21.6 percent of the gross domestic product. The report, the first of its kind in Japan, found women doing 85 percent of this unpaid work.[18] Surprise.

Since the dawning of the industrial age, women have rarely been in charge or managers, so it is not surprising that work which is acknowledged, recorded, and valued is the traditional "men's work" rather than "women's work." Only in the last few years have statistics been disaggregated by gender to try to ascertain women's contribution, along with a movement by economists to try to understand the "care economy," that portion of production devoted to nurturing and maintaining life.

Rewards for women's work lag far behind those for men. Even though 40.6 percent of the workforce in Japan is female, individual women's earnings average less than 60 percent of a man's earnings. Estimates range from 50 to 60 percent.[19] In the United States, the ratio of women's earnings to men's earnings "rose" to approximately 76 percent in 1995, partly as a result of men's decline in earnings. In Japan as in most countries, a majority of women are working but are not earning incomes comparable to men (see Table 1.6).

What kinds of work do Japanese women do? Women are now found in all industries in Japan, with some industries having a higher proportion than others. Even traditional, exclusively male domains are being breached. Women broke an ancient taboo in 1992 by working on construction of a tunnel. In Japan the belief that women should not work on tunnels because their very presence was a bad omen had been upheld until then by the construction industry. The woman who worked on that first tunnel in 1992 received broad media coverage as another barrier fell.

Table 1.6 Ratio of Women's to Men's Salaries

	United States (%)	Japan (%)
1980	60.0	53.8
1985	68.2	51.9
1987	69.1	52.3
1990	70.2	50.7
1995	76.0	51.9

Source: JETRO, *US and Japan in Figures*, 1997.

Women have recently been accepted into the Self-Defense Force, as the national police force or army is called. Fifteen female officers of the Maritime Self-Defense Force sailed around the world as part of a navigation exercise in 1995 on the training vessel *Kashima,* which had to be specially designed to include women. The second Japanese astronaut to circumnavigate the planet was a woman and she was also the first Japanese to do so a second time. Women own and operate all kinds of businesses, from restaurants to trading companies, to retail stores, to moving companies, to the manufacture of ceramics for high-technology products. Over 50 percent of women employees are found in manufacturing, service, wholesale, and retail trade. Increasingly they are being recruited for finance, information, and new service industries and are starting their own such businesses. The opening of one very male sanctuary—sumo wrestling—has recently received international publicity, but the first women on the trading floor of the stock market, described in the same article, will probably have a more lasting impact.

One widely accepted stereotype, which supports the national values and goals, is that Japanese women work only until they find a man, then quit to get married and raise a family. Major corporations hire attractive, bright, marriageable women who hopefully will become wives of the salarymen with whom they work and then retire. Since the working lives of salarymen with an intense work focus leave little time for courtship, the company tries to take care of that as well.

Male executives have repeatedly told me, "We can't have women managers. They leave to have babies." The truth of this assertion can be questioned. At the national level it is contained in what I call the myth of "Japan's M-shaped curve." Often I was referred to the M-shaped curve as proof that Japanese women predominantly leave work at ages twenty-eight to thirty-four to have children. Both men and women cited this tendency as justification for the paucity of women managers and for relatively lower salaries for females. This was usually accompanied by a statement about the uniqueness of Japanese women's employment patterns and the folly of comparing Japanese women to women in other countries, and was filed away as another example of the belief in Japanese uniqueness to be tested, if possible, against known research, like intestines that can't digest foreign beef or rice, or use contraceptives tested in other countries.

In fact, the M-shaped curve of Japanese women's employment rate does indicate a decline in the percentage of women working during the child-rearing years, thirty to thirty-five, but with women returning to work at forty to forty-five, or at the time of children's school matriculation (see Figure 1.3).

As can be seen from the historical charting, however, the M-shaped curve has both risen and flattened over time. In the last decade a higher proportion

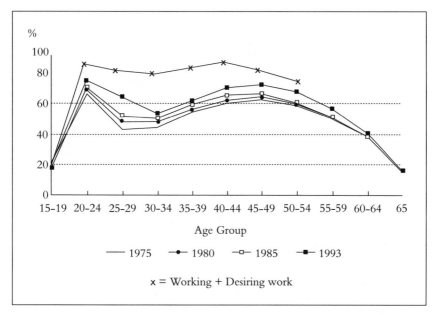

Figure 1.3. Labor force participation rates of Japanese women in 1975, 1980, 1985, and 1993. Labor Force Survey, Management and Coordination Agency, 1986, 1994, and Japan Institute of Women's Employment, 1992, Tokyo, Japan.

of women have been working, the decline in numbers of women working during childbearing years has decreased, and the period away from work has shortened. Even at the lowest point of the curve, more than 50 percent of Japanese women work. When nonworking women desiring work are added to the Japanese chart, the participation rate at the highest point, ages twenty to twenty-five is 86.9, and at the lowest ages thirty to thirty-five, is 81.8. That is, at the lowest point 81.8 percent of women are either in the labor force or would like to be, and the M-shape disappears.

This is not dissimilar to the trend in the historical chartings of women's labor participation rates in the United States. The uniqueness at a given point in time fades with historical perspective.

Historical male labor force participation rates are included in the United States graph and indicate a slow convergence toward the female (see Figure 1.4). The shape of Japanese male participation rates is similar but declines sharply at fifty-five rather than sixty-five years.

Using international comparisons, again we find that Japan is not unique. Participation rates of working women for Japan, France, West Germany, and the United States are plotted in Figure 1.5. While Japan's M-curve is the most pronounced, the rates fall within the same population, with Japan's participation rate actually rising above the others by the middle and late forties, while

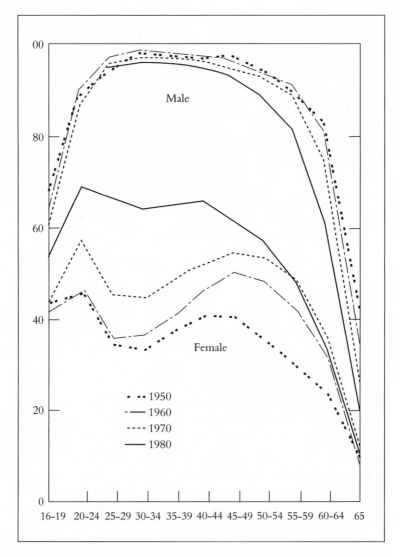

Figure 1.4. Labor force participation rates of women and men in the United States in 1950, 1960, 1970, and 1980. United States Department of Labor, Washington, DC.

at the lowest point on the curve, ages thirty to thirty-four, more than 53.5 percent of Japanese women are working.

The M-shaped curve does describe the societally "appropriate" career pattern for Japanese women: to work from graduation until marriage, followed by full-time child rearing and a return to work in their middle forties. Hence perhaps the pervasive insistence on the pattern's strength and uniqueness.

While this belief that Japanese women work only until marriage, retiring until their children are through school, is commonly held, only 33 percent of

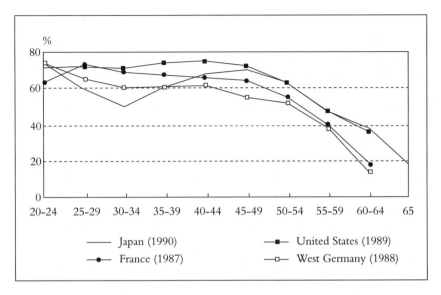

Figure 1.5. Comparison of female labor force participation rates in Japan, France, the United States, and West Germany. International Labor Office, ILO, Geneva, Switzerland.

employed women were single in 1995. In reality, more than half of Japan's working women were married, with an additional 9.1 percent widowed or divorced, and more than half of women with children under age twelve were working (see Table 1.7).

So much for the myth of unmarried women as the majority of working women in Japan. The myth supports the values of Japanese society, assigning women full-time to the wife-mother role. But at the same time the economy also depends on women's labor for its high productivity, another deeply held value. These conflicting values must be acted upon by women and reconciled by society, which often chooses to ignore the dilemma created for women and the nation.

Japanese women work both full-time and part-time. Part-time, or *pato,* the *katakana* Japanese version of a foreign term, is officially defined as thirty-five hours or less per week, but hidden hours or even overt work requirements often bring this total far beyond the specified limit. Some part-time

Table 1.7 Marital Status of Employed Women

Single	33%
Married	57.8%
Widowed or divorced	9.1%

Source: *Labor Statistics* 1994, Japan Ministry of Labor 1995.

workers work more than 40 hours a week. The real difference between *pato* and full-time workers is in salary, bonuses, and benefits, with part-time employees receiving considerably less of each, and usually no bonus or benefits. Part-time employees provide an expendable workforce that can more easily be shifted with fluctuations in business, thus requiring less investment and commitment from employers. This buffer is a major component supporting the cherished lifetime employment and seniority-based rewards system of the salaryman.

Statistics for women as part-time workers vary, but official government figures say women represented 68 percent of all part-time workers, or 6,920,000 out of a total of 10,150,000 part-time workers in 1996. At the same time, 25.5 percent of all female employees were categorized as part-time, and part-timers constituted 15.1 percent of the total labor force. One of the fastest-growing types of business in Japan recently has been companies that provide temporary staff at all levels, which during the downsizing of Japanese corporations has gained impetus placing both males and females. For women returnees to the labor force, part-time work has the advantage of greater control over hours. Many women, however, were heard to complain that it was the only option available to them.

Tax incentives allow a wife to make 1 million yen annually ($10,000 at exchange 100 yen = $1) before she and her husband must pay taxes on her income and she must be taken from his benefits package, or vice versa for the husband, although no statistics on husbands in this category are available and no examples were mentioned. This situation was referred to as the million-yen wall. In addition, the husband can claim his wife as a dependent for a spousal deduction of 300,000 yen until her income exceeds the 1 million yen and the husband also continues to receive household benefits. Given the prevailing high tax rate, the cap on income before taxes provides a strong incentive for wives to work part-time when this luxury is an option. Indeed, a woman would have to make considerably more than 1 million yen to make her work monetarily worthwhile. Combine the tax situation with the facts that women carry the major household responsibilities even when working and that women's average salaries are considerably less than men's, and part-time work becomes a logical choice for many women.[20]

Why do women work? The reasons women state for working are diverse. A *Survey on Women's Lives and Work* by the Prime Minister's Office in June 1992 found the following:

Women's Reasons for Working

Supplementing the household budget	41%
Money to spend as I choose	36%
To make a living and save for the future	34%

Getting satisfaction from work	31%
Broaden horizons and make friends	30%
★ Multiple Response questions	★

A popular belief is that women work for fashionable clothes, travel, and self-indulgence until they can get married and be supported by a man. The reality is that women work for a variety of reasons, many of the same reasons men work as indicated by men's responses to the same 1992 Prime Minister's Survey.

Men's Reasons for Working

To make a living	87%
It is the expected thing to do	46%
To save for the future	39%
Getting satisfaction from work	36%

The largest group of both women and men work because their income is needed. As in the United States and around the world, a proportion of women support themselves and their children. In other circumstances women's earnings are essential as a second income for the household, given the high cost of living in Japan. For younger couples, it is often assumed the wife will work to continue the standard of living to which both have become accustomed in Japan's affluent society. Some women work because they get satisfaction from work, want to use their talents, and like having an income. Differing from men, a large proportion of women said they worked because it provided an opportunity to expand their horizons and make new friends.

Several recent books on women in Japan argue that Japanese women have the best of all worlds. When compared with Japanese salarymen, Japanese women usually have more freedom and, some suspect, exert a degree of expert and subtle manipulation to keep the husband hard at work to pay for that freedom. The thesis states, "Now is a golden age" for Japanese women in contrast to Japanese men. Women can work if they want, or they can be full-time wives, mothers, and homemakers when they so choose and spend their leisure time in self-improvement or playing golf, practicing ikebana, or going to the theater and *pachinko* parlors.

Certainly this may be true for some Japanese women, but the women managers I interviewed did not fit this description. Most worked because their income was needed. Some emphasized the stimulation and satisfaction of their work. Others felt they were contributing to a better life for their families and their communities.

For some, a career had not been a conscious choice, but having begun work after leaving school, they had found the income welcome and the work interesting and challenging, or they didn't want to be quitters and so continued to work. The successful women who reported that they had not made the choice to work until well into their careers raise important issues for today's young women who, as they begin their first job are confronted with a long-term decision about whether they want a clerical or career job under the current two- or three-track system.

Many of the women interviewed told of the difficulties of working—child care, problems of adjustment at home and work, criticism from family. They discussed the barriers for women in society and at work, the demands of Japanese business life and family responsibilities. A few stayed out of the workforce for several years after marriage, but not one said she would have preferred to be a full-time homemaker without the experiences she had at work.

Recognizing significant barriers to management in established corporations, many women in Japan, as in the United States, have become entrepreneurs, starting their own businesses. In 1996, 5.7 percent of all heads of companies in Japan were women, in businesses ranging from small shops to major companies. While this statistic is often dismissed as limited to small home businesses, that is not the case. Women do own many small and medium-sized businesses, but women-headed businesses also include the largest publishing company in Japan and one of the most prestigious fashion houses, as well as moving companies, database, information, and research services, high-technology materials and manufacturing, management and financial service firms, franchises, food services, restaurants, and retail stores.

Women are, as they have always been, involved in the production of goods and services and national wealth, but now they seek also to have their opinions counted, to influence events, to be involved in setting priorities, in effect to be managers and leaders. Increasingly, women are demanding that their voices be heard in decisions about their own lives and the world's resources. The desire to influence the events and circumstances of one's life is bubbling to the surface for women around the world, and Japan is no exception.

Concurrent economic, demographic, and social trends have quietly created dramatically different lives for Japanese women, as they live longer, marry later, have fewer children, and spend longer periods of their lives alone, or at least without a husband. Technology and longer lives free women to consider expanded options, with new choices, possibilities, and problems. The changes in women's life cycles also stimulate changes in the roles they choose and are required to take in society, with important ramifications for family life, education, and the world of work. Japanese women have valid reasons to prepare themselves for long lives with a greater degree of independence, whether by necessity or choice.

The role of manager is a relatively new modern role for women, often seen in Japan as in direct competition for full-time commitment to home and family. Women in Japan who are managers or want to be managers are in the vanguard of social changes. Change, especially change in status and gender roles, is associated with challenge, anxiety, and resistance, all of which confront Japanese women managers and the nation today. Women managers' careers, lives, opportunities, problems, and responses illuminate critical areas of social change.

This chapter sets the stage for looking at the career and life paths of Japanese women managers. It serves as a prelude to examining their lives and careers for clues to how they were able to transcend barriers, powerful stereotypes, and socialization to become effective managers and leaders. A surprising discovery was a pattern of events in the early lives of women managers that created conditions for adult success. The next chapter reveals these formative events of childhood and early life.

2

Growing Up Japanese and Female

Women Managers' Early Years

Given the enormous obstacles that Japanese women encounter in their male-dominated world, what has helped the successful women transcend these barriers? Some fascinating patterns emerged from my research. As reported in their interviews, success began early. Each of the women managers interviewed was asked, "What helped you to succeed?":

> From my childhood I was always ambitious. My mother knew education is very important even for a girl. She was forty-four when I was born, and maybe she was living through me.

> Since I was a child, my parents encouraged me always to improve myself. Unlike other traditional Japanese parents, they never told me to be feminine or obedient, but just to care for others.

> I was brought up that way. My parents took a "let-alone" policy to bring up their children. They respected and left complete freedom and self-responsibility to me and my brother in deciding for our future. It made me have more choices in my life rather than the limited choices if I had followed the traditional social norm.

> Selection from women managers' answers to
> question "What helped you to succeed?"

The conditions contributing to success began with birth—where, when, and to whom—and with early childhood experiences. My research revealed

38

life patterns with common threads. Some pieces of the patterns were initially surprising and puzzling, but they made complete sense as they fell into place in the context of the environment, culture, and economic conditions.

The women's answers revealed life patterns that both reflect and deviate from traditional gender role socialization. Beginning at birth, socialization conveying gender messages is transmitted to children by family and society. Actions, words, approval of desired behavior, and disapproval for undesirable behavior teach children "proper" behavior, first within the family and later in the broader social milieu. For successful Japanese women, their early experiences were an important key to success.

As outsiders to industry, government, and corporate culture, women need an extraordinary conjuncture of personal and environmental factors to succeed. Women are marginal to these systems in the sociological sense, that is, they are on the edge and not in the mainstream. As minorities and outsiders, women need unusual circumstances simply to enter. Success and survival require strategic acuity. Some strategies for entry and survival used by the successful women were consciously defined, planned, and operationalized. Others evolved from a woman's life experiences, situation, and status. This chapter focuses on factors in family, early lives, and socialization that differentiated successful women. The patterns emerging from their histories provided clues to their ability to move beyond tradition.

The era of their birth was a determining factor for all, with both positive and negative implications. This is not surprising, since external events impact all of society, and opportunities for women have been different in each historical period. For many of the women managers, their early years included unusual and powerful external events. The women born between 1925 and 1946 all mentioned the impact of the war and postwar occupation as key formative influences on their lives.

One-third of the women who participated in my research project were born prior to 1945. This age cohort was predominant in the first interviews (see Table 2.1) because they most clearly met the initial criteria of success.[1]

The fact that successful managers were in their late forties, fifties, and sixties was not unexpected. The route to upper management is time-consuming, and this is consistent with other industrial societies, especially more traditional ones.

In recounting the story of her life, each woman in this age group men-

Table 2.1 Age Distribution of Women Managers in Interview Sample

Age	20–30	30–40	40–50	Over 50
Number of Women	15%	25%	26%	34%

tioned the war and postwar military occupation, which were more seminal for some than for others but significant for all. The upheaval and chaos of the war and postwar years temporarily suspended prescribed norms of behavior, including gender role behavior. Survival was the issue, and everyone worked at whatever needed to be done. The social chaos of turbulent times required new behaviors and provided an opportunity for girls to move beyond traditional roles. Examples from their stories illustrate the power of those experiences.

Memories of War Years

Scene: Japan 1945

The sky is red with flames, the road is jammed with people running from the heat and terror of the fires. The six-year-old girl is frightened, dazed, and confused. She has fled from her home with her family—her mother, father, brother, and sisters—to escape the devastation wrought by the flames of the firebombs. She has become separated from her family in the crush of people fleeing the city and now is alone and frightened as night begins to fall. The year is 1945. The place is near Nagoya, Japan. Yuri, the little girl, has spent her entire childhood in this picturesque, very old, traditional town, Kinawi City. An idyllic country setting, the town had become the site of a munitions factory for the war effort, making it a prime target for Allied firebombs. That night the city burned down completely, and as the family fled, Yuri was lost and separated from the rest of her family.

Shaking with fear and cold, her thoughts that night were on life and death. She vowed, "If I can live today, if I can live until morning, I will go the United States and talk about this experience and insist on peace." She distracted herself by making plans to do this. She thought, "To go to the United States, I must study. I will have my own job and I will go to the United States." She thought of all these things during that night.

In the early morning hours Yuri's mother and father began their search for their lost daughter among all the dead bodies along the riverside. Believing that she had been killed, they had little hope of finding her alive. Miraculously, she had survived among the dead bodies, and there was great rejoicing when they spotted her. In the midst of the devastation they gave thanks for her life.

That wartime scene seems very remote from the sophisticated elegant setting in which we sit as I interview Yuri Konno in Tokyo. She sits opposite me in her office above the fashionable Aoyama district of Tokyo, lovely and serene in a designer suit, surrounded by all the accoutrements of power and wealth. The little girl is now the president of several companies, a member of influential government economic boards and commissions, and a true "woman of the world." The horror and fright of her experiences from that night in Nagoya are still very much a part of the woman, though. She describes that night as if it occurred yesterday, and she attributes part of the motivation for her lifelong commitment to work for peace in the world to that experience. Her resolve to work to ensure that war does not come again to her country or to the world, and to care for the children of the world who are in need has roots in that night.

The little girl did go to the United States. She went first on a Rotary scholarship in high school. Later, in 1964, she was chosen as a guide in the Japanese Pavilion at the International Exposition in New York City. While there, she chanced to meet a journalist on crutches. Incredibly, the man had been a pilot in one of the planes that bombed the munitions factory near Nagoya. In the recognition of their shared experience, he cried. She cried. They became good friends, and she again affirmed her vision to be a bridge between Japan and the United States so that communication might prevent such horror from taking place again.

Life Without a Father

Another of the women managers I interviewed had different experiences during the war and postwar years, but her life was also profoundly affected by these events. Mitsu is the same age as Yuri. Her father was a doctor conscripted to serve in Manchuria in Japan's expansion to China. As the war ground on, Mitsu and her mother and brother were evacuated home to Japan, but her father remained in Manchuria to care for the troops. At the end of the war, there was no word from her father, and he was presumed dead.

Life for the family in Tokyo was extremely hard, with no father and no money. Mitsu's mother, who had never worked and had no skills or training, was forced to do manual labor and cleaning to earn money for her family. Mitsu, seeing her mother's pain and difficulties, touched by her mother's exhaustion and red hands when she returned to their home late at night, vowed that she would never find herself in her mother's position. She would prepare herself to earn an income. She would have a profession and be able to take care of herself, her mother, and her family if necessary. This was a new insight and resolve for a Japanese girl brought up in a traditional well-to-do, professional family. And she maintained her resolve. Later the family learned that her father was alive, but it was several years after the war before he was able to return to Japan and join them.

After he returned, he encouraged both his daughters and sons to go to the university. Mitsu thought she would become a doctor like her father, but even though the national universities were now open for women, medicine was still considered a man's profession. Since there were few openings in medical school and women were discouraged from entering, she instead majored in science, later becoming a laboratory scientist, marrying a doctor, and parenting a doctor son.

Rather than practicing her science, however, Mitsu was one of the first women to enter the civil service by examination and start on the management track. The track was difficult for a pioneer woman in the civil service, but she persevered, living through a hazing apprenticeship in which she was expected to serve tea to her male coworkers and even her male subordinates the second year. Her graceful exterior was buoyed by her determination to succeed, to have a profession, and not to be dependent on society as her mother had been when her father was thought lost.

Mitsu successfully rose through the civil service ranks to become a deputy minister of labor, studied in the United States, and served the ministry in various positions in Japan, as representative to the United Nations and in posts around the world. Then she once more became a pioneer by resigning from government service before retirement age while still young and productive. She accepted a position as president of the Body Shop, Japan, a company introducing environmental concepts and new products successfully to Japanese people.

Achieving her goals of competency and self-reliance, Mitsu was also one of the women who lived the traditional roles of doctor's wife, dutiful daughter-in-law, and mother of a son who also became a doctor. While the women in this age group had parents who generally espoused quite traditional values, each of the women chose her own path to achieve her life goals. Some, like Mitsu, combined all, but in their own way. Others were pioneers in their lifestyles as well as in their professions.

One of the successful women managers interviewed in this age group chose to raise her daughter alone without marriage, and she successfully combined her career with motherhood. She attributed part of her determination and perseverance to the necessity to provide an income and life for her daughter. As she said, there were times when she might have chucked all the problems and difficulties of a career in a man's world for a life of travel, creativity, and pleasure, but there was always her daughter to consider. So she continued to work and became a pioneer and leader in her field.

Manchurian Childhood

During Japan's expansion into China, many Japanese families of businessmen, professionals, and military officers were transferred to Manchuria. A childhood in Manchuria and experiences in the war and immediate postwar years were influential to another of the women as she built her career. Ichiko Ishikawa was born and spent her early years in Manchuria, where she and her family witnessed alternative ways to live and different ways to rear girls and boys. She remembered her mother's horror at the practice of foot binding as seen in older women. On their return to Japan her mother reinforced the cosmopolitan experiences by teaching her daughter that she need not become a traditional Japanese housewife. Her family training and experiences inspired her to use her talents and abilities to make the world a better place in which to live. This socialization served her well as she climbed the corporate ladder as a pioneer in retailing and marketing.

Ichiko worked her way up the ranks from saleswoman to buyer to marketing manager, eventually becoming the first Japanese woman president of a department store, the venerable Takashimaya Department Store. She attributed some of her achievements along the difficult path to success to her mother's teaching that she need not adhere to the social norms of the traditional Japanese but could do what she wanted. The route was not easy, but it never is for a pioneer. Ichiko managed her career, sometimes carrying her babies with her to work on the subway when there was no caretaker, working the long hours required of executives, traveling the world in search of fashion, fighting for what she knew women wanted in department stores, and learning to ignore and parry the expected sexual harassment of women, which was considered normal at the time. During this time, she edited a book, *Think Like a Man, Work Like a Dog, Act Like a Lady*,[2] whose title conveys the philosophy that carried her to success. She adapted to the male-dominated world, worked harder than anyone else, and acted like a "lady."

Within the postwar world, each of the women managers created a career and lifestyle to fit her own unique abilities and needs. Even though all were of the same era, each carved her own route, slightly different than other women managers. The more traditional view of how women should succeed is described by Yuriko Saisho, another successful Japanese woman manager in this age group, in her book *Women Executives in Japan: How I Succeeded in Business in a Male-Dominated Society*.[3] Yuriko was one of the women who had been unprepared for the working world. Forced to support herself in the devastation following the war, she chose to work in advertising and marketing. Hard work, determination, and the evolution of Japanese business contributed to her becoming a successful international businesswoman, the chairwoman of Nippo, a large marketing and advertising company. Chapter titles in her 1980 book include "Standing on My Own Two Feet" and "We're Women, So We Try Harder," with advice similar to that in books published in the United States in the 1960s. Her advice to women was to "be ambitious, but without sacrificing womanly qualities." That suggestion sounds somewhat quaint today, but it embodies the fears, even now, of both women and men that successful women may lose their "womanly qualities," however they may be defined.

Life on the Home Front

A story that more closely follows Japanese feminine tradition was told by an amazing woman in her seventies. Born to an affluent, high-status family, she had been trained and was skilled in the womanly arts of ikebana (traditional flower arranging), embroidery, and Japanese painting. She had lost her young husband and her family in the war and felt she had no marketable skills with which to take care of herself.

The woman found work with the occupation army, eventually landing in the commissary, where her beautiful embroidery made into pillows, furniture covers, and decorations were popular with the wives of soldiers stationed in Japan. Ready-made clothing was not available, so anything that helped the home seamstress was in demand and especially useful in those postwar years. It was necessary to make do with what was available for clothes, and meager decorations were appreciated. She began teaching classes in embroidery and traditional painting and improvised tools to help in sewing and handiwork. Her first customers were American, since Japanese women considered her work old-fashioned. Later she patented her tools and developed a profitable business manufacturing and distributing these items abroad and in Japan, where they are now popular.

Wartime Propaganda

Another woman who traced her career choices to events of the war years is Hariko Watanabe, a respected and well-known television executive who now produces television workshops and trains women for roles in television. Hariko was in the second grade during the war when the teacher instructed the students to change a passage in their books that was critical of the Japanese army. Having been reared in a scholarly family, in which learning and knowledge were venerated, she was outraged by this censorship, even at such a young age. She vowed that meddling with the truth would not happen again if she could help it. When the war ended she worked for a scholarship to attend a well-known journalism school in the United States, and she has dedicated her life to the search for truth and knowledge and to transmitting valid information to the public, sparing no nation's foibles. She was honored for her work, especially training and supporting women in the media, with a national award in 1992.

The women who experienced the war and occupation years and the deep changes wrought in the structure and fabric of their society told me many stories about changes this era had brought to their family and working lives, such as the right to vote, to enter the national universities, and to run for political office. While it brought pain and poverty to some, it also gave them the opportunity to dream of accomplishments not even considered previously. The women who lived through the war and the immediate postwar years were profoundly influenced by those events and their repercussions in the ensuing years. They followed their dreams, and they also remembered how things had been before and how much better life seemed now. Men who lived through the war and postwar years were sometimes surprised when I told them of the depth of the war's effect upon women and the profound changes it had wrought in their lives. The men also had been affected by the war and its consequences, but the structure of their lives had not changed as completely as it had for women who lived through those years. Expanded horizons and heretofore unthinkable possibilities created profound shifts in the lives of this generation of women.

Japanese society after the war was "unfrozen" in the sense used by change theorists, that is, the existing rules for how to behave, think, and feel were temporarily upended. The prevailing prewar beliefs in the divinity and infallibility of the ruler and the state were toppled, and the postwar chaos created an opportunity to view the world and life in new ways. Traditions were quickly reasserted, but with the brief pause came an opportunity, particularly for women, to experiment with new ways of being in the world and to discover new possibilities for work and family life. These women's stories illustrate the complex interaction of environment, person, and culture in the creation of leaders and managers.

The birth date of a women manager placed her in a particular moment of history, with external events influential in determining new possibilities and options. For the younger women, many of the advances appreciated by the older women were taken for granted—the ability to attend the college of their choice, to vote, and to inherit property. One advance had occurred within their memory, the passage of the equal opportunity legislation, and women in their early thirties spoke of that law as crucial to their being hired.

In many respects the stories of the women in the first age cohort, in their late forties and older, were the most dramatic because of the extensive changes they experienced and witnessed. The enormity of world events surrounding their lives stimulated concomitant changes in family and work. Their childhoods had been disrupted by war and its aftermath. The routine events of childhood, school, and home disappeared, if only temporarily. The women of this age were clear that the revolutionary changes in the world had profoundly influenced choices in their lives. Independence and self-reliance had been forced upon them at an early age. Most were imbued with traditional values and yet saw these values challenged and in turmoil. They struggled, and they still struggle, with the meeting of old and new. The divorce rate of this age group has increased at the highest rate in Japanese history, as these women have expanded their lives while their husbands' lives narrowed over the years to a company life. These women helped coin the phrase "big garbage around the house" to refer to husbands who retire at fifty-five, an unheard-of attitude toward husbands for their mothers. The women managers in this sample did not follow the pattern of more frequent divorce, but their family lives were less traditional than those of their mothers.

The women in the middle age group, thirty-five to forty-five, are not as numerous in the ranks of management. Most had lives that were more settled and optimistic. These women are among those labeled by some social analysts as the most privileged women in the world. They were born at a time of economic recovery and enjoyed a degree of affluence hitherto unknown. The increasing wealth of society and the availability of labor-saving household appliances and consumer goods were theirs to enjoy. Most married at the "proper time" and felt they probably could work or stay at home as a homemaker and mother. They have leisure, and they have the means and time to participate in activities and hobbies at their pleasure while their husbands, the salarymen, work the long hours necessary for success.

Women in this age group thought they could choose to stay home when their children were born, and then also choose to return to work after their children were grown, but this has proven difficult and sometimes impossible. It is not easy to return to work and find a management position in one's thirties anywhere, but it is especially difficult in Japan.

The youngest age group of women managers (twenty-five to thirty-five) had different stories to tell. Many have lived outside of Japan either as students or as family dependents of businessmen and bureaucrats. They have grown up with television opening the world to them. Their lifestyles, their fashions, and their outlook are international. They are the ones who told me of their frustration on finding the equity they had experienced in the university to be nonexistent in the world outside, which they found still dominated by males.

These are also the women whom Dr. Sumioka treats for "June blues" when they come up against the "glass ceiling." Their expectations are different than those of their mothers. They are disappointed in Japanese men of their age, whom they consider "immature and spoiled." Most are impatient at the slow rate of change in the Japanese business world. Their greater awareness of possibilities in the wider world sometimes leads them to overestimate the changes in other countries, but that doesn't stop their push for change in their own lives. Among this group are many of the women who are leaving the corporate world and starting their own businesses in greater numbers, a development parallel to that in the United States, where the highest growth rate for new businesses is occurring in women-owned businesses.

Many of the younger women seem to confine their activities to their own age group and are isolated from older successful women. But they were eager to learn about Japanese women who are successful and who have combined success with satisfying lives and families. The focus groups in which we brought together successful women of different ages were very popular. Generally, the younger women are not willing to lead the life of the stereotypical Japanese *sarariman,* the Japanese word for salaryman, but they do want to work and use their talents professionally. They do not want to sacrifice their lives for either work or family; about that they are clear.

While individual lives and experiences of the women in each age group follow different patterns, common threads ran through the age cohorts, from young women to those in their nineties and all the ages in between. They are curious about the global world, excited about the expanding role of Japan, and concerned about whether they will be able to achieve their visions in what all agreed is still a male-dominant world.

Patterns

In addition to the era of birth, other patterns from early family life emerged from my research. The central patterns were mother's influence, family structure, birth order, travel and life outside Japan, and education. Not all the factors were present in each woman's experience, but at least one, and usually more, was present. The demographics of the sample and the distribution of life patterns among the women managers are discussed more fully in chapter 5. These factors are also compared with what is known about the lives of successful women leaders in the United States.

Contradictions are immediately apparent in the lives of successful women managers. Their lives don't fit the accepted pattern of Japanese society. Something in their lives or in their circumstances puts them slightly outside the normal cultural conditioning for young girls, factors that allow them to be less bound by the restrictive gender roles normally placed on female children. And yet each must find her place in that society in order to develop the self-esteem necessary for success. To achieve their goals, they must understand and fit into the society sufficiently to work and receive the support they need. The successful women were both outsiders and insiders—outsiders in order to transcend the rigid socialization, and insiders in order to be managers. Balancing the insider and outsider roles is difficult, particularly in Japan, where appropriateness and fitting in are valued.

Women who succeed as managers and become leaders in male-dominant societies worldwide are a minority, both exceptions and exceptional. They are marginal in the anthropological meaning of the term; that is, they do not conform to the average, to the expected roles and values of their culture. Marginal may apply to those at either end of the continuum, to the most successful and the least successful. In common practice, it is used with a negative connotation to refer to those who have fallen to the bottom of society. The term is used deliberately here for those who have managed to succeed, who are at the top end of the continuum, with the intent of emphasizing that these successful women do not fit accepted social norms. Another term, "liminal," referring to the point where one perception or condition blends into another, perhaps more accurately connotes this outsider and insider condition. This protocol is consistent with recent anthropological research.[4]

Each women manager has had to surmount the barrier of a socialization that restricts girls to the narrow range of activities deemed feminine, and that by implication restricts boys to a different narrow range of activities: women to the roles of wife and mother, and men to the role of breadwinner. As long as the strict delineation of roles is prevalent, transcending social pressures and expanding one's own life requires special circumstances and/or conscious effort by both men and women.

Mother's Influence

A pattern of formative influences shared by the majority of the women managers related to the role of their mothers. The mother's influence took different forms but was always a component of their life stories, not surprising since Japanese mothers are renowned for their nurturing and the identification of children with the mother. Takeo Doi considers this identification and indivisibility a key factor in understanding Japanese behavior, which he has termed *amae,* in his oft-quoted book *The Anatomy of Dependence.*[5]

All the women's stories contained a remembrance of a happy early childhood. At first this seemed surprising, especially for those born in the difficult war and postwar years. The description was consistent, though, with my observations of Japanese families. Babies and small children are rarely heard crying in Japan, and they usually seem happy and quiet. They are given attention and physical contact, and often are carried on their mother's back as she goes about her daily activities at home or in the subway. In Japan one can buy jackets that fit around both mother and baby. Sometimes a rather large child can be seen on the back of what looks like a tiny, frail grandmother, but the appearance of frailty can be deceiving in Japanese women. It is only later, at age four or five, depending upon the family, that children are strongly disciplined and socialized. These early experiences of contact, love, and approval must have been maintained even during the difficult war and postwar years and have contributed to the self-confidence of the women managers. That self-confidence is essential as the women refute social norms in their careers, while a strong sense of self helps alleviate the loneliness of being an outsider.

The mother's influence on these women took at least three different forms: as role model, as encourager, and as negative role model. Examples of each follow.

1. Mother as Role Model

One woman recalled in an interview:

> My family had a lumber business in Central Japan, and everyone worked in the business. My mother took care of the books for the business, and my brother and I were expected to watch out and care for ourselves at an early age and to clean up in the store as well. We played in the store before we started to school. I always assumed that a family shared business and house-hold tasks. Only later did I notice that not all my friends' families were that way, although we did have some friends whose families also had businesses.

A woman physician told of how the medical practice of her father and grandfather was in a clinic next door to their house. Her mother was the nurse and office manager. The whole family was involved in making the medical practice work. She knew all her life, she said, that she would become a doctor and heal people. These women all assumed that women worked.

Another of the managers interviewed had come from a medical family but had not been so closely connected to the practice. Her mother, however, had also been the office manager. All the children in the family had their jobs to maintain the home and office. As this woman explained,

> I remember having a small broom when I was probably four or five years old, before I went to school. My job was to sweep the front stoop and steps, and I remember distinctly the pride I took in having the corners of the doorway completely clean when my mother inspected the house. Later we were allowed to work in the clinic to clean and sweep and then still later taught to sterilize instruments. That was a great honor to have that task. I don't remember that there were different jobs for the boys and girls. The assigned job depended on the age and strength of the child.

She always thought that everyone in a family, including the women, worked at the family business as well as at home management. Her brother became a doctor, but she majored in home economics and eventually became one of the first female consumer affairs managers for one of the largest electronics companies. At some point she must have decided she didn't want to be a doctor. Both of her brothers became doctors. Neither of the sisters did so, but the difference in choice of careers for boys and girls was not the result of early chores and conditioning. The parents had been different than their neighbors and had sent the children to a private school in which girls and boys were taught to take care of themselves and do the house maintenance jobs as well as attain high scholastic achievement. Her mother had been the oldest in her family and had also helped in the surgery of her father; in fact, the medical practice they now operated had belonged to her mother's father. Her mother's brother had not been interested in the medical profession and is a well-known author. So, in effect, her mother had carried on the family tradition by marrying a doctor and running the clinic.

Ryo did not marry a doctor but instead married a financial manager who is now the president of his own company. In talking about her experiences she reflected, almost as if not having thought of it before, "Maybe I didn't have to be in the medical profession or marry a doctor because my brother became a doctor. I suppose my mother's taking over my grandparents' practice made it easier for my uncle to be a writer, and my mother was happy working with people in the clinic." Ryo's sister is a successful architect. The entire family have created lives outside the traditional pattern of family and gender. Their home was outside of Tokyo, and I asked if that made it easier than if they had been brought up in Tokyo. She said, "perhaps," but didn't feel the city was a key determinant. More important was the family history of service and healing for both boys and girls.

2. Mother as Encourager

Some mothers were intent on giving their daughters opportunities to do what they themselves had not been able to do. They had been forced to forgo chosen paths, because of family or social pressures, circumstances, or expediency. These mothers encouraged their daughters not necessarily to be what the mother had wanted to become but to persevere in whatever they wanted to do. A few of the women had not been aware of the subtle messages of encouragement from their mothers until they described them to me.

> My mother had been an excellent seamstress before she married my father. She had liked making clothes and seeing them make women happy. She gave it up when she married my father, but she often talked about her life when she was a seamstress and went to tea houses to meet with customers. She wanted me to have an education, even though I was a girl. She thought that would give me more choices when I grew up.

> My mother worked in a bank before she married my father, and while she never talked much about her early life, she very strongly encouraged me to continue my education, to have independence, to see the world and not be limited by marriage.

My mother always wanted to be a teacher, but she had to quit school and work so that her brothers could go to school. She always told me to work hard and stay in school so that I could teach and help other people.

3. Mother as Negative Model

Some women who described their life experiences had watched their mothers' lives and struggles and determined that their own lives would be better. They vowed not to endure what they felt their mothers had to endure. Some had seen their mothers helpless in the face of the father's death, illness, the war, absence, or unemployment. Others had witnessed a mother's subjugation to an unkind husband.

A prominent example of this pattern can be found in the life of Fusae Ichikawa, a pioneer who dedicated her life to fighting for women's rights and women's suffrage. Fusae Ichikawa was motivated by her mother's difficult life to try to change the lot of women. In her autobiography, Ichikawa said she determined to improve women's lot when she saw her father's cruelty to her mother, and the difficult lives of the other women around her.

Later, in a visit to the United States as a young adult, she saw that women's lives could be different than her mother's life and those of the other women she had witnessed in her childhood. She lived from 1892 to 1981, and in her lifetime, which extended through several distinct eras in Japan's history, was elected to the Parliament in the House of Councillors in five out of six attempts. She was elected when women were given the right to vote in the first postwar election. She was elected twice with the largest number of votes ever received by a single candidate in Japan. Her life was devoted to protecting the rights of women, giving women the vote and civil rights.

External events created difficult lives for the mothers of several women I interviewed. Two of the women whose stories were told earlier in this chapter promised themselves they would never be as desperate as their mothers had been after the war, with no skills and no preparation to make a living in the world. Each determined to prepare to take care of herself. They worked hard and persevered to receive a university degree and enter professions before marriage.

Shizue Kato, who introduced Margaret Sanger and birth control to Japan, describes in her autobiography how she was motivated by the coal miner's wives she saw in her childhood, who were exhausted by childbearing and hard work and died early. She saw her mother giving them help, and she later endured humiliation and censure to make birth control available to women in Japan. Her mother served as positive role model, while the examples of the difficult lives of the coal miner's wives gave further stimulus as negative models.

Birth Order and Family Position

The importance of this category proved to be the most surprising when it became apparent on analyzing the data how consistently it appeared. The majority of the successful women managers grew up without older brothers. They either had no older brothers, had no brothers, or had older brothers who, for varied reasons, were not regularly present in the women's early lives. Several who at first said they had older brothers later revealed complicated family patterns. In one, an older brother was twenty years older, the son of a first marriage, and she had not met him until she herself was twenty. Another woman's older brother died before she was born. The pattern was consistent and surprising. On reflection, however, it makes complete sense and will be explored in depth later.

Birth order emerged as a critical factor in the patterns of successful Japanese women managers, but with its own twist. The most prominent pattern was not being firstborn but it was the absence of older brothers in their early years. Some were firstborn, but not a majority.

Only a few of the women managers did not fit this pattern. The exceptions proved to be youngest children with both male and female older siblings. One described herself as "spoiled," with more freedom than her older siblings. One said she was "not conforming," which seemed to mean not forced with such vigor into the prescribed rules for girls. Each of these women had been almost forgotten, as one said, and allowed freedom to play and spend their time as they chose, rather than spending the majority of their time learning "girl" household tasks. One explained the situation by saying her parents already had a boy and another girl to fit the ideal or appropriate roles and therefore didn't need another example, so her behavior was not closely monitored. One said that her parents were over forty when her brother was born; when she was born three years later, they were so happy to be able to have a second child that both she and her brother were treated as treasures without distinction.

Birth order has been named as a success factor for both women and men in the United States, with women firstborns and only children having an edge in earlier studies of successful women. Frank Sulloway's recent book, *Born to Rebel*,[6] is based on an extensive statistical analysis of twenty-five thousand people, covering the globe and history. Motivation for the research grew out of his interest in Charles Darwin, whose unwillingness to accept establishment theories and the science of his time allowed him to venture out on the fringes, find his own answers, and develop his theory of evolution.

Sulloway's research on birth order builds on earlier research on family structure, postulating that the process of finding and creating a role for oneself in the early family of origin has lasting effects on the nature and permanent life stance of children. His research posits that younger children born into an existing family structure, with each member already having a defined role, tend to reject the established structure to create a satisfying place for themselves. This often translates later into the rebel, the creator of new theories, new kingdoms, and new ways of viewing the world. The research validated his thesis that birth order combined with the tendency to divergence explains younger children's predominance as leaders of rebellions. At this moment in history, Japanese woman managers are rebels in an establishment that allocates management to men; consequently, the managers who were youngest in the family fit Sulloway's definition of leaders of rebellions.

An absence of brothers in the women managers' early lives was the most striking pattern, true for 93 percent of the women managers interviewed. At first the significance of having no older brothers was not obvious, but when it began to appear so consistently among the women's stories, it was exciting to look at each new set of data to see if the women had older brothers. The importance of this absence of brothers in their early years became increasingly apparent as the interviews proceeded and was the most consistent pattern found among successful women managers. I began to hold my breath as I asked about each woman's birth family. For one reason or another, the majority had been without brothers, either because they had none or because the brothers were absent for a variety of reasons for significant portions of the women's early lives.

A few women had brothers who were much older or younger, so that they were not around during the early formative years. Three described older brothers who were frail and sickly. Two had brothers who had been sent to the country to get well. Several were the oldest in large families, so they had lived some years without brothers and in their older status were not required to be subject to the boys in the family. For others, the family consisted of only girls.

Without older brothers, the women had not been consistently restricted to "girls' roles" in relation to "boys' roles." The absence of older brothers allowed them to escape the constant subtle socialization and comparisons of male and female gender roles and the strict delineation between boys' and girls' roles and tasks in the home. In a society with strict hierarchies, roles, status, and rules are transmitted most powerfully in early childhood relationships. The significance of an absence of brothers in the early family lives of the women managers for the development of leadership capabilities and motivation is fascinating. How this background affects their lives will be described in their words and the implications explored in subsequent sections.

Early studies of achieving women in the United States found the dominant mode to be only or oldest child. While the Japanese women talked about having been allowed to do things usually reserved for boys, the majority were not "only child." They were girls without older brothers in their formative years.

One such woman remembered with great pleasure flying kites with her father, an activity usually limited to fathers and sons in Japan. Her family had consisted of two girls, followed by a long interval before her brother was born when she was almost eight. She recalled:

> I remember spending what seemed like all day Sunday flying kites with my father. The kites became ever more elaborate, and I learned to be quite expert at flying them. It was so exciting, and I remember the feeling of happy exhaustion coming home holding my father's hand and telling my mother about my feats with the kite.

Another spoke fondly about fishing with her father.

Several, whose fathers had worked at home, had followed them around, as recalled by a woman whose father was a doctor and another whose father was a craftsman. This pattern was seen in the lives of a large number of the women. They had not been limited to "girl" tasks or "girl" play, either because they had no brothers, their brothers were much younger, or for some reason were not present in the girls' lives. One woman had a brother who was twelve years older than she and already away at school when she was born, so she didn't see him on a daily basis.

Sumi had an older brother, a younger brother, and two younger sisters. Both of her brothers were frail, whereas she was strong, robust, and healthy. She recalled:

> People were always saying, what a shame that I wasn't a boy because I was the strong, healthy one. I also was talkative and stood up for myself. My grandfather, whose visits were a big occasion, would often say to me, "what a shame that you aren't a boy." My mother would find a chance to whisper in my ear when this happened, which it did often, that I was just right and it was wonderful that I am a girl.
>
> I used to stand up to my grandfather when he told me I was bad, or told us a story that I thought was not right. He said I was not a proper girl and would never find a husband. I was too strong. My mother's whispered reassurances are probably why it didn't destroy my spirit. Even though she didn't stand up for me publicly, she let me know that it was all right for me to be as I was. When I was about eleven or twelve, mother told me that when she had my brother to continue the family line, her father had really paid attention to her for the first time in her life. My mother had been the third child in a family of eight, with two older brothers. My grandfather had lavished all his attention on her brothers from a concubine and had paid no attention to her as a child, and she had longed for his love and attention. But she said she was glad I was a girl and glad I was able to speak up for myself.

The support and silent approval from her mother had been crucial for Sumi to continue to be strong, and to live with her grandfather's criticism. Her father had been considered a "modern boy" when he married her mother, and although he also was supportive of Sumi's speaking out, he often was absent. A childless neighbor couple had adored her, and when the grandfather was expected to visit, her mother often suggested that Sumi visit the neighbors, who gave her complete approval.

Before the war, Sumi's father had been a Mitsubishi executive, and her early years were spent in China, free from the intense social pressure of family and society and with no one to correct her speaking out. It was natural that she should also go away to the university and eventually marry a non-Japanese man. She hadn't consciously thought about whether or not to marry a Japanese man, but having a foreign husband was quite natural for her. She is now a writer and television producer. The hurt of those long-ago days was transformed into creativity and success, but when she recalled her grandfather's criticism of forty years ago and the earlier comments that she should have been a boy, her voice sounded sad and a shadow passed over her face.

Kiyoko, another general manager, also had an older brother who was frail and sickly in childhood. He had gone frequently to stay with grandparents in the country because the "air was fresher and better for recovering from ill health." His absences left her without male comparisons or rivalry, not necessarily from her own parents, who held progressive views, but from other relatives and friends.

Yuki's only brother was born when she was three, and she remembers railing at her mother about the unfair privileges her brother received. When she learned about the patterns of successful women without older brothers, she agreed that she probably would not have noticed the unequal privileges if he had been the elder. Each of the women had not been discouraged in her childhood from activities normally reserved for boys, and had in fact often been encouraged to be active and accomplished in doing what they wished and engaging in activities like kite making, fishing, and playing ball. One said that girls' day was only one day of the year, but the games they played were all year long, indicating their balancing influence on her self-image.

Socialization conveying gender messages is transmitted to children beginning at birth. First in their own family and later by a broader social milieu, actions, words, approval of desired behavior, and disapproval for undesirable behavior teach children their "proper" behavior. The phrases "good wife, wise mother" (*ryosei kenbo*) and "self-sacrifice" are powerful components of the early gender messages transmitted to Japanese girls. This ideal for the appropriate female gender role is illustrated by Haru Reischauer's description of a "proper" woman in late nineteenth-century Japan. Her book about her own

Japanese and American heritage describes her paternal grandmother, Masako, whose influence was important for the family and future generations.

> As a proper wife of a samurai, Masako took complete control not only of running the large household but also of caring for the children. Matsukata (grandfather) was the finance minister of Japan and Masako the finance minister of the Matsukata family. Masako was a remarkable person in her own right. She was the eldest daughter of one of the highest-ranking samurai of Satsuma. Despite all the work of running this large household Masako found time to be a companion to her husband, taking daily morning walks with him.
>
> For all her outstanding qualities as a household manager and wife, Masako is best remembered as having been a wonderful mother. She had been raised in the strict samurai code of regarding jealousy as the worst of all feminine vices, and she lavished on the children of her husband's concubines the same love and care she gave her own children. Yet she was a strict mother, though she exercised her discipline in a gentle way, never scolding or showing anger. In accordance with samurai custom, she was harder on the girls than on the boys. She had them perform menial jobs, such as polishing the floors of the long wooden hallways with bags of rice bran or cleaning out toilets, all to help prepare them to become good housewives.
>
> The children all felt closer to Masako than to their father. Affairs of state naturally took him away a great deal, and as is still common among urban Japanese families, the mother was very much the center of the family.[7]

While this ideal may not be the present operative model, vestiges of this ideal woman still influence the socialization of girls in Japan. A "good" Japanese wife in the nineteenth century was strong, as she is today. She was a good manager of the home, and a companion and listener for her husband when he wished her company, but never demanding, and never jealous of her husband's activities. Reinforcing these criteria and supporting the socialization of women was the fact that from the thirteenth to the nineteenth century women were not allowed to divorce their husbands, while men could easily divorce their wives for any of seven reasons contained in Japanese codes influenced by Confucianism and handed down from the eighth century. Valid reasons for a man to divorce his wife included disobedience, sterility, lewdness, jealousy, leprosy or other serious illness, stealing, and talking disrespectfully.

With the ease of divorce under these criteria, the divorce rate was higher in the nineteenth century than today, about 2.8 per 1,000, compared with the current rate of 1.6 per 1,000 that is worrisome to the government. A civil code of 1898 allowed Japanese women for the first time to seek a divorce for three reasons—cruelty, desertion, or serious misconduct. A husband's adultery was not grounds for divorce, even though a wife's infidelity might be. Some men today might wish for a return of the nineteenth-century grounds for divorce.

Women's legal rights were changed with Japan's 1946 constitution. Divorce, inheritance, and property rights were made more equitable for women. Ideals for gender role behavior do not change as quickly, though. Attitudes about proper behavior for women and men are so deeply embedded in family relationships, child-rearing practices, and education that only a conscious effort to increase awareness, combined with strong social pressures, can bring change.

This chapter has explored factors in the early lives of Japanese women managers that contributed to their success. External events that required new responses, the influence of the mother, birth order, and the absence of brothers in these women's early lives were important. Each of the successful managers had one or more of these conditions in their lives, allowing them to transcend socially prescribed rules of "proper behavior" for girls. Of these factors, the absence of brothers was the most consistently present. Without brothers, the women had been encouraged to be more active and to do things that women with brothers generally had not done. Since my research focused on successful women, it is not possible to say what percentage of women who do not succeed as managers have older brothers. However, this pattern found in the majority of the successful women is striking.

This chapter began by noting that the conditions contributing to success began with birth and early childhood experiences. Actually, success factors can be traced back even further to creation myths, beliefs about how the world began, and the historical and prehistorical roots of masculine and feminine orientation and gender roles. Successful women are inhabitants of a place in time, and they are members of a broader culture with roots in antiquity. The influence of historical roots on the definition of gender roles, dominance, and status is explored in the next chapter, which compares the historical evolution in Japan and America.

3

Sex Roles, Creation Myths, and Worldview

Japanese and Western Historical Perspectives

In primeval times, women were one with the sun and truth of all-being. Now we are like pale-faced moons who depend on others and reflect their light.

Raicho Hiratsuka, feminist literary circle,
SEITO journal, *Blue Stockings*, 1911

Beginning my research on women in management, I realized it was necessary to learn more Japanese history in order to understand women's roles and the evolution of today's women managers. History as bestowed to each generation constructs, and is a construct of, a society's values, and in turn becomes a tool to maintain the status quo. Roles of women and men in all cultures are socially constructed and have antecedents in historical roots.

Japan's Historical Roots

History, culture learning, and research data come from unexpected sources and in a variety of forms. Arriving in Japan, I was indeed blessed to be given a wonderful interpreter of Japanese culture, who appeared magically in the first week of my Tokyo sojourn. This fairy godmother was an amazing woman in her eighties who speaks English as an American, Japanese as a local, and moves easily between Japanese and Western culture.

An early lesson that proved invaluable came during one of my first Japanese meals. When served my rice, I looked for the soy sauce that is ever-present in American Asian restaurants. She said very quietly, "Japanese do not put anything on their rice. Japanese appreciate the delicate flavor of the rice, and children learn at an early age that it is to be savored and not altered with additions." I did learn to savor the delicate and varied tastes of rice and at least did not make that particular cultural faux pas among other Japanese. She saved me from other embarrassing situations as I checked with her when I had questions.

Later she elaborated on the reasons for the difference between the Chinese mode of eating rice, putting flavorings and additions in and on their rice, and the Japanese emphasis on unadorned rice. The Japanese custom dated back to ancient times.[1] After rice was introduced from China and became the staple and sometimes the only food available, it was highly valued, honored, and savored in its delicate natural variations. The war in the 1940s, she added, had reinforced the value of rice, as it was again often the only food available in the latter days of wartime and recovery, when everything was scarce and rationed.

From those simple but important early experiences, my learning about the omnipresence of tradition and history in Japan grew. Emiko Ohnuki-Tierney's book *Rice as Self*[2] contends that rice represents the Japanese self as that self undergoes various historical changes. Rice remains immutable while not only its meaning but its materiality has changed. Learning the symbolism of rice was relevant to understanding the emotions attached to trade discussions when Japanese rice appears threatened. National identity is intertwined with rice, and the farm lobby's power is augmented by the emotionality stimulated for all Japanese by any perceived threat to national self-sufficiency. A sense of history and origins infuses current Japanese life and culture and is necessary to understand women in management today. While history and legend may be varied to suit the purposes of the user, the basic framework is shared throughout the society.

In Japan, history is particularly important not only because the past influences the present but also because the Japanese, in common with other Asian nations and in contrast to Americans, carry a deep sense of history. References to history are routinely used to explain contemporary events not only by scholars but in everyday conversation. Even the most resistant of the younger generation in Japan are constantly made aware of their history. The official calendar in Japan is based on the empires of Japan's history. Each time the current date is written, the name of the empire is evoked.

The current period is called *Heisei,* the era of Emperor Akihito, and dates from the death of his father, Emperor Hirohito, in 1989. Emperor Hirohito's era, the *Showa* era, dated from 1926 to 1989. The date reminds one of the era of Japanese history. In order to translate a particular date into an international document or compare dates in international documents, there is a reminder of where it fits in world history. For instance, the year 1941 would be written in Japanese as *Showa* 16, 16 years after the beginning of Hirohito's reign. In this way Japanese people are constantly reminded of their history, of who was emperor in the time period, and how Japanese history relates to that time period for the rest of the world.

While the Western dating system relates to a historical event, the birth of Christ, and reminds us that we are basically a Judeo-Christian civilization, that fact is not often made explicit. Only rarely is "anno Domini" written after the year, and we don't need to translate to another date because our dating system is shared with the rest of the English-speaking world. The Japanese are reminded each time they date something of the names of their empires, and that they are unique and different from the rest of the world. The dating system is still another element that emphasizes the nation's distinctness and reinforces the widely held belief in a unique, homogeneous society.

Another example of historical present can be found in the numbering system for buildings in Tokyo. Buildings were numbered by the period in which they were built, making the system absolutely unintelligible to foreigners. In a city noted for its efficiency and productivity, this instance of history taking precedence over efficiency often brings a smile, even as it provokes intense frustration. In a similar fashion, Japanese history contributes to understanding otherwise incomprehensible paradoxes facing women managers in Japan today, as well as management styles, business, and organizational culture.

The earliest records of Japanese history come from a third-century Chinese document, *Gishi Waijin Den*. That document described Japan as a tribal society, living by agriculture and fishing, with rice introduced to Japan from China in the second or third century B.C. The tribes were said to have distinct class divisions and were led by both male and female chiefs with religious status.

Female Heroes, Leaders, and Gods

Evidence of prehistoric society in Japan indicates that, like most prehistoric societies, it was probably matriarchal. One tribal group, ruled by Queen Himiko, appeared to have authority over the other tribes. The country itself was called the "queen's country" by the Chinese, giving credence to the concept of a nonpatriarchal society, with women rulers.

The supreme god in Japan's creation myth is the sun goddess, Amaterasu, whose full name is Amaterasu Omikami, or Great Heaven Shining Mother. Japan is one of the few cultures for whom the Sun is female. She is the ancestor of all Japanese people, and from her the imperial household is said to descend in an unbroken line. The Japanese creation story has Amaterasu Omikami sending her grandson to populate the land of plentiful reed-covered plains. She sent with him the three sacred treasures—mirror, sword, and cashew-shaped jewels—the sacred symbols of the emperor.[3] As Motoori Norinaga proclaimed,

The special dispensation of our Imperial Land means that ours is the native land of the Heaven-Shining Goddess who casts her light over all countries in the four seas . . . making our country the source and fountainhead of all other countries, and in all matters excels all others. Our country's Imperial Line, which casts its light over this world, represents the descendants of the sky-shining goddess.[4]

In contrast, the Western world has no extant female gods to consciously or unconsciously affirm women's power and suitability for leadership. The major elements in both the Islamic and the Hebrew/Christian creation stories are male, with the female subordinate and created from the male. Saint Thomas Aquinas in the thirteenth century avowed, "As regards the individual nature, woman is defective and misbegotten"[5] and an orthodox Hebrew prayer to be recited daily says, "Blessed art Thou O Lord our God, King of the universe, who hast not made me a heathen; . . . a slave; . . . or a woman.[6] Only recently have feminist scholars reexamined biblical traditions and found ancient documents that reveal women spiritual leaders in the Judeo-Christian tradition. These feminist findings are still controversial and are not accepted by many traditional religious bodies. While Native American legends and creation myths include a feminine role, they have not yet become a firm part of America's national cultural heritage.

Japan's first official histories, *Kojiki, Record of Ancient Matters*, a.d. 710, and the *Nihongi, Chronicle of Japan*, a.d. 720, introduce the Empress Jingü, who is thought to be a composite of several real-life women rulers and mythological shamans embodying the female leadership in Japan's past. Women priests were influential. The temple at Ise is still honored as the temple of the supreme goddess, *Amaterasu*, the ancestor of the emperor line, and her temple designated for the emperor's family.

Eight women emperors, or *tennö*, have reigned in Japan in recorded history, compiling a total of ten reigns, two having reigned twice. One empress successfully led her troops into battle against Korea at a very difficult time in Japanese history when wars seemed constant. The Empress Jitö is credited with having shaped Japan's history in the seventh century. First as a wife, she dedicated her loyalties to her husband/uncle against her emperor father. Then she reigned in succession, as empress and partner in joint rule, as empress dowager for her son, as the forty-first *tennö* herself, Empress Jitö, and finally as ruling ex-sovereign, *dajö-tennö*, for her young grandson. This precedent of succession that she established was followed by many of the powerful male emperors.

Prehistoric Japan was also most probably a matrilineal society, like most early societies before the role of the male in procreation was fully understood. Property rights were transmitted from mother to daughter. Husbands either went to live and work on the farm of their wives or lived in a separate male community and visited regularly. This gradually changed as the influence of Buddhism and Confucianism from China and Korea infiltrated the islands, beginning in the sixth century. The change from matrilineal to patrilineal was gradual and discontinuous, with spiritual and secular power remaining in the earlier Shinto goddesses and priestesses alongside the growing male hierarchy for several hundred years. The Goddess of Creation, Amaterasu Omikami, survived as the ancestor of all Japanese, as did some of the other goddesses. Vestiges of the old system of matrilineality can be seen in the custom of *yoshi,* adopting a daughter's husband who takes his wife's family name and family succession.

In the West, the Neolithic goddess cultures were obliterated much earlier in European prehistory. Marija Gimbuta's research places the Neolithic matrifocal society from 6000 B.C.E. (before the common era) to 2000 B.C.E.[7] The collective societal memory of feminine goddesses had been buried and denied in Western culture until archaeological diggings in the twentieth century began to unearth a matrifocal society and re-create history.[8]

In contrast to the historical record of women in Japan, some powerful women in Europe were labeled witches and agents of the devil in the fourteenth to seventeenth centuries and later in America. Considered dangerous, many women were sought out and burned at the stake. In the Puritan culture of Massachusetts, they were considered agents of the devil and subjects of the Salem witchhunts.[9] Later the frontier ethos and the cowboy/pioneer/settler tradition defined women's place as home and hearth, bearing children and guarding the family home, required to be strong and resourceful. But no matter how strong, women were secondary, dependent on men and considered their property. In the more recent Tokugawa period in Japan (seventeenth to nineteenth centuries), commoners, as opposed to samurai families and aristocracy, had less rigid gender divisions, with wives working the family farms and shops, and husbands as well as other relatives engaged in child care and housework.

History as Bestowed

Growing up in the United States, it is easy to escape a sense of the nation's history as a whole. United States history consists of regional histories. The history of the American continent told most commonly in United States history books dates from the coming of Europeans to the East Coast of the continent. The Pilgrims and the Puritans are commonly viewed as the progenitors of America. While evidence of early human populations in North America is being discovered on both coasts, and has been shown by carbon dating to be from more than 40,000 years b.c.e. their existence has not routinely been taught as American history. The major historical events recounted by all schoolchildren are the voyages of the Pilgrims to escape religious persecution; the war against the British to gain independence in 1776; the Civil War, which freed the slaves and preserved the Union in 1865; the conquering of the Indians; and the two world wars, which brought the United States abruptly into the greater world scene.

As a native of California, I most thoroughly learned a history that focused on the western region: the Spanish conquistadors and their scouts, the Catholic priests who established missions from Mexico to northern California. Mission visits were routine for all history classes. The Pilgrims, the lives of the founding fathers, and the Civil War were a continent away. Later, living in Hawaii, I discovered a Polynesian historical heritage influenced by British and American settlers and missionaries. In the Pacific Northwest, French fur trading and explorer heritage is combined with stories of the brave settlers traversing the Oregon Trail. These histories provide a different heritage for each region. A common element in American history is a yearning for the wide-open spaces of the vast continent with unlimited resources and a frontier, pioneer spirit.

It is interesting to compare the stories of the early histories of Japan and the United States. All national histories seem to begin at a point that is convenient for the tellers of history and the times in which they live. Japan's national identity has been linked closely to a myth of homogeneity, so that the diversity of early settlers was generally ignored in historical accounts. Modern historians are resurrecting some of that diversity, recognizing that transmigration and settlements in Japan came from the north, south, east, and west. The recognized indigenous people in Japan, the Ainu, are a dwindling group in modern times, but knowledge of the Ainu civilization is only now being included in Japanese history.

Likewise, the United States had not included the civilizations of its earlier inhabitants in traditional histories, preferring to begin historical accounts with the arrival of European settlers and explorers rather than the civilizations of the American First Peoples. The last decades of the twentieth century have brought a recognition of a much older historical base in the United States and an attempt to integrate this base into our heritage. In the strong urge to start afresh in the New World, early settlers erased the collective memories of other civilizations that might have antedated their arrival and wrote a history beginning with themselves.

Because of its vast spaces, the American culture could more easily tolerate and even honor diversity within a shared framework of democracy. As communication and travel became easier, it would have been impossible to maintain a myth of homogeneity. Integration of new people and ideas no longer occurred through conquering territory but through settlements, home-steading, and cultivation. The melting pot image could not hide the diversity as it became more obvious and eventually part of the American cultural symbol. Japan's size, comparable to that of the state of California, and its concentration of population in discrete areas made it easier to construct and maintain a myth of homogeneity, which is only now being deconstructed.

Japanese analysts of America seem always to be struggling to understand and define a unitary identity comparable to their own. To my surprise, I found that the America identified by Japanese usually is that of the eastern seaboard, although in a recent Japanese university entrance exam on American history that asked where the first American colonies were located, several students, in all seriousness, identified "Beverly Hills," at least recognizing a western part of the United States.[10]

The Frontier Mythology

Until recently, American popular culture has glorified the Old West, with its pioneers and cowboys, and has viewed the Indians as savages. The frontier spirit may be America's strongest historical perspective with its heroes the conquerors of territory and people as embodied in John Wayne films. The vision was of an unending land to the West to be conquered, as expressed in the phrase "Go west, young man." Women must still recover from the popularization of that model. The difference between the "masculine" model of conquering nature and a "feminine" model of harmonizing with nature is profound.

Western tradition has a few heroic women—Cleopatra, Joan of Arc, the first-century British queen Boadicea, Elizabeth I, Catherine the Great, and the biblical Hebrew prophetess Deborah, who presided over a peaceful forty years. But none are from the United States, where to this day there has not been a woman president although we may be getting close. In the world of industry, where power is now seen to lie, there have never been more than one or two women heading Fortune 500 companies, the largest major corporations in the United States.

Myths unify nations and societies, and both the United States and Japan are in the process of redefining and integrating disparate myths. Words, forming the myths of a society, both reflect and create the culture, as nations evolve and change. The telling of a nation's history and historical perspectives play importantly as the "received truths" of each generation. A scenario for understanding the creation and maintenance of patriarchy in the Western world has been described by Gerda Lerner:

Men and women live on a stage on which they act out their assigned roles, equal in importance. The play cannot go on without both kinds of performers. Neither of them contributes more or less to the whole; neither is marginal or dispensable. But the stage set is conceived, painted, defined by men. Men have written the play, have directed the show, interpreted the meanings of the action. They have assigned themselves the most interesting, most heroic parts, giving women the supporting roles.[11]

Culture is the medium in which roles are defined and assigned to men and women. In the Japanese memory bank, there is more recent knowledge of women as leaders, as heroes, and as rulers than in the American. We do not have that historical affirmation of women and power in the United States. The significance of historical and mythical women leaders has the potential for both positive and negative impact for today's Japanese women.

The knowledge of women heroes allows a glimmer of affirmation for the legitimacy of feminine power. When the highest god/creator is feminine, defining power exclusively as the domain of males becomes more equivocal and must be guarded and defended forcefully. Women's power must be denied with greater fervor, especially if individual women succeed in contradicting the established patriarchal social order. Women who aspire to leadership in a society that acts with a patriarchal script may encounter very negative reactions. These contradictions of the historical and spiritual knowledge of feminine power with present-day male dominance create strange paradoxes and customs, while the gleam of feminine possibility hides in the dimmest recesses of the memory bank for both men and women. Just as in modern Western organizational theory, more of the "feminine" values were embraced even though the early practitioners were mainly male.

In a recent book, Leonard Shlain postulates that a feminine way of seeing the world is based on images, whereas the masculine way is based on language.[12] He expounds a controversial theory, that the Jewish nation invented the alphabet as a means to separate themselves from the goddess cultures of the day, to unify and bring together a "rag-tag group of ex-slaves" into a nation. The common identity they espoused was monotheistic and patriarchal, to differentiate it from the multiple goddesses and gods worshiped by the Greeks and Romans. In Shlain's theory, the alphabet and writing created a unique, common masculine identity supporting a disavowal of the goddess culture from which the Jewish nation emerged.

Following this line of reasoning, an interesting proposition would be that the Japanese, Chinese, and Korean nations, in retaining iconographic writing, with imagic thought, may not have had to eliminate the goddess culture so completely. While the logic of the alphabet has been the basis of scientific advances, iconographic thinking and perception are recognized as essential to the new sciences, information technology, and creative innovations, perhaps auguring a latter-day recognition and valuing of the feminine. Confucianism, with its hierarchical male dominance, was a later import to Japan. Today's forceful denial of women and the feminine in management may be related to their dimly remembered power.

Borrowing and Adapting, Conquering and Being Conquered

Japan has always followed an "accretionary approach." Carefully selecting and importing other cultures all the while carefully leaving Japanese culture unaffected. Viewed positively, the accretionary approach accepts foreign culture and absorbs it, while preserving the principal Japanese identity. Viewed negatively, it includes no true appreciation of foreign culture.[13]

Japan's long tradition of borrowing the best from other cultures and civilizations and adapting the imports in very Japanese modes is relevant to understanding the country today. The ideas, technology, religions, materials, and resources of other civilizations were all fair game. Many of the forms and infrastructure of early Japan were borrowed from China, the most advanced civilization of ancient times. China's religion, arts, food, and technology were adapted to the needs of Japan's geography, climate, and people. Each became uniquely Japanese, sometimes more beautiful and complex than the original, with its foreign origins submerged and barely recognizable. Japanese art is distinguishable from Chinese and Korean art, but common roots are often evident.

The Japanese writing system, *kanji*, was adapted to the Japanese language from the Chinese as an exclusive male prerogative. Women created a simplified system based on women's language, which made writing easier than the unwieldy iconography of the Chinese writing system awkwardly adapted to the Japanese. One of the world's first novels, *The Tale of Genji*, a story of court life written about A.D. 1000, was the work of a woman, Lady Murasaki (Murasaki Shikibu).[14] It is a rich source of information about life in this era. While men were writing *monogatori,* or stories, as the *Tale of Genji* was, they tended to fall into a prescribed style with which all men were familiar. Women's writings were less restricted and could be more creative. Women artists and writers were limited to the elite, wealthy class, who had enough leisure time to allow learning to write and create art, but it was also true that only wealthy men had the leisure to develop writing competencies.

Over the centuries, Korea was also a source of ideas, technology, and people. Korean ceramics were highly valued, imitated, and adapted for the Japanese people and their soil. Korean artists were brought to Japan to practice their arts and teach Japanese artists, creating a unique Japanese ceramic style. From these centuries of borrowing and adapting, it is not surprising that in the present day the Japanese have well-honed skills for adapting and improving on the technology and philosophy of other countries. Such skills have served the Japanese well as they developed their electronic and automobile industries with increasingly sophisticated manufacturing processes. Higher-technology industries have evolved, and while there is concern now about creativity and innovation in Japan, the skills of adapting and improving also contribute to innovation.

The early borrowing and adapting often occurred by force as neighboring countries waged wars of conquest for scarce resources in the region. The boundaries with China, Japan, and Korea have fluctuated over the centuries as one or the other of the three was victorious. Historians have described the phenomenon as waves of mounted invaders going in both directions from at least the second and third centuries. Large mounds in the Korean tradition are found in the western areas of Japan, indicating long-term residence and concentration of wealth and power.[15] In the other direction, Korean craftsmen, whose descendants still remain, were taken as prisoners in conquests by Japan and brought forcibly to teach their crafts.

Raiding each other's countries by legitimate or illegitimate forces continued into the twentieth century. Over centuries of invasions and counterinvasions, an identity with the cultures and customs of their neighbors developed, along with deep suspicions. The societal forms that developed to survive and adapt in this world were feudal, maintained by a military aristocracy. The successful warlords reigned and extracted tribute from the countryside and the conquered, rewarding their soldiers to keep the loyalty of the samurai and warrior class. Class roles and boundaries became highly developed, as a tool to maintain order. Confucian doctrine, with its formal rules, was a useful import to support the validity of a strict hierarchical society and rigidly defined classes.

The Heritage of Feudalism

In Japan the Tokugawa era, beginning in 1600, is noted for ending the nation's internal and external wars. As in feudal Europe, the general population, exhausted from wars, appreciated the absence of war when one lord successfully conquered the smaller fiefdoms and imposed an armed truce. People gave obedience, sometimes willingly, sometimes reluctantly, to the most powerful warlords. Feudal Asia was roughly parallel in time to feudal Europe, but the Asian form of feudalism was more complex and highly evolved, and it continued into the nineteenth century, deriving structure from the sophisticated and hierarchical Chinese civilization.

After conquering most of Japan, Tokugawa successfully created national government structures, sealed the nation's borders, and banished foreigners to prevent foreign colonization of the country by either trade, conquest, or the Christian religion. The only exception was a small community of Dutch traders confined to the tiny island adjacent to Nagasaki. During the Tokugawa era, the samurai lifestyle required the wives and families of regional samurai leaders, or *daimyo*, to remain as permanent hostages in the capitol, Edo (Tokyo), while the men returned in alternate years to their estates to bring back tribute (*Sankin kotai*). These prolonged absences meant that samurai wives were single-handedly responsible for home and family affairs for the largest portion of the time, but samurai wives were not considered leaders or even valuable workers. The influential role of mothers has always been recognized, but mothers have remained subordinate in the power structure.

Commoners during the Tokugawa era, on the other hand, had a much less gendered division of labor. The family business, farm or merchant, was the focus of life, and both men and women participated in productive and reproductive work as it was done in and for the household. Recent writing indicates that men participated in household labor and that women certainly participated in the productive work of farming, weaving, and selling merchandise.[16]

The reopening of Japan and the ending of the Tokugawa era isolation from the Western world came more than two hundred years later, in 1858. The arrival of Admiral Perry's "black ships" *(kurofune),* with their display and use of foreign armed might and technology, forced the opening of Japan's borders to the outside world. This traumatic event was indelibly etched in the national psyche. Some current analysts attribute Japan's attempt to create a twentieth-century empire, the East Asian Co-Prosperity Sphere, in part to memories from that earlier event and a determination not to be invaded, again either intellectually or physically.[17] The Western world's forced entry in the nineteenth century, combined with internal pressures toward change, precipitated the beginning of the Meiji era in 1868. The emperor was returned to power, enthroned in Tokyo, and his role was used by the successful junta to consolidate power. Japan leapfrogged across centuries to advance successfully into the industrial age as it responded to the crisis of identity wrought by the forced entry of foreigners, with their superior technology and power.

The Meiji era originally brought an opening of women's horizons and great hope for bettering the quality of women's lives, as well as the lives of the whole population. Recognizing the need for haste to match the technology and power of the West, of which they had been unaware, and which had now been forced upon the country, all Japanese, including women, were encouraged to contribute to the development of Japan. Women were asked to participate in bringing science, technology, and education to the nation.[18]

This opening for women's expanding roles was short-lived as Japan moved in a different direction to develop and consolidate its national life at the beginning of the twentieth century. Women once again were given supportive roles as keepers of the home and were not encouraged to participate in intellectual, political, or external affairs. In fact, they were pressured to stay home, out of public life, and to retreat from education, professions, and fields they had been encouraged to enter at the dawn of the Meiji era.[19]

Hierarchies, Status, and Religion

Some Japanese observers comment that Japan is still a feudal society but that now the lords are the corporations. Indeed, it is striking to visit an old cemetery, as I did in the hilltop monastery city of Koyasan, and see the evolution from family graveyard plots, especially for samurai and elite families, to the corporation plots, where the largest recent monuments carry the names of corporations with the corporate elite. It is considered an honor to be buried in the corporate grave site, rather than in the family site, at least for some. For others, the family and corporate site are the same.

Temples and shrines in Japan provide an opportunity to observe some of the modern-day practices that have evolved from the multiple roots of Shinto, Confucianism, and Buddhism. When the Japanese are surveyed about their religion, the total choices selected are twice as large as the population sampled, with the majority of Japanese declaring more than one religion. It is said that Confucianism pervades Japanese ethical values, Buddhism is the religion for death and funerals, Shinto for marriage. All three religions tend to emphasize universal relationships—to nature and to other people, with the universe, with the group, with family. Shinto is a religion of the continuity of life and nature in the universe, the veneration of ancestors linking past and present; Buddhism provides a more structured framework for relationship to the universe, all living creatures, and a possible afterlife; and Confucianism has specifically defined hierarchies for family and national life, the deference of subject to ruler, child to parent, wife to husband, and female to male.

Western religions, in contrast, postulate a personal one-to-one relationship with god and emphasize the individual, in whom the forces of good and evil battle for dominance. Spiritual life in Western religions may be pursued in a group, but in the final analysis it focuses on each person's responsibility for finding individual salvation.

Japan provided an opportunity to experience the profound difference in worldview each perspective fosters, to realize the implications of a Japanese tendency to look to the group for identity and meaning, whereas Western socialization first encourages an individual identity and subsequently encourages connection with the group. Each perspective is the result of complex interactions supported by culture, religion, and family. Experiencing the subtle difference of the two perspectives on daily decisions and actions was an important part of my learning in Japan.

Group orientation is often expounded as the most important aspect differentiating Asian culture. The group versus individual stereotypes are just that, stereotypes, that serve as a beginning observation. Seen on a continuum from individual to group, Eastern and Western orientations *tend* toward different poles, but the lines are not straight, and the global economy, communication, and changing lifestyles have narrowed the distance.

The nature of the land and geography, historical necessity and preference, as well as religion fostered the group orientation in Japan. Less than 15 percent of Japan's land is arable, with steep volcanic mountains and canyons to the sea. Although richly blessed with beautiful scenery of mountains and ocean vistas, the country is not rich in resources. The paucity of land requires intense cultivation and group collaboration to survive. Historically, agriculture developed later in Japan as wetlands rice was introduced from the southern part of China in the first and second centuries. Temperate climates, abundant rain, hard work, collaboration, and development of skills made Japan a productive agricultural country in spite of its minimal resources.

Later these attributes of hard work, ingenuity, and group cooperation applied to agriculture in order to survive seemed naturally adapted to industrial productivity. Successful productivity in Japan has always used group cooperation to a degree unknown in the Western world. Cooperation, one form of which is the well-known industrial *keiretsu,* continues to keep Japan productive today. The cooperative form that developed over centuries of history is natural to the Japanese culture, whereas it must be learned and superimposed in modern Western society, whose historical emphasis was on the individual conquering the world, the wilderness, nature, and other enemies. The close relationships in Japan extended to politicians, bureaucrats, and industrialists, but they excluded women. This system has been productive for the economy but not without increasingly obvious dangers. Corruption crises in government and businesses illuminate the dark side of such close collaboration and the danger of entrenched, unquestioned power relationships and exclusivity.

The hierarchical nature of society, adherence to precise rules, and role definitions for the players are often cited by women as among their most important barriers to leadership and management. The structure is also contradictory to the need for creativity and innovation in Japanese industry. While group cohesiveness, cooperation, discipline, and a well-defined and carefully adhered-to structure have contributed to Japan's productivity, they also provide powerful resistance to change even in the face of crisis.

Women and men interviewed about prevailing gender attitudes often blamed Confucianism for the male dominance and rigidity of Japanese society. Confucianism, with its precise definitions of the distribution of power, of roles, of women subordinate to men, is an understandable target. However, with additional probing, people may blame feudal history. Confucian doctrine is seen as just another tool used to perpetuate the dominant status of the role played by men. Religions are adapted to the needs of a country. Confucianism in Korea, influenced by the patriarchy of Christianity, has supported an even more pronounced hierarchy with males in the dominant roles, whereas in China, Confucianism has confronted the egalitarian doctrines of communism and come to an uneasy truce. Vestiges of the Confucian hierarchy in China are revealed in the obvious predominance of men in the ruling group and in the instances of female infanticide and abortion under the one-child policy. Ambivalent attitudes in Japan are revealed when the same people who blame Confucianism for the difficulty of making change are grateful to Confucianism for the greater order and productivity of Japanese society in relation to Western society.

Current experiences, perceptions, actions, and policies are all influenced by Japan's religion, its still-recognized matrifocal roots, its group orientation, the density of its population, the skills of imitation and adaptability for survival, the consequences of succeeding waves of war with neighboring kingdoms, as well as vestiges of feudalism. The path from primeval times, when women were one with the sun and the truth of all-being, leading to a present where, as Raicho Hiratsuka's poem says, women are like pale-faced moons who depend on others and reflect their light, has been a circuitous one. Historic factors may assist in understanding apparent contradictions in Japanese business and management as we move to the drama of corporate life and view the "man's world" of modern corporate Japan in chapter 4.

Part 2

THE DRAMA OF CORPORATE LIFE

Roles, Actions, and Status

4

Otoko Shakai, A Man's World

Organizational Culture and Work

> We live in the age of corporate organisms. Though no formal announcements have been issued, it's becoming harder to ignore that they have wrested control of the earth from *homo sapiens* and supplanted us as the planet's dominant species. It is the multinationals, government bureaucracies, religious hierarchies, military bodies, et al., not individual humans, that generate our era's character, its patterns of wealth and poverty, its technological progress and ecological peril, its entertainment and political agenda. They have, in short, taken over and nowhere more so than in Japan.
>
> David Kubiak, *Kyoto Journal,* 1990

David Kubiak's whimsical description of Japanese corporations anthropomorphizes corporations, giving them a personality, a purposefulness, and a life of their own, which may not be as ridiculous as it seems at first reading. Corporations as institutions have distinct characteristics. They are entities, not quite human, able to affect people's daily lives with products, by-products, policies, and actions, and their personalities are created by the blending of people, purpose, industry, location, history, and era.

To become managers, women must be members of such entities or organizations. As social systems, organizations exist to accomplish work that can't be done by individuals alone, encompassing most projects in the present-day world. Members engage in patterned activities that are interdependent and focused on a common goal or desired outcome. Social systems are fuzzy sets, as defined by Lotfi Zadeh,[1] requiring both quantitative and qualitative measures to understand and evaluate them.

A systems view provided a framework for my research on Japanese women managers to examine relationships between organizational cultures, individuals, and environments. This view serves as a reminder that each element, each event, in the system is interdependent with any change causing reverberations throughout the system. System models, at their best, compel an awareness of the reciprocal nature of all the elements in a system, an organization, corporation, or family. Figure 4.1 depicts, in a highly simplified fashion, the system elements of individual, organization, and society that are relevant to Japanese women managers.

Cultural Guidelines

Chapter 2 described patterns in the early lives of individual women that determined their viewpoints, motivations, and life choices and influenced their ability to succeed as managers. This chapter examines organizational cultures in Japan and their effect on women managers. Culture helps to make sense of the world. Cultural guidelines help members adapt to the demands of a changing, complex, seemingly uncontrollable external world, allowing them to function without having to think about each specific action. Within the

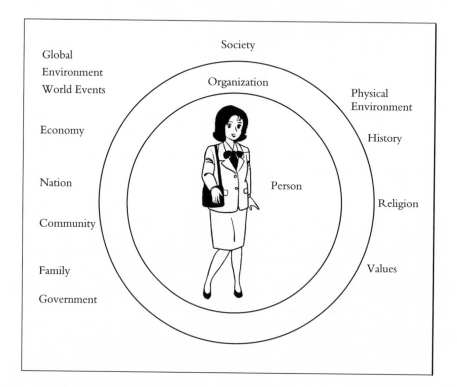

Figure 4.1. A systems view of the world of a manager.

group, it is safe to assume that other members will also abide by the implicit rules. Members trust that they can depend on the group's reactions and support if they act according to the shared rules. This shared culture pulls people with diverse needs, values, and styles together into a cohesive social unit.

A culture is defined by groups of people who share common assumptions about what constitutes the truth and the nature of reality. These shared assumptions guide behavior, feelings, and actions, and influence what is valued and what is forbidden by the members of the social system, whether it is a nation, an industry, a corporation, or a family. Culture also defines the boundaries: Who and what are a part of the group, and who are not. Insiders are defined as those within the boundaries who follow the cultural norms, while outsiders do not.

Although not using the word "culture," Chalmers Johnson has emphasized the importance of organizational culture to an understanding of Japan:

> Institutions are not just rules of the game. They are places infused with values, places where people spend their time working, where they compete with each other. Institutions have lives of their own. And if you want to understand Japan, you'd better understand the unique character of Japanese institutions.[2]

The unique character of Japanese institutions grows out of national values reflected in the norms, roles, and behaviors that are encouraged or denied. Unspoken but powerful rules growing out of values govern daily life, work, and the relation between the sexes, allowing people to live without always thinking about rules and relationships. Politics, history, and ideology all contribute to shaping this culture on an ongoing basis with images, ideals, and representations of women and men. Common customs in Japanese industries distinguish them from their American counterparts. Relative to other industrialized nations and from the outside, Japanese organizations appear more consistent, but each organization still develops a unique culture. Culture constitutes the glue that holds people together, not necessarily articulated but known by all members in good standing. One definition of a leader is a person who defines reality, the sum of all these shared assumptions, and convinces others of that definition, in effect shaping the culture.

Japanese Organizations and Management Styles

> Corporate environment is so close knit that outsiders find it difficult to enter. Japan's economy looks like a seamless block to foreign eyes, but even Japanese have difficulty doing business with each other. Any line of industry has its own culture and so does every company.[3]

Just as myths and beliefs unify national cultures, organizations develop their own rules, myths, and beliefs to unify the culture, so that if a man introduces himself as "Okomoto, from Mitsui" people have a picture of who he is and what general behavior to expect. Present-day Japanese corporate practices are commonly thought to have their roots in ancient culture. While this is partly true, many practices are of more recent origin. Lifetime employment policies, often attributed to samurai loyalty to the lord, actually grew out of the period of labor unrest in the 1950s, developed by corporations seeking stability and loyalty in their workforce. Seniority-based reward structures are related to lifetime employment. Also in support of company stability, the Japanese labor market is characterized by company or enterprise unions, with little industry-wide interaction or bargaining power.

Japan's postwar economic miracle required the development of organizations, structures, and infrastructures that could quickly and effectively mobilize and utilize people and maintain productivity over an extended period. At the macroeconomic level, collaborative industrial organizations of contractors and subcontractors with close business and government cooperation characterize the Japanese economy. This form developed during Japan's rapid industrialization in the nineteenth-century Meiji era, out of such common-sense arrangements as sheepherders who supplied a lord's textile company beginning their own business and continuing to supply only the lord's company, remaining loyal and considered a part of the company "family."

Growing out of this kind of collaboration, the *zaibatsu,* in the form of tightly knit interlocking company structures, were the major engines supplying Japanese military and industrial prewar and wartime production. Disbanded in the postwar occupation, many re-formed as the current *keiretsu.* The only thing in American industry that compares to the workings and power of this type of intricate collaboration in Japanese industry is the American military-industrial complex, where the characteristics of Japanese industrial policy can be found. The close, tightly held relationships between defense industries and the military, the retirement of military officers into the industries with which they have worked, the secrecy and autocratic methods of decision making, and the belief that only military people can understand the issues have parallels to Japanese industrial policies.

Borrowing and adapting from Western management theory and practice, and building on the remnants of Japan's prewar industry, uniquely Japanese management styles and organizational structures have evolved. Japanese managers effectively used W. Edwards Deming's theories of total quality management, neglected in America, and his advocacy of labor management cooperation that accelerated productivity in Japan, another example of the Japanese learning and successfully adapting foreign ideas and products.

At the microeconomic level, Japanese organizations are flatter than American organizations and tend to be rigidly hierarchical, with fewer layers between the top of the organization and the bottom. Although many American companies moved in the direction of flatter organizations as they restructured and reengineered to cope with a prolonged recession, American organizations still have a higher ratio of managers to workers. As of 1994, 12.8 percent of the workforce in the United States were managers, while only 3 percent of the workforce in Japan were managers (see Table 4.1).

The larger number of American managers are usually middle managers or vice presidents in one form or another. Most Japanese organizations have only one vice president, while American organizations have a plethora of vice presidents, executive vice presidents, senior vice presidents, deputy vice presidents, assistant vice presidents, and so forth. Sony, for instance, was considered to have a more westernized organizational structure, with four vice presidents instead of one for its Japanese organization until a major restructuring divided the organization into eight companies, each with its own president.

Similar to boards of directors in the United States, directors of Japanese corporations guide policy making, but directors are employees of the corporation, and managing directors are operating managers. The distinction between line managers and staff managers is more clearly drawn in Japan than in the United States. Line managers supervise people who are actually engaged in the production or service of the company. And the closer the function managed is to the core business of the company, the more likely the line manager is to be a candidate for top management.

In the United States, it is also important for managers to have line management experience, and the core function has evolved from production to finance to marketing, with variations by industry. One problem described by Japanese women managers is being stuck in staff or advisory management positions with few direct subordinates. In 1995 Sony promoted its first woman manager to a line management position, as head of the marketing division, considered an important breakthrough by women.

Table 4.1 Percentage of Workers Who Are Managers

	United States	Japan
Total	12.8	3.0
Male	14.0	5.0
Female	11.4	1.0

Source: U.S. Dept. of Labor, 1994; Japanese Ministry of Labor, 1994.

Clues to Corporate Culture

Japanese corporations are generally seen as a man's world, *Otoko Shakai*. What aspects of organizational culture determine whether it is a man's world, friendly or unfriendly to women? This chapter seeks clues to Japanese organizational culture that are relevant to the success of women managers. An observer trying to understand a culture looks for clues to discover the culture's implicit and often unspoken rules.

Shinji Kirimura, an executive of a large Japanese company, Furukawa Electric Company, said he had been asking himself, "What kind of society have we made for ourselves? and, What are the norms of our society?" He answered, "In the old days society was centered around the aristocracy, then came the feudal warrior society, and later the military took charge. Each historical period had its own set of values. At the present time companies play the leading social role." And in each era, males have dominated.

Historically, women's contribution to the Japanese economy was in agriculture and production. The textile industries were predominantly staffed by women workers, who often lived in dormitories nearby, their lives completely controlled. Women were concentrated in primary industries and unpaid family work. Office work was men's work until mobilization for war required replacements by women. The occupation of office lady, or OL, as it is usually called, is a postwar phenomenon. Office ladies were hired at age eighteen or nineteen and left the company five or six years later to get married, ideally to a coworker. Considered temporary labor, they were limited to the domestic zones of companies, the copy machine, the tea area, and the word processors, doing clerical and serving jobs and thought of as "office flowers," *shokuba no hana*, who bloom and disappear at age twenty-nine at the latest. Office ladies are still important components of Japanese business culture, but they are increasingly controversial in the light of women's changing roles.

The *Asian Business Journal* surveyed women managers throughout Asia about companies and locations they judged best for women.[4] Japan was ranked one of the less desirable countries for women managers among all the countries surveyed. The most "woman-friendly" country was Hong Kong, followed by Singapore and then the United States. Japan ranked twelfth, after China and before only South Korea, Germany, India, France, and Indonesia. The difference between the top three countries and the rest was significant. Organizational cultures in Japanese companies were seen as difficult for women to enter and strewn with barriers for women managers.

The field of anthropology has developed tools for deciphering cultural rules, norms, and values when observing another culture. Organizational behavior is the area of management that draws on these tools to study behavior, culture, and values in organizations. Understanding organizational culture helps managers create more effective organizations. Tools from the disciplines of anthropology, psychology, and sociology are used to understand organizations, to diagnose problems, and to work with people to improve operations.

Clues to organizational culture are often implicit, taken for granted, and unrecognized by the members. Asking the questions that are not usually asked about ordinary day-to-day corporate life shines a spotlight on how people behave in the organization and helps bring to awareness the embedded nature of culture. The goal is to discover and understand the organizational culture and then to use the understanding to create effective organizations (see Table 4.2).

Organization charts provide clues to organizational culture. Japanese organization charts are not widely distributed, a first clue to an assumption that they are not exactly public knowledge. When available, the charts are often presented vertically, with top management on one side of the page and workers at the lowest levels across from them on the other side of the page (see Figure 4.2). In contrast, Western organization charts traditionally are printed horizontally, with top management at the top of the page, moving through management levels to the workers at the bottom of the page. The arrangements convey different views of the organization and management.

Table 4.2 Clues to Organizational Culture

ARTIFACTS
Visible signals
    How do people dress?
    Where are desks, offices and/or parking spaces?
    How do people talk and address each other?
    Who sits where?
    Who has tea/coffee/lunch/golf/dinner/drinks with whom?

VALUES
Ideals influencing decision
    Who are the heroes?
    What are the organization's favorite stories?
    Which topics are stressed in making decisions?
    Which behaviors are punished?
    Which behaviors get rewarded?
    How does one get and keep power?

UNDERLYING ASSUMPTIONS
    What is real?
    How are time and space structured?
    What makes people tick?
    How should people interact with the environment?
    How should people relate to one another?
    What do we really think about ourselves?

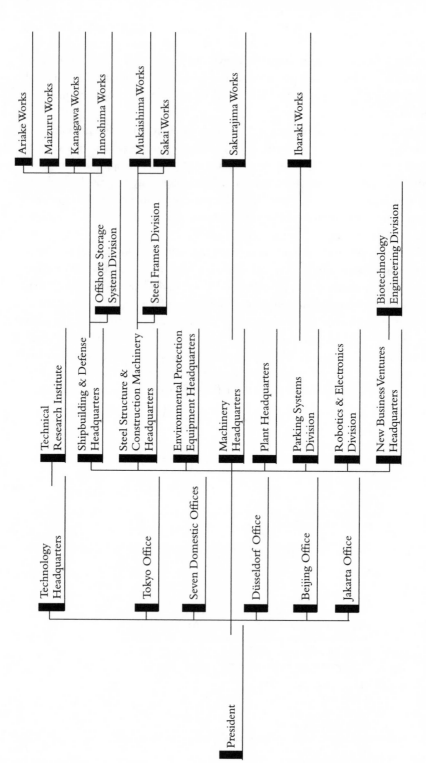

Figure 4.2. A Japanese organization chart indicating levels of management horizontally, rather than vertically. Hitachi Zosen Annual Report, 1993.

Status and Class Clues

In Japanese organizations there is an assumption of each person's appropriate place and value in the organization. The prevailing belief is that the nation is a one-class society, even though in actuality class and status exist and are widely recognized by all Japanese. When surveyed, the majority of Japanese say they are middle-class (94 percent), even though there may be large differences in wealth, income, and status. Less than 1 percent of Japanese people said they were upper-class, and only 5 percent considered themselves lower-class. Again, it is important not to stick out.

There is, in actuality, less difference between salaries of top management and workers in Japan. Chief executive officers of major Japanese companies receive about 25 times the pay of the average worker, while American CEOs receive 157 times the average wage of the American worker and the differential goes as high as 500 times as much, according to a Towers Perrin study of 1992.[5] Top management in Japan, usually the oldest men in the organization, receive status and deference by virtue of age and position, and are rewarded with attendant benefits of car and driver, golf club memberships, or luxury business travel, rather than the large wage differentials found in American companies. The Japanese hierarchy is very clear, with great deference to top management, but fewer layers between top and bottom than in organizations in the United States. A strict hierarchy does prevail, which is a benevolent patriarchy when functioning at its best, an autocratic dictatorship when not. Always at the bottom of the hierarchy are the service and clerical workers, the office ladies.

Mean annual salaries in Japan are higher than in the United States. Japanese salaries have both salary and bonus components. The bonus is an important part of the salary, theoretically linked to the performance of the company and the unit. In practice the bonus is relied upon by employees and has consistently risen until 1992. The recession years provided shocks when some bonuses decreased. In 1995 the average total wage in Japan was $30,020, while in the United States it was $22,667.

Japanese management style is described as bottom up. Middle-level and lower-level managers are often the initiators of policies, with the process of *nemawashi*[6] bringing out everyone's thoughts or consensus before presentation to top management, who then announce the agreed-upon decision. The process emphasizes the importance of consensus and involving everyone before decisions are made. *Nemawashi,* an aspect of well-known lore about Japanese management, is sometimes blamed by outsiders for the tediousness and difficulty of doing business with the Japanese.

The human resources department (*jinji-bu*) is the most important functional area in Japanese organizations. This department provides the only entry point into corporations during the April hiring period for graduates, makes the initial hiring decision, and is central in subsequent decisions about transfers and promotion. Thus, given the prevalence of lifetime employment, it determines the present and future structure of the organization, a very powerful role. In contrast, the status of human resource departments in the United States has been subordinate and ancillary to the directions of functional departments. A recent survey of American businesses indicated that human resource departments are usually not brought into hiring decisions until after the decision has been made by the functional manager.

Another clue to Japanese management style can be found in the layout of the typical Japanese office, which is striking at first visit (see Figure 4.3). One large office generally serves for a department or a division with as many as two hundred people, with the top manager seated at the back of the office and the remainder of the staff arrayed from back to front in order of rank, with the lowest-ranking office ladies, at the front. Only directors and managing directors have private offices, justified by their external liaison functions, and they usually spend the majority of their time on the floor with employees rather than in their offices. Everyone's activities are visible, making office secrets difficult.

Managers are able to see all employees and the contents of their desks. In a letter to an advice column in the Tokyo newspaper, a new worker lamented that a coworker had moved his desk files because she couldn't see the boss clearly and had to look around them, and that she had repeated this maneuver several times. The advice was to comply with the coworker's desire, which was described as legitimate. While the office arrangement makes it easier for workers to share work and communicate, the arrangement also contributes to the long hours worked. There is a reluctance to leave before coworkers or the boss, whose desk affords a view of all.

The long hours of Japanese workers, while a cause for both envy and recriminations from other nations, are not necessarily productive. Time spent waiting for one's superior or coworkers to leave may be simply "busy work." While the productivity of Japan's manufacturing industries is among the world's highest, the productivity of white-collar Japanese workers is among the lowest. The 1990s recession has brought publicity to this segment of the workforce, which economists have labeled the "working unemployed." Estimates have placed the number of excess white-collar workers as high as four million. The norms of lifetime employment and seniority-based, rather than merit-based, pay make it difficult to evaluate or terminate office workers.

Socializing and continuing work discussions at lunch or dinner and during after-hours drinking are customary. The after-hours drinking and dinners are notorious among foreigners, whose endurance is often tested, but for the

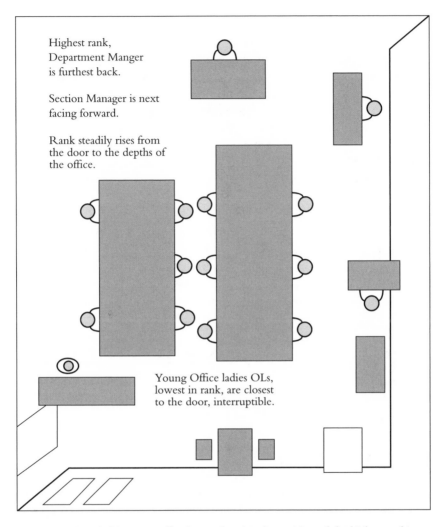

Highest rank,
Department Manger
is furthest back.

Section Manager is next
facing forward.

Rank steadily rises from
the door to the depths of
the office.

Young Office ladies OLs,
lowest in rank, are closest
to the door, interruptible.

Figure 4.3. A typical Japanese office layout showing the position of the highest ranking manager furthest back and the lowest in rank closest to the door.

Japanese these less-formal times provide an opportunity for forthright communication and disagreement, unthinkable at the office. This camaraderie often extends to the golf course on the weekends. After-hours socialization is more difficult for women, because of other responsibilities and personal preferences. Confusion reigns among Japanese men about the "right" way to relate to their female colleagues in what had traditionally been an all-male sport. Publications and magazine articles abound, purporting to teach Japanese men how to "relate" to Japanese women in a karaoke bar or restaurant, but the questions remain. Professional women and younger male managers are questioning the necessity of the long evening "meetings." A few have minimized them, but change is always difficult. An encouraging sign is that required socializing has become a legitimate topic for discussion, even though it remains a part of the "Japanese way of doing business."

Understanding cultures requires observing both explicit and implicit behaviors, paying attention to what people say and what they actually do. Sometimes rules are spelled out explicitly in company handbooks or media "how-to" publications. More often a variety of clues must be sought to discover organizational culture. The rules or norms may be spelled out when norms and values are changing, or when it is felt that the rules are not shared by all the members of the group. As an example, Keidanren, the powerful economic organization to which all large Japanese corporations belong, issued a publication entitled "Rules for Corporate Behavior" in 1992, when international criticism was being aimed at the ethics of Japanese companies. The need for some national response to criticism stimulated an explicit statement of rules. Keidanren's Corporate Behavior Rules, called "The 7-5-3 rules," provided specific guidelines for corporate behavior. Seven covered corporations' social roles, five covered rules of fairness, and three specified top management obligations to conform to international cultures.

Dress Codes

Another example of an explicit statement of norms is found in the instructions to graduates, new employees, and potential employees in Figure 4.4. The figure illustrates norms of dress and behavior that young Japanese men and women should follow to succeed in organizations, reflective of prevailing norms or rules of dress and behavior in Japanese companies; they are adapted from a publication by the Japan Management Association.

Graduates refer to the suggested dress as their "recruit suit." While "Dress for Success" seminars had a vogue for American women and men striving to succeed in the 1970s, the norms of dress were never as clear or uniform as in Japanese companies. United States norms varied widely among industries and geographic regions. Even the well-known standard dress of dark suit and tie, exemplified by the frequently satirized norms of the IBM Corporation, were supplanted as the corporation evolved in the 1990s. Regionally, the aloha shirt and muumuu worn in offices in Hawaii on Aloha Friday are a far cry from the banker's three-piece suit on New York's Wall Street. Such diversity is not seen in Japan.

Proper Grooming for Women

- Hairstyle should match office atmosphere
- Beware of bad breath
- The trend is to brush your teeth after meals
- Work cosmetics are different from after work
- Of course you must use some cosmetics
- Accessories coordinated
- Use subtle colors
- Use clothes appropriate for time, place, and occasion
- Use light colors for manicure
- Watch for runs in stockings
- Heels must be in good shape
- Use standard shoes

Proper Grooming for Men

- Hair clean cut like a freshman
- Drandruff is a symbol of dirt
- Watch for dirty teeth and bad breath
- Don't use the same handkerchief as yesterday
- Be careful of how you tie your necktie
- It is not fashionable to wear a gaudy necktie
- Are your shirt cuffs worn?
- Fashionable clothes are of no use if they aren't clean
- Are your pants well pressed?
- Beware of the smell of your socks
- Are your shoes dirty?

Figure 4.4. Dress codes and grooming rules are well defined for Japanese young people aspiring to careers. These rules are available in numerous popular publications as well as company manuals. Adapted from a Japan Management Association publication, Tokyo, Japan, 1996.

Acculturation and Training

Another cultural clue is found in the legendary loyalty of Japanese employees to their companies. This loyalty can be attributed to organizational culture directly reinforced by national culture. Japanese organizations use a variety of methods to acculturate employees. *Shanai gyoma*, company events or rituals, are effectively used to support the shared culture. A hiring ceremony, or *Nyūsha shiki*, is held each April to welcome new employees, and the president always attends to urge them to become effective employees and responsible members of society. Then everyone joins in the *shakai*, the company song, which is sung at all company events.

American companies might envy the orientation programs for new employees, which are equivalent to intense and lengthy team-building retreats of three to four months, usually including rigorous physical tests of endurance and strength requiring team cooperation. Explaining the power of corporate norms in Japan, Shinji Kirimura of the Furukawa Electric Company said,

> From the moment employees enter a company, they are sucked into its current. In the case of a large enterprise young men and women just out of university enter fresh and are soon dyed the color of their company. Company values are stamped onto them in the process.[7]

Thomas Rohlen, an American professor of anthropology, participated in a three-month training program for new male recruits to a bank and rightly described it as a total immersion into the company culture, with Zen meditation, military exercises, and physical, intellectual, and spiritual programs contributing to the socialization process.[8] Only two weeks of the training were actually related to jobs at the company, and it was these two weeks of training that included new women recruits. This training is a powerful socialization to the culture, molding the type of person the company wants as an employee.

New employees go through the training as a group, and each class or team develops its own strong group identity. Each person hopes to be promoted and become a top manager, but in the team spirit, if the star is not oneself, then the hope is that one's team members will make it to the top. Continuing training for both new and old employees emphasizes team collaboration.

Other tools that reinforce the culture are the *Shakun,* the corporate articles, which specify desired mental and spiritual attitudes and which are recited daily in the morning assembly in some companies. A New Year's party, *Shinnenkai,* is traditional on the first day of work in the new year to pray for renewed prosperity. Again the president attends. Everyone sings the company song and participates in the toast. The *Shasho,* or employee badge, is worn on the lapel to identify an employee and reinforce the sense of belonging to the culture.

The ritual exchange of business cards, or *meishi,* reinforces the identification with company culture. The cards are exchanged on meeting, examined carefully and respectfully to ascertain the role and status of each person, and then arrayed on the meeting table as reference. This serves a very useful purpose for foreigners as well to help remember new names. Employees introduce themselves by their personal name and their company name, with the two seeming to be pronounced as one, for example, Nakamura of Sumitomo. Sometimes the company name is given before the employee's family name, especially for companies with high status and prestige value, identifying the person as belonging to this "important company."

The company invests heavily in each recruit, so an employee who adheres to the norms and rules of company culture can be reasonably confident of secure employment and promotions at regular intervals. The expectation is that *he* will rise and be rewarded in direct proportion to his age and length of service (seniority-based rewards and promotions, *nenkyö-joretsu*). Fitting women managers into this well-defined, traditional company culture can be, and for many companies has been, a real challenge. Some have deemed it impossible even before trying.

Heroes and Management Styles

Rising from the bottom, or *hira*, rank-and-file worker to management, the three most common levels of management in Japanese industry are *kakarichö, kachö* and *buchö. Kakarichö,* or section chief, is the first management level or first-line supervisor. The second, *Kachö,* is translated simply as manager, and *Buchö* usually as general manager. The number of people at each of these levels in 1994 was:

Buchō	356,470
Kachō	822,810
Kakarichō	809,640
Total Managers	1,988,940

Various suffixes are added in Japanese to indicate different gradations, but statistics on management generally are given for these three categories. *Jichö,* for example, is deputy director. *Jūyaku* is a director, *kaichö* is chairman of the board, and *shachö* is usually translated as president.

Literal meanings of some management terms are as follows:

Kaisha is company.
Kaichö, then, is the head of company.

Shiten is store or branch.
So that *shitencho* is head of branch
Ji is next to.
Jichō is next to the head.
Kachuzuki is attached to, or sideways, i.e., attached to a *kachō*
Madogi-wa is window person, i.e., someone on their way out.

Who are the heroes? Preferred styles of management are another indicator of organizational culture. In Japan today, managers' styles are sometimes
compared to the methods of famous warlords whose names immediately
evoke a colorful image of the type of management employed. Three common examples include the most famous warlords. The Tokugawa Ieyasu
style is named for the general who founded the Edo shogunate, which
wielded power for 250 years. This type of manager waits patiently for the
right chance, as expressed by the following haiku:[9]

> The silent bush warbler
> Let us wait
> Until it sings.

A second style is named after Toyotomi Hideyoshi, who initiated a new
political system in Japan and believed strongly in his own abilities. He dealt
with all challenges in a firm and positive manner. His haiku is as follows:

> The silent bush warbler
> I'll try to make her sing.

A third style is that of Oda Nobunaga, a famous military general who
is credited with bringing peace to Japan in the age of warring states. The
strategy he employed was to get to his enemies before they could get to him.
His haiku is:

> The silent bush warbler
> Let us shoot it down
> Before it can sing.

Poetic metaphors such as these provide clues to the culture of the organization, who the heroes are, what is valued, what works, and prevailing attitudes. Shared phrases and associations reinforce the organizational culture.
Corporations are one of the last bastions of male heraldry and dominance in
both Japan and the United States. In Japan, corporate leadership is heir to the
samurai tradition. The feudal lords are the corporate leaders, as illustrated by
the descriptions of types of managers. Several women managers averred that
Japan is still a feudal society. The corporation has taken the place of the
samurai lords.

Clues to Masculine and Feminine

Such traditional cultures are committed to the status quo and invest a great deal in harmony and stability. Women are seen as disruptive of this type of status quo and harmony. On the other hand, not disrupting the status quo has high costs. A quotation from *Blueprint for a New Japan,* by Ichiro Ozawa, describes succinctly the opportunity costs of unquestioned maintenance of the status quo:

> An economic and social framework that emphasizes cooperative, long-term relationships may become nothing more than a closed society, one that bars foreign companies or any other outsiders from entering.[10]

With this statement Ozawa brings into question two icons of the Japanese economy and nation—close group identity and lifetime employment. When carried to the extreme, these characteristics create closed systems that do not allow new life to enter, with the inevitable consequence of atrophy and death. Ozawa's statement is particularly significant, since he has achieved power and prominence by virtue of this system. Now he is describing the dark side of the cultural norms of long-term relationships and the close, cooperative, homogeneous group.

Traditional Japanese organizational culture was defined by and for men, and women must choose whether to try to enter and adapt, try to change the culture, or create their own organizations. Changing the culture is an uncharacteristic alternative for Japanese women or men, exemplified by the folk wisdom "The nail that stands up gets hammered down." It is difficult for women to enter and adapt because they do not "fit" the prescribed roles, or, at least, the stereotypes of women do not fit.

Some fields are considered "women's work" and others are considered "men's work." The definition of men's and women's work varies by country and national culture, as well as by type of industry and organization. What makes a profession or industry "masculine" or "feminine"? Writing and literature have long been considered "feminine" professions in Japan. Traditionally, women have been encouraged first to become mothers and housewives, but have not been discouraged from becoming writers, secretaries, and more recently office ladies, all considered temporary, interruptible, and appropriately serving positions. In the United States, older women recall when the only career options open to them after high school were teacher, nurse, and librarian. Communist Russia and the former Soviet Union considered medicine a female occupation, and 80 percent of the doctors were women, compared with only 5 percent in the United States at the same time. The profession of medicine, however, had a lower status in the Soviet Union than it had in the rest of the world, a characteristic common to majority female professions in industrialized societies.

While living in India I was surprised to see women carrying bricks and mortar for construction of buildings while dressed in gorgeous full skirts embroidered with coins. Hod carrying was considered a "woman's" job in that part of India, and the tribal women wore their family treasures of coins and jewelry while working, their person being the safest place for treasures in their nomadic lives. Never having seen women at this job in the United States, I had assumed that only men could do it.

A well-intentioned male colleague briefed me about the extreme sex segregation he observed in Japan, with women confined to feminine fields like fashion, cosmetics, and entertainment. Sex segregation does prevail in Japanese industries, and women *are* in feminine fields, but they are also found in every industry and profession, although their representation is small in some industries. Half or nearly half of workers in the wholesale, retail, finance, social services, and agriculture industries are women. Women in management, on the other hand, either are not in some industries or else there are too few to be measured. The largest number of women managers in Japan are in the wholesale and retail industries, consistent with common expectations, but their representation in construction and finance is less intuitive.

With voices that are different, women may be denied entry to some industries, shunted to invisible areas, or restricted to decorative roles as office flowers rather than being allowed to demonstrate and test their productivity. Men, as well as women, are restricted to narrow paths in companies with closed cultures, but the original narrow paths were designed by and for men. The culture no longer fits all men, if it ever did, but men have been heavily socialized to fit.

Using the clues to culture stated previously, my reading of clues to organizational culture in the United States and Japan based on observations and a literature search are summarized in the Table 4.3. Another person who reads the same clues might come up with a different interpretation, but a few of the more obvious artifacts, values, and assumptions were chosen to illustrate clues in each culture.

The fit between an individual with unique background and skills, and the organization, with its culture and prescribed norms, determines the success of the individual, the organization, and the economy. The complex interaction between organizational culture, national culture, environment, and individuals creates the mosaic of economic and personal life. Examining these interactions can provide insights into how organizations evolve, change, become more effective, or disappear. The cultures of some organizations are more supportive of women in management than others. Systems with open or

Table 4.3 Clues to Organizational Culture in Japan and the United States

	Japan	United States
ARTIFACTS		
Dress	Prescribed; don't stand out	Varies with field—creative, old-line, technology, etc.
Transport	Subway, taxi	Private car
Car	Status symbol	Essential, foreign Mercedes Benz, BMW has status
Office	Group	Private
Social	Business associates	Separated from business
Party	Restaurant	Home
Distance	High until insider	Close, but sharp boundaries
Language	Formal	Informal
Home	Separate, haven	Open boundaries
VALUES		
Heroes	Emporer, samurai	John Wayne, self-made man
Money	Not visible	Status symbol
Rewards	Group approval	Money, office, accouterment
Punishments	Stand out, withdraw support	Ignore, criticize, withdraw rewards, fire, let go
Evaluation criteria	Seniority, fit in, qualitative	Job performance, production, statistics
Education	High value	Espoused, but self-educated has high status
ASSUMPTIONS		
Definition of reality	Group-defined, authorities	Self-defined, test
Structure of relationships	Hierarchical. Blood *Jinnyaku*	Egalitarian. Choice
Structure of time	Lifetime, antiquity, job completion	8-hour, quarterly, twentieth century, immediate
Verifiability	Tradition, custom	Pragmatic. Does it work?
Gender roles	Explicit: male-dominant, female-subordinate	Espoused egalitarian, hidden male-dominance assumptions

permeable boundaries are more open to women, and they are also more open to innovation and creativity. Given such a well-defined "man's world," the search for women managers might seem overwhelming. The next chapter confronts powerful stereotypes to describe how and where they were found.

5

The Search for Successful
Japanese Women Managers

Research Confounding Stereotypes

There are no women managers—just office flowers.
Senior male communications
industry executive, sixties

Women can't be managers. They leave to have babies.
Male utilities executive, fifties

In many cases, it is more difficult for women than for men to
achieve success and balance it with quality of personal life as
the system and the mentality of the society is still in transition.
Thirty-year-old female corporate executive

Given the prevailing male-dominant culture of Japanese organizations, the
belief that there are no women in management is not surprising. The questions I was most often asked about Japanese women managers were "Are
there any?" "Are they married?" and "Where are they?" The questions reveal
widespread assumptions: first, that there aren't any women managers; second,
that if women are managers, they aren't married; and third, that the women
are not really managers. Finding women managers was part of a research
process that involved extended interviews of the women alongside data gathering on the economy and culture. This chapter's goal is to confound stereotypes I encountered by describing women managers, their lifestyles, their
family status, and the industries in which they are found. In the very process
of seeking out women managers, I gained insights into who they are and
how they became managers that lend depth to the quantitative results. The
research process is set forth as part of the basis for evaluating the findings.

The degree varies, but in every country of the world today men are considered the natural leaders. Some women do succeed and attain leadership in the most discriminatory societies. My ongoing interest has been to understand how these women become successful leaders where the prevailing culture does not support or value their participation. Women who have successfully transcended formidable barriers to become managers are impressive and worthy of attention, breaking traditional gender role stereotypes and becoming agents of social change. Cultural differences provide an opportunity for sideways viewing of the ways in which women and minorities, outsiders to the traditional power structure, become successful. Placing women managers within the context of differing cultural assumptions may yield fresh insights into unquestioned assumptions about gender and management by helping to diffuse the emotionality that often surfaces in discussions about gender and the roles of women and men.

Women in Management

Trends indicate a slow rise of women in management in industrialized countries. For example, labor force statistics indicate that the situation of women managers has improved in Japan, Korea, and the United States over a decade, but women managers still represent a small minority and still are outsiders in each country. More women are working, but they are not being promoted. The United States approaches parity in the number of total managers, but senior executive positions remain elusive (see Table 5.1).

The small proportion of working women who have made it into the ranks of Japanese management are an elite group, but their numbers are in-

Table 5.1 Percentage of Women as Workers and Managers

	1981 (%)	1995 (%)
Total labor force		
Japan	34.1	40.6
Korea	37.5	40.4
United States	43.0	46.0
Total managers		
Japan	5.1	8.9
Korea	0.1	0.2
United States	27.0	43.0
Senior executives		
Japan	0	0.1
Korea	0	<0.1
United States	1.0	3.0

Source: ILO *Yearbook of Labour Statistics* 1996, Geneva, Switzerland.

creasing. In 1997 approximately 300,000 women were classified as managers in Japan, up from 130,000 women in 1983. A 1991 survey by *Diamond,* the weekly business magazine, found 50,000 women with the title "shacho-san," or company president, up from less than 15,000 in 1981. Fifty-five percent of all Japanese businesses have a woman manager, 38 percent have women first-line supervisors or subsection heads, 19 percent have women section heads, and only 7 percent have one or more women department heads.[1] The higher the management rank, the fewer the companies with women.

In order to become managers, women must insert themselves into traditional management culture and penetrate the boundaries of the insider group or, alternatively, create new roles for themselves outside the traditional structures. In Japan, all of this must be done in a context in which being an outsider is particularly difficult. When achievement is not encouraged for women, powerful motivators and forces are necessary to catapult them beyond accepted gender norms to success. My research was designed to learn about those forces for successful Japanese women managers. How women transcend barriers to entry and become "insiders" or succeed as outsiders is important to learn not only for women who wish to become managers but also to contribute to an understanding of change and innovation.

My earlier research in the South Pacific[2] revealed that "ascribed status" was related to women's ability to transcend the socialization of the female role and achieve success in the male-dominated public arena in traditional Pacific societies. Ascribed status in Fiji is that of a chiefly class. The chiefly tradition requires leadership and responsibility for one's clan from both men and women born into chiefly families. Women, given the title *Adi,* as well as men, *Ratu,* assume responsibility for their village and clan. Girls of the chiefly class were not given the limiting socialization of girls outside the chiefly class, which imprinted early deference to men. For example, men in the village are always served meals first, followed by the male children, then the female children, and finally the women if any food remains. One Fijian woman manager recalled always sitting next to her grandfather, the chief, at meals when in the village. Because of this, women reared as *Adi* were not bound by the prevailing gender definitions and, given their strong sense of responsibility and vision of service to their village, achieved influential positions in society.

Building on the South Pacific and American findings, I initiated my research in Japan by adapting the interview structure and survey questionnaires and using grounded theory methodology and life histories. As a beginning, it was necessary to define the parameters by asking, "Who is a manager?" and "Who are *successful Japanese woman managers?*" The word "manager" is itself built on the word "man," and the usual definitions of manager exclude women, with traditional management texts based on a male model.

This book views a manager in less gender-specific terms as the person who brings together necessary resources to achieve desired objectives. A manager focuses the energy of a group and mobilizes resources of money, people, information, plant, equipment, and markets to accomplish goals. Scholarly definitions of managers may emphasize the operational aspects of the process and assign the visionary goal setting and motivation to leaders. The distinctions between the two are arbitrary and are highly dependent on the perspective of the writer. Henry Mintzberg's observations of a large number of managers found the essential functions of a manager to be interpersonal, informational, and decision making.[3] For the purposes of this book, "manager" and "leader" will be used interchangeably, except when referring to a specific position of manager.[4] The Japanese women interviewed for this book meet the definitions of manager as they successfully direct organizations, carry on business within the national and international economy, and handle affairs of state, of corporations, of small home businesses, and of families.

Criteria for Success

Japanese criteria for success were necessary to choose women deemed successful by Japanese standards. A preselected sample of successful women managers was found in the members of *Keizai Doyukai,* the Association of Corporate Executives, which is one of four powerful industrial organizations in Japan. Before the war the Japanese government sponsored industrial and trade organizations in order to promote and guide industrial development. The postwar government has a very close, "democratic" relationship with the industrial organizations, which are now quasi-private.

Outside of Japan, the best known of these organizations is *Keidanren,* an abbreviation of *Keizai Dantai Rengo-kai,* or Federation of Economic Organizations. *Keidanren* is an umbrella economic organization whose membership includes all the major corporations of Japan. Building on several economic and industrial organizations that were active before the war, *Keidanren* was established in August 1946 and now includes approximately one thousand corporate members. Its goal is to "maintain close contact with public and private sectors at home and abroad, to find practical solutions to economic problems, and contribute to the sound development of the economies of Japan and countries around the world."[5] Research, conferences, and policy recommendations to the government on behalf of industry carry the voices of business. While *Keidanren* does not have official government status, the organization, because of influential corporate members, wields a great deal of political clout, with its reports and recommendations often found in the international press.

The other major Japanese economic organizations are *Nissho* (*Nihon Shoko Kaigi-sho*), the Japan Chamber of Commerce and Industry; *Nikkeiren* (*Nihon Keiei-sha Dantai Renmei*), the Japan Federation of Employers' Associations, composed of regional employer and trade associations, concerned with labor relations; and *Keizai Doyukai*.

Keizai Doyukai differs from the other organizations in that its members are individuals, the owners or heads of corporations, rather than corporate affiliates. It was established in 1946 by a few leading management figures from industrial and financial circles with the original purpose of renewing old business ties and reconstructing the Japanese economy. Now the organization is considered a "Key Club of Power," according to Dow Jones, striving to bring corporate executives together to focus on the national economic interest. The association had been strictly a male club until 1986, when the first women were invited to join. A potential member must be nominated by two current members and then approved by the association. Entry is difficult, and members have been chosen by the nation's top executives as their peers. In 1993 there were twenty women out of a total membership of two thousand.

My research began with these recognized leaders, women executives judged as successful by their colleagues to become members of this venerable Japanese organization of executives. The women members of *Keizai Doyukai* include the presidents of three successful information systems corporations; the former president of one of the most prestigious department stores, *Takashimaya;* the current ambassador to Kenya and Uganda, who had previously been an assistant minister of labor; the owner-founder of a well-known, successful children's clothing chain; a bank, and a prestigious law firm; an internationally famous fashion designer; an art gallery owner; officers of department stores and of a successful "cram" school; a manufacturer of plumbing supplies; and presidents of three successful fashion businesses and a food services corporation. Truly, these women meet Japanese criteria for successful executives.

Having chosen the population of women managers with which to begin, the next challenge was to enter their world for interviews. Making connections and establishing credibility were essential, with personal contacts crucial in Japan. Sponsorship of Fulbright Scholars, an assistant minister of labor, introductions from a former diplomat in Asia, and references from known Japanese, such as Haru Reischauer, proved the key to arranging interviews. For several of the interviews, the process required being questioned by several layers of management before making my way up to the woman executive. After my first discouraging months of seeking interviews, the interviewees began to enthusiastically provide names of other successful women managers and business owners. It soon became evident that the sample must be expanded. I had worried about the paucity of women managers, but as it turned out the challenge became limiting the size of the sample while still including representative women. The research eventually included over 160 women executives in industry, government, politics, media, the arts, and education, with the basic skills, attributes, and leadership abilities needed for management similar across this spectrum of settings. Research on the overall situation for women in management in Japan proceeded concurrently with the interviews.

As the research progressed, it became apparent that the opinions of younger women and men must also be heard in order to understand the context for women in management now and in the future. So junior executives, younger women and men, as well as the successful women managers were interviewed, as were faculty and administrators in educational institutions that were in touch with student trends. Finally, male executives and men who work and live with women managers provided another essential perspective. A sampling of male managers, from managing directors to supervisors, as well as coworkers and spouses, contributed unique perspectives.

Era of Birth

Selected on the basis of their achievements, women managers fell naturally into three age categories, with different world conditions influencing their lives. Their stories reflected the impact of world events on options, expectations, and life choices. The majority of the managers were over forty-five, consistent with career paths for men and women requiring decades to become successful. The women in this age group were influenced most by World War II and the events of the immediate postwar years. A Japanese phrase, apparently common in the 1950s, was that two things had gained strength in Japan following the war: women and stockings.

The women in each era had unique histories, as the examples in chapter 2 indicate, with the histories of those who lived through the war years the most dramatic. Not only did the war and its immediate aftermath have a profound effect on the women personally, but the structure and environment of government, laws, education, and work were all in flux and being questioned. This age group included the first women to vote in Japan, the first to enter the national universities, and the first to have rights guaranteed by the constitution. The women whose formative years were influenced by the events of war and postwar turbulence are now in key management positions.

While interviewing successful women managers in their midforties, fifties, and sixties, I was often introduced to young women moving rapidly upward in the business and organizational world. In their late twenties and early thirties, they had grown up in a world where the concepts of rights for women and individual rights were taken for granted, seen as a part of the culture.

They entered the best universities and traveled abroad both with parents and alone, to school, for pleasure, and for work. Their working lives began with, or were influenced by, the passage of legislation in 1986 guaranteeing equal access to employment under national law, and they were influenced by changes taking place in the United States, Europe, and around the world. The International Decade of Women was declared in their college or early working years. They labeled themselves as first wave, second wave, and third wave, depending on how long after the passage of the equal employment opportunity law they entered the workforce. The first wave began work immediately after the passage of the equal employment legislation in 1986, the second wave the next year. Since all companies in Japan hire college graduates in April of their graduation year, the concept of succeeding waves of women is an accurate description.

The early twenties generation presented still another culture, having grown up in an affluent and internationally powerful society, and seeing few limits on their lives and work. Most went to college and chose to work, but they expressed strong reservations about the narrowness of the salaryman life. Their parents had wanted to give their children everything they themselves had missed. These women often found the stories of the older women managers of struggle and deprivation strange and exotic. In turn, some older women managers complained about the lack of motivation and work ethic of younger women, not understanding their casually leaving a job, moving among jobs, or taking time off for extended study and travel.

Missing were women in their late thirties and early forties. There was usually a pause as people tried to think of women in this "in-between" age group. Mitsuko Horiuchi, councilor for women in the Prime Minister's Office, was the first woman I met in this age group. When I asked, "Where are all the women your age?" she answered without hesitation that they are home, taking care of children. The 1970s and early 1980s spawned a movement in Japan comparable to the 1950s in the United States. As the damages of war mended and the society became affluent, young women were encouraged to marry early and return home. The parents of women now in their thirties and forties had lived through the difficult war and postwar years and wanted the "good life," as they remembered it, for their children. Part of that remembered good life had included homemakers, full-time wives and mothers, taking care of the house and children while men, the samurai economic warriors, went off to battle the corporate world. The media and government were active in supporting this ideal with a back-to-the-home movement. A nonworking wife again became a prestige symbol, contributing to a large dip in the 1980s for the "M-shaped curve" of women's labor participation rate, constantly cited as the career path for Japanese women.

Mitsuko Horiuchi, an exception in this age group, had not intended to have a career, only to work after graduation from university until she married and began her family. But she had started work in the Ministry of Labor surrounded by women who had successfully carved careers for themselves while married and having children, and they assumed she would continue to work also. She said she became identified with this group that was supportive of women working and found herself continuing to work after marriage and then children, enjoying it and finding challenge and satisfaction. Most of her friends, even those who had taken career track jobs after college, stopped work when they married. Many of them quit intending to return later, but most had not returned. Thus the paucity of women managers in this age group.

The Economy and the World

The complex web of interactions between the historical age, with its unique set of events and influences, and each woman's individual life circumstances and history, as well as the evolution of national and corporate cultures and the influence of international trends, all contribute to a woman manager's ability to succeed. The state of the economy is inseparable from the role and position of managers, especially women managers. In Japan women's entry into the workforce, as well as into leadership and management position, was accelerated by a booming economy and the demand for skilled labor. Later women's participation decreased slightly as households became affluent, with labor shortages a countervailing force that allowed women's labor force participation to increase slightly each year. As the economy soared in the "bubble years," women were once more recruited as temporary buffers; they complied because, for many households, affluence was offset by the rapidly rising cost of living.

In 1992 the proportion of female university graduates finding jobs in the April hiring period exceeded the proportion of male graduates for the first time in history. Then the "bursting of the bubble" created yet another economic cycle for women and corporations. The hiring rate for women fell precipitously as the economy headed downward, and it continued to fall even when the recession seemed in abeyance. Few career track women were hired in the 1993 hiring period as major companies hired men over women, foreseeing a period of restructuring and downsizing.

Internationalization of the Japanese economy on both the demand and the supply side has had a mixed impact on the hiring and promotion of women. Production facilities in Asian countries have tended to concentrate on male managers, with a reluctance to dispatch women in management positions to developing countries. However, two of the women interviewed reported successful experiences in Asia and hoped their good experiences would encourage companies to send other women overseas because of these women's positive impact on employee relations and customer service.

Even though the number of women is few, Japanese companies in Europe and the United States have found a positive advantage in public relations and community image when they send their talented women to these areas. Several women interviewed had gained valuable experience and skills through their overseas assignments. The language and communication skills the women brought, as well as the public relations benefits, advanced the progress of the women and the companies. Another international avenue for Japanese women, discouraged by life in Japanese companies, has been to seek and find their fortunes in Hong Kong and other Asian countries.

The United Nations has used the international talents of Japanese women effectively. Ambassador Ogata, the United Nations high commissioner for refugees, is probably the highest-profile Japanese international woman manager. Her competency, skill, and communication talents have endeared her to both the Japanese and the international community. While she provides an excellent role model for Japanese women, she is not the only Japanese woman in leadership in the United Nations. In fact, the United Nations is the only organization in which there are more Japanese women than men in management.

The rigid structure of the Japanese employment system has served to the advantage of women leaders in international organizations, with men reluctant to leave career tracks for international service, fearing a loss of promotion opportunities and the benefits of the lifetime employment system. Japanese international aid agencies, both government and private, have benefited as they attract women university graduates who see more equal opportunities. The first Japanese to attain the position of vice president of the World Bank from within the bank, rather than by bureaucratic appointment, is a woman, Mieko Nishimizu, one of four female vice presidents of the World Bank.

Antecedents of Change

Younger women managers were aware that they had benefited from legislation and a general societal thawing of attitudes toward women's issues. They recognized the importance of events providing openings and opportunities into which they were prepared to jump. Many women who are now managers acknowledge a debt of gratitude to their foremothers, who pioneered new roles for women. Three of these women, whom I was fortunate to interview, are inspiring not only because of their achievements in the face of great odds but also because, at age eighty or over, they are active, interested in world events, and still speaking about the necessity to expand women's role.

Ayako Ishigaki, born in 1903, an author and the president of Yamagato School of Fine Arts, hosted a community dinner for a group that had traveled to Taeji for a conference entitled "Families in Transition." A tiny figure in elegant designer clothes, she graciously talked about her own life and visions even as I worried whether I was selfishly taxing her energy, since she was recovering from a broken rib. Her life is controversial in Japan because of her strong antiwar stance in the 1930s, but her many books have been read by a large audience and have influenced Japanese women. She translated Pearl Buck's books into Japanese, and her own 1955 article, "On the Housewife," questioned the social meaning of the full-time homemaker.

Yoshi Matsui, president of Chacopaper Company, insisted on keeping an interview appointment even though she was recovering from a cancer operation. She is already eighty, yet her interest in the situation of women managers today is surpassed only by her excitement about her work and her embroidery patterns, which she hopes to collect for a book.

Shidzue Kato, born in 1897, remains an activist for women's rights, family planning, and reproductive freedom. A politician and author, she gave the opening speech at another "Families in Transition" conference in 1992. The story of her life, *Facing Two Ways*,[6] documented a nation and its history so well it was used as a text by American occupation planners. Her recent thoughts about the situation of Japanese women and men on her hundredth birthday are quoted later in this book, as she still urges women to fight, if need be, to have their voices heard.

The hundredth anniversary of the birth of another pioneer Japanese woman, Fusae Ishikawa, was celebrated in 1993. A fighter for women's suffrage and a member of Parliament, she lived to the age of eighty-seven and never stopped fighting for equitable solutions for women's issues and against political corruption. Participating in the celebration of her hundredth birthday with women for whom she had been a mentor and role model was inspiring and an impressive learning experience. Her lifelong efforts working for women's rights influenced those who knew her, as well as younger women who have only read about her work.

Work and Family

Another stereotype of Japanese women managers is that they have had to forgo marriage in exchange for success. This was not true of the women I interviewed. The majority of Japanese women managers in this sample were or had been married. The unmarried were mainly twenty to thirty years old. As shown by Table 5.2, only 7 percent of the women over forty-five were single.

Only three of the women over forty who had never been married de-

Table 5.2 Age and Marital Status of Women
Managers Interviewed

	Over 45 (%)	30–45 (%)	20–30 (%)
Married	84	50	50
Widowed, divorced	9	4	0
Single	7	46	50
Children	55	15	0
% of those married with children	60	28	

scribed being single as a choice. The fiancé of one had been killed during the war, and she had been engaged a second time to a diplomat who died of a tropical disease. Another said she had "forgotten" to get married as she became absorbed in her work, and gradually the men her age seemed less interesting. Another had a long-standing relationship with a man about whom she cared deeply, and one said her fiancé had been killed in an auto accident. Only one said she had decided not to marry because she thought it would be impossible to have a career and marriage. The managers' marital status is consistent with Japanese government statistics of 1995, when less than one-third of working women had never been married. It differs, however, from the stereotype of Japanese women managers and is consistent with the high value placed on marriage and family by society and by the women interviewed. They saw marriage and career as complementary, not either-or, choices.

For all the women interviewed, their career path included a family path. Whether married, with children, or single, they had considered family and career options together. Balancing work and family was not separated and was seen as an inevitable challenge of a career. Sixty percent of the women over forty-five who were married had children. For those between thirty and forty-five, 28 percent of the married women had children, and more anticipated that they would. Some with children had continued to work with only the required six or eight weeks leave at the time of birth. Two had taken several years' leave and then had returned to work, one to her previous job and one to another related job.

Several of the women credited their husbands with encouraging them when they had been ready to give up their jobs. Participation of husbands in child care was a success factor cited by a number of the women over thirty. Only one mentioned her husband's help with housework, an activity that apparently is less common for men than child care. Twenty percent of the women credited the support of their mother-in-law for help with housework and child care. One mother-in-law had cared for the manager's children for six months when she had to go away for training. Several of the older women lived with parents-in-law, relieving them of responsibility for housework and cooking because the mother-in-law managed both, an option that is no longer readily available.

Single women talked of their parents, with whom two lived, taking responsibility for them as they aged. All were concerned about the future care of parents-in-law or parents. Most male executives interviewed did not talk about their families, wives, or children; when queried, they said they had taken for granted that they would follow the traditional path, marry and have children with a wife who would take responsibility for family. This may be one factor that contributes to the confusion felt by younger men. They have neither the psychological preparation nor the skills for a different path.

Where Are Women Managers?

The Japanese women managers interviewed for this research were represented in all the major industries except mining and agriculture. Table 5.3 shows the percentage in each of the standard industrial categories.

Almost 23 percent of the women managers interviewed were in the wholesale and retail industries, where the largest number and proportion of both women managers and workers are found in the Japanese workforce, as shown in Table 5.4.

Women constitute half of the workforce but only 12 percent of the managers in the wholesale/retail industry. One-third of all women managers are in this industry, which includes department stores, wholesale and retail trading houses, restaurants, and hotels. Examples of such companies in the research are the department stores Takashimaya, Isetan, and Seiyu. Takeshimaya is a prestigious department store (*departoo*) in Japan, with branches extending throughout the world. The Seiyu Limited, a conglomerate of supermarkets, department stores, and information and financial services, is considered one of the more women-friendly Japanese companies, providing child care and family leave even before required to do so. Others included JC Foods Company, a successful food production and distribution business founded and headed by Merle Aiko Okawara.

The conception that Japanese women managers are to be found only in the feminine industries is a widely held stereotype. Official statistics list Japanese women managers in each industry category except agriculture, mining, and utilities. Two Japanese women managers interviewed were in the utilities industry, as defined in the official statistics, but apparently their numbers were too insignificant to be shown. Perhaps they were the only two.

Table 5.3 Industries of Women Managers Interviewed

Industry	Women Managers (%)
Retail	22.6
Services	22.6
Manufacturing	6.7
Finance	2.7
Transport	2.0
Construction	0.7
Utilities	0.7
Government	12.7
Media	9.3
Education	8.0
Arts	8.6
Science and health	2.0

Fashion, textiles, and cosmetics, considered feminine industries, do include some very successful women managers. The Body Shop has achieved renown for its natural products, based on beauty secrets collected around the world by the company's founder, Anita Roddick, and also for its vision of the planet. The company commits a percentage of its profits to environmental causes, and its packaging and marketing materials are recyclable. The company is the fastest-growing cosmetic franchise in the world. Mitsu Kimata left a position as deputy director in the Ministry of Labor to take on the project of developing the Body Shop in Japan, which she heads.

Table 5.4 Percentage of Japanese Women Workers and Managers by Industry

Industry	% of Workers	% of all Managers	% of Female Managers
Wholesale, retail	50.0	12	33
Manufacturing, production	38.8	6	19
Construction	16.3	8	14
Finance, insurance, real estate	44.9	8	14
Community, social, personal services	48.3	8	14
Transport, storage	16.1	6	5
Agriculture, forestry, Fishing	46.2	0	
Mining, quarrying	16.7	0	
Utilities	15.1	0	
Total	40.7	8	100

Adapted from *Labour Statistics,* Ministry of Labour, Japan, 1995; *Yearbook of Labor Statistics,* ILO, Geneva, Switzerland, 1995.

In the fashion industry, Hanae Mori is the dean of Japanese fashion designers whose internationally known house began in the 1950s with the design of costumes for the fledgling movie industry. Now the Hanae Mori Group has over twenty companies, with at least fifteen hundred employees. Other Japanese women have found their own niches. Familiar, Ltd., designs, manufactures, and distributes children's clothing from its Kobe headquarters, with an elegant children's department store on the Ginza and stores in Honolulu and San Francisco as well. Another woman, Reiko Sudo, began a textile and fashion boutique, Nuno, collecting natural fibers from around the world and encouraging the resurgence of native Okinawan banana cloth for beautiful home furnishings and designer clothes. The high proportion of women workers in agriculture and manufacturing in Japan was surprising. Women are not, however, managers in the same proportion in those fields.

Women managers and workers in the United States are shown in Table 5.5 for comparison by industry. Interestingly, the United States construction industry has the lowest percentage of both women workers and managers, whereas Japan has a higher proportion of women managers. The construction and services industries in Japan had the highest proportion of women at department head rank. Slightly more than half of the Japanese women managers interviewed were in the first three categories: retail, services, and manufacturing. The next highest categories were government, education, media, and the arts which constituted 39 percent of the interviewees. Portions of the latter three categories are included in official statistics under services and wholesale, retail in an arbitrary classification, depending on the major empha-

Table 5.5 Percentage of Women Workers and Managers in the United States by Industry

Industry	% of Workers	% of all Managers	% of Female Managers
Social services	59.4	49.8	43.6
Finance	53.3	48.5	21.1
Wholesale, retail	47.1	43.1	15.1
Manufacturing, production	33.3	28.5	11.3
Transport	29.8	35.4	4.3
Mining	15.7	23.0	.4
Agriculture	21.1	22.0	.4
Utilities	21.3	21.8	.7
Construction	8.5	14.7	2.2
Total	45.1	41.6	

Adapted: *Yearbook of Labour Statistics,* ILO, Geneva, Switzerland, 1995.

sis. Here they are separated for discussion because of different histories, organizational cultures, and paths to management.

The women managers in the service industry were found in businesses ranging from the Japan Management Association, where Tomiko Suzuki is manager of the International Division, to Dial Inc. developed by Yuri Konno into one of the foremost information services companies with an enviable database derived from its beginnings as a phone consulting and information service, providing answers to questions about daily living. Women managers interviewed were from translation services, consulting companies, executive search firms, and manufacturing, communications, construction, and transportation companies.

Penetrating Masculine Domains: Construction and Transportation

When her husband's trucking business was threatened during the oil crisis, and idle drivers and empty trucks needed to be employed, Chiyona Terado founded ART Moving Company, making it the first company listed under "Moving" in the phone book. Moving companies had always been considered a sideline in the transportation industry, but her innovation resulted in one of the best-known moving companies in Japan.

A former flight attendant became a Japan Airlines personnel manager. Another Japanese woman, Mieko Otsuka, founded and heads a successful executive charter jet company, Circle Rainbow, in Hawaii, catering to the tastes of both Japanese and American executives. Mieko came to America to obtain a commercial pilot's license, which was not available at the time in Japan, and stayed to meet a need she recognized.

While construction is often seen as an especially masculine industry, it has 14 percent of all women managers and several at department head level. Kajima Construction Company, one of the largest construction companies, had a woman copresident. Two women managers from the construction industry were interviewed.

In the field of finance, women control the purse strings in Japan, with a husband's salary going directly to his wife, now often by electronic direct transfer, bypassing the husband, who receives an allowance for spending money. Thus women are a strong force in the financial world, controlling personal and domestic consumption, savings, and investments. But on the level of public finance, both national and international, Japanese women have not been visible. The first to recognize their value were foreign banks and financial institutions.

Citibank Japan has nine women vice presidents, of whom two were interviewed. Foreign banks in Japan learned early that while it was difficult to hire top male university graduates, they could hire the best women graduates who did not receive satisfactory offers from Japanese companies. Learning from them, Japanese banks also promoted women, and several now have women branch managers.

One of the interviewees had been a manager at Shearson Lehman and left to form her own companies. Kiyomi Saito told of trying to lease her first office and being told that her father would have to sign the lease. Even though she had been a well-paid manager for twenty years, she was a single woman and thus considered a credit risk. The financial services company of which she is president, Pont Du Gard Company, has done well, and she has diversified into management consulting, information services, and writing. Women in financial services in Japan said, "How can you trust women with personal income, savings, and investment, if you can't trust them with financial management?" A parallel phenomenon with a similar rationale was seen as American women demonstrated for reproductive freedom, asking, "How can you trust me with a child if you can't trust me with a choice?"

Voices of Women

Writing has traditionally been an acceptable profession for women in Japan, but not as managers of communication and information businesses. Now this has quietly changed, with women managing a variety of communication and information businesses, several in top management. Sawako Noma is president and CEO of Kodansha, Ltd., the largest publishing company and one of the top three hundred companies in Japan. Miriam F. Yamaguchi is director of Taoko Weatherhill, another large, prestigious publishing company.

Among newspapers, *Asahi Shimbun* has the reputation of being the most liberal of the daily papers and has a number of women in management positions. Chikako Takahashi is director of the international division and the first woman to sit on the board of directors. She began as a reporter in 1960, when twenty women entered the company together. Three remained to celebrate their thirty-year anniversary. They went through the typical path for journalists, being transferred to hardship posts and writing stories that more senior employees didn't want.

Of the other two, Ruriko Horie is a senior staff writer and fashion editor. Yoko Sato was a senior staff writer who became involved with women's concerns and the comfort women issue. She felt that her activist feminist articles made her unpopular with management and prevented promotions, but she stayed until retirement in 1994 and now heads a consulting company. She commented that "women are creeping into the corporate ranks, and the bottom of the pyramid is becoming thick, but promotions are not assured." All three women balanced family and journalistic life and felt the understanding of family issues made them better reporters. By 1994 there were a total of 150 female professionals at *Asahi Shimbun*. Their influence is felt as sexist language is screened more carefully, more articles of interest to women are found in the front pages as well as in the society and home pages, and a "Women and Work" page is now a standard feature. Women are moving up in other newspapers as well. A managing editor of the *Okinawa Times* is a woman, and *Yomiuri Shimbun* has many women journalists.

Television is one of the few areas that appear less sexist in Japan than in the United States. Of the flagship evening news shows of the five commercial networks, three have female anchors. In the early days of television news, the women were "hai-hai girls" for a man, that is, they would smile and say, "yes, yes," when the men talked. Now the majority are competent, hardworking professionals, with minds and opinions of their own. A simple and obvious reason is the ratings race. Women have brought higher ratings, the lifeblood of television.

In fact, when Nippon Television's nightly news, "Today's Events," had falling ratings in 1990, the network brass decided to change their usual dual anchor format of male and female anchors. It was assumed that the respected male journalist, Yuichi Aoyama, would get the job, but to everyone's surprise his partner, Yoshiko Sakurai, asked for the assignment and got it. As a graduate of the University of Hawaii and a former Tokyo correspondent for the *Christian Science Monitor,* she speaks English fluently and has more international experience than any of the men. The bold move paid off in large ratings increases. At forty-nine, Sakurai is clearly in charge, with "hai-hai boys" to complement her. Connie Chung, take note. Chung's reputed $2 million salary, about ten times more than the salaries of newscasters in Japan, was envied, but not her callous treatment by the network.

Credit for the influx of women newscasters is partly due Hariko Kojima Watanabe, president of HKW Video Workshop. She trained women to do news and economics shows, campaigned for their recognition, and served as a role model, for which she received an International Award for Outstanding Achievement in Journalism in 1991.

A number of women have gone from television to successful careers in business and government. Kaori Sasaki, interviewed as the president of UNICOL, a consulting company, and as founder of the Vision network for women. was a television commentator and personality in an earlier phase of her career, as was Noriko Nakamura, the president of another network JAFE, Japan Association of Female Executives, as was Naoko Doi Banno, president of Career Strategy, Inc., as were women Diet members.

The advertising industry was an early convert to women professionals when it recognized that women were major consumers and corporate success required an understanding of what women wanted. While women were first hired in staff or advisory positions, they have since infiltrated at all levels. Naoe Wakita is president of Dentsu Eye, a division of Dentsu Inc., the largest advertising agency in the world, and she is the first woman to sit on the corporate board. Dentsu Eye is a successful company that is majority female. Four women managers interviewed worked in other divisions of Dentsu and Dentsu Human Development Institute, a research arm, as well as the president of Dentsu Communications, Inc. in New York City.

Women have least representation in large, traditional corporations and trading companies. Toyota Motor Corporation and Nissan Corporation each has one woman manager at the department head level. Fuji Xerox, a less traditional company whose president is considered progressive, has more women managers, of whom two were interviewed. IBM Japan is noted for its progressive policies toward women, and although its parent company is American, it was quick to assure me that it is a Japanese company. Its personnel policies specifically set forth gender equity goals, and manager rewards are linked to success in developing women subordinates. Workshops for both women and men and merit evaluation are all a part of the stated policies to encourage competent women, which was confirmed as practice by two women interviewed.

Government

The government bureaucracy was the earliest and best employer and incubator for Japanese women managers. Civil service examinations, with hiring and promotion based on merit and open criteria have provided more equal opportunity. The Ministry of Labor has been in the forefront of developing women managers. A Women and Children's Bureau was created within the Ministry of Labor by the occupation forces in 1946, strongly suggesting it be headed by a woman. The ministry has continued to hire and promote women. Ten of the women managers interviewed had spent early years at the ministry, with three still there. Ryoko Akamatsu, minister of education, ambassador to Uruguay, ambassador to the United Nations, deputy minister of labor, and president of the Japan Institute of Women's Employment, began her career in the Ministry of Labor. Ginko Sato, who began in the Ministry of Labor and was appointed ambassador to Kenya and Uganda, is now the first woman commissioner on the Securities and Exchange Surveillance Commission, an important role as the market reels from corruption scandals. Former Ministry of Labor managers are representatives at the United Nations and the Prime Minister's Office, director of the Tokyo International Labor Office, a vice governor, and president of the Body Shop.

The Foreign Ministry hired career women in the first years after the new constitution, one of whom became an ambassador, but then ensued a gap of twenty years in which few women were hired until the passage of the Equal Opportunity laws. So after the first career appointment from within, women came from agencies other than the Foreign Ministry for diplomatic appointments.

The Ministry of International Trade and Industry (MITI) is considered a male stronghold, but it has fostered women managers as well. In 1994 the ministry had eight women department heads. Yoriko Kawaguchi, now a director at Suntory, and Harumi Sakamoto, managing director of the Seiyu Ltd., were both managers in this ministry before retiring to corporations. Fusae Ota, who when interviewed was director of the research division, is now a line manager of the housing division.

Academia and the Arts

The academic world has many competent women professors and teachers but few in decision-making positions. Less than 5 percent of college presidents in Japan are women. Tsuda University, one of the oldest women's universities, has long been the exception. Akiko Minemoto, who has a Ph.D. in monetary economics, is the president of Tsuda Jukukai Institute, the umbrella organization for Tsuda University and its related educational institutes. Tsuda University, the first institute of higher education for women in Japan, was founded by Ume Tsuda on her return from an American education in the Meiji era. Yuriko Ohtsuka, vice president of Meikai University, was formerly president of Tsuda University, its first married woman president. Before her tenure, marriage was prohibited for a woman president of Tsuda. Even a progressive women's institution was not immune to the stereotype that marriage and management are mutually exclusive. In April 1997 a major breakthrough came when Masako Niwa was named president of Nara University, making her the first woman to head one of the ninety-eight national universities.

Several of the women managers interviewed had graduated from Tsuda University, to which they attributed some of their ability to think for themselves and stand against convention. Over the last decades, subject majors for women at Tsuda and other universities have changed from an early emphasis on the humanities to include the spectrum of social sciences, math, and natural sciences.

Women have slowly infiltrated the fields of applied science and medicine. The second Japanese astronaut and the first woman Japanese astronaut, Chiaki Naito-Mukai, is a heart surgeon. Women interviewed were psychologists, obstetrician-gynecologists, economists, and physicists. Hiroko Sue Hara, professor of sociology at Ochanomizu University, has published widely on women's issues and is one of many qualified women professors in all fields, sociology, literature, psychology, law, mathematics, and science. Fumiyo Uchiyama, is a professor of applied physics at Tsukuba University, one of several. Overall, less than 6 percent of full professors at the university level were women in 1997. Mizue Maeda is director of the National Women's Education Center, under the Ministry of Education, providing resources and opportunity for research and dissemination of women's studies and related topics throughout Japan.

The arts have always been acceptable for women as dilettantes and docents but not as directors or managers. Women like Dr. Hiroko Nishida, chief curator of the NEZU Institute of Fine Arts, and Mazako Shimizu, curator of Setagaya Art Museum, are changing that. Author and artist Mayumi Oda, whose goddesses first introduced me to Japanese women's history, now concentrates on political activism related to nuclear issues. Tatsuko Ogihara is general secretary of the Noh Laboratory Theater. She was the first outsider to manage a Noh company, a role that had always been considered the duty of the wife of the leader. Now all Noh theaters have professional managers, but she is the only woman.

New Types of Business

New types of business have attracted women. One example is network marketing, the term used to describe a business form that uses the tools of networking for the distribution of its products and services. While the corporate structure follows fairly traditional models, the network distribution system relies on networks of people to market and sell the product. Each distributor recruits other distributors, for whom the original recruiter has responsibility for training and oversight and receives a small percentage of profit from the sales of the people recruited. Success requires efficient systems of communication, consistent motivation of distributors, and efficient product delivery. Japan's emphasis on personal relationships and the inefficiencies of the national consumer products distribution system have provided fertile ground, allowing the few companies that have been allowed entry to grow and prosper.

Amway and Avon have the most experience with this form of marketing and have made inroads into the consumer products industry. At a recent international conference of Amway distributors, one Japanese woman was quoted as saying it is not unusual for women marketers of Amway to make more than corporate executives. When questioned about her own earnings, she said in very Japanese fashion, "It's not correct to boast and brag, but my earnings are high." The extent of market share and profit going to these distributors is difficult to ascertain, but the corporate groups of each company speak glowingly of their Japanese markets. Amway Japan had a 20 percent growth rate in 1992 to reach a declared income of about $400 million, ranking 136 on the *Business Today Tokyo* list of the three hundred largest Japanese companies.

NuSkin is another network marketing entry to the Japanese market. Its marketing focus on natural products and health will provide an interesting competitor to the growing number of retail outlets marketing with a similar emphasis. The majority of distributors are women in all the network marketing companies in Japan. Their ability to quietly market to their friends and acquaintances at home has given them a decided advantage. Perhaps that is another reason that the woman interviewed did not wish to have her income disclosed. The industry has provided women a unique opportunity to earn incomes approaching those of their male peers, while maintaining images of feminine roles and a feminine industry. Knowing that high profits may attract more traditional businessmen, invisibility is an asset and a shield that contradicts the sales promotion techniques used in the United States to advertise and give public recognition to high earners. Cultural adaptations are essential in all industries.

From manufacturing to the arts, to entrepreneurship, science, communications, technology, and services, Japanese women have quietly but steadily made their way into management. This chapter has summarized industries in which women work and manage, the research process, and characteristics and family status of the women managers. The next chapter probes more deeply into the sometimes lonely and thorny paths that women traversed to management, exploring limits and the barriers they surmounted as they entered traditional positions or forged unique roles for themselves.

6

Paths to Management

Broken and Straight

Women don't know the sweet taste of success. Only the fear of taking the heavy responsibility is imagined, and thus women often run away from success. We need more models.

Interview with successful female media executive, fifties

Success for me seems like being able to do what one likes to do with happiness given the job satisfaction, fair evaluation, fair opportunities, and support. It is more difficult for women as the system and the mentality of the society is still in transition.

Interview with thirty-year-old female corporate executive

The views of these two women managers capture hopes and fears of many Japanese women who aspire to management today. As the older woman said, women are bombarded with messages about the high costs associated with success, and very few have tasted the sweetness of success. The younger woman manager would like to find job satisfaction, support, and fairness, but she sees the system and the mentality of Japanese society as "still in transition" and more difficult for women than men. She articulated views expressed by many other young women in interviews. They find their lives and the demands upon them to be very different than their mothers' lives and yet, they say, society's traditions and values are "stuck" in a time warp from their mothers' generation. Calm exteriors were occasionally breached by frustration at "the way the world is," but more often they focused on how to adapt or what to do to make it in the system.

Transition Persons

Women managers are in the middle of a changing world, an evolving global economy and workforce, and they exemplify the dilemmas of those in transition. A "transition person" is in the eye of change, adapting, following, and creating change, and thus the object of intense scrutiny, criticism, and approbation, both from those who seek change and from those who resist change.

In her first solo news conference as first lady, Hillary Clinton termed herself a "transition person." With her own professional life and successful career before and during her marriage, she is different than previous wives of Presidents who, nominally at least, followed the more traditional pattern of full-time wife or "wife as career." This is especially true in contrast to her immediate predecessor, Barbara Bush, the "mother figure" of many Americans. Hillary Clinton's lifestyle more closely resembles the present lives of younger American women, the majority of whom do work. She challenges deeply held values about "woman's place" simply by being who she is, stimulating heated emotions and debate often tangential to the topics she discusses.

Young Japanese women are similarly "transition people." Through their lifestyles, ideas, and popular culture, they serve as catalysts to remind traditional society that life is changing. Japanese women managers of all ages are "transition people." They are creating social change simply by being where they are and doing their work successfully. They are changing the images of both women and managers, putting in question deeply held assumptions about life and work. Working women are acceptable, and within the norms, since women constitute 40 percent of the workforce, but managers are outside current norms, with only 1 percent of working women in management.

Ambivalence, frustration, and resignation are not unexpected responses as Japanese women struggle to find success and happiness in a different mode. A professor in her early forties lamented, "I enjoy what I'm doing. I would be a full professor with a larger research budget if I were a man, but I'm able to teach subjects that interest me and make a living wage. My mother is proud of me, but she asks each time we are together about men in my life. She won't relax and be really happy until I'm married."

Crown Princess Masako epitomizes these dilemmas. Her Harvard and international experiences combine with an elite Japanese education and family to form the ingredients for success. She also fits the pattern discovered for successful women managers, having no older brothers. Before her marriage in 1993 to Crown Prince Naruhito, she was on the "fast track" in the Foreign Ministry as a trade specialist slated for top diplomatic positions. In her first solo news conference as crown princess, in December 1996, she revealed some of her feelings about her role. "While there are various ways of thinking with respect to how a woman should act, how do I find a proper balance between the traditional role of the crown princess and my own personality? I make strenuous efforts," she told reporters. "While placing importance on those old things that are good, is it not also important to take into account the demands of a new age?"[1] With those words she articulated the key to what many Japanese professional women are experiencing as they try to balance the past and their futures.

Then to illustrate the strength of the establishment tradition and the dilemmas she faces, the Household Agency, which micromanages the imperial household and its public relations, issued a more acceptable version. It translated her comments as: "With respect to myself, the question is probably one of finding a point of harmonious balance between a traditional model of a crown princess and my own self. I do not think it is simply a question of whether or not I am, for example, modernist or conservative." Her words were passed through the screen of acceptable utterances, filtered and sanitized, to fit what the agency, the guardian of tradition, defined as appropriate, just as it attempts to manage her life.

Different Paths

As Japanese women combine new roles, such as manager, with the traditional "good wife, wise mother" role, they take paths less traveled and not necessarily comparable with the male archetype. They are forced to clear away barriers and nonessentials and to develop their own compasses and maps to find the way. Diverse strategies brought women into the positions of power they now hold. Chapter 2 described early experiences that were important to successful women managers, especially the absence of older brothers. This chapter looks at later formative experiences. Awareness of alternatives to the prevailing social rules was deemed important by women who succeeded and transcended restrictive norms in adulthood, whether the awareness was gained from birth order and early family experiences or later education and experiences.

The previous chapter told where women managers are. This chapter will examine how they got there, defining benchmarks along the road, and identifying the characteristics of planned and seemingly unplanned journeys as well as wrong turns that ultimately led to success, noting social supports and rejections along the way. Some women used consciously defined and operationalized strategies, while others "backed in" to success with less conscious strategies that grew out of life experiences, situations, status, and events.

Straight Path to Power

As a bureaucrat who was highly educated and highly qualified, it was a career track and I knew that I would go up.

Female government executive, sixties

The path taken by this government executive is deemed the appropriate one by the norms of organizational culture described previously. She graduated from the prestigious University of Tokyo (Todai) in the top of her class and after graduation joined the Ministry of Labor, where she was promoted regularly, eventually becoming director of the Women's Bureau. Along the way she married and had a son, taking the minimum maternity leave allowed.

This path is considered the appropriate one for a manager and the one taken by most men. One should work hard and compete to enter the best universities, compete and use connections for a job in a top corporation at graduation, and once hired be assured of lifetime employment with rewards and promotions linked to seniority. This typical male executive path may have started as early as kindergarten, with cram schools available to help parents and children gain admittance to the best schools, coaching them on what to wear, instilling discipline and self-confidence so that the child will make the right impression for kindergarten or elementary school.

For each step along the traditional path, books and cram schools purport to prepare the child and family to fit, and therefore to proceed up the path. All lead to the goal of the "right" university, Keio, the University of Tokyo, or Waseda, where after an April graduation the lucky graduate may reasonably expect to be recruited and hired by one of the major corporations. Then ensues a subsequent steady, predictable path, following the corporate guidelines up the seniority ladder and finally retirement at age fifty-five or sixty. Not all men follow this exact route, and certainly not all make it to the top, but men are supposed to follow this clear, well-defined path. Women traditionally have not followed or been guided into this path, and have not been programmed for this route to success from childhood as men are.

In reality, few women start from the bottom and reach executive positions.[2]

Ichiko Ishikawa, the president of Takashimaya department stores, was one of the few women who followed the traditional path, starting in sales, learning about all the departments, and becoming a buyer and eventually president. Similarly, several of the successful women in journalism had been hired on graduation from the university and worked their way up. When hired, they were warned they would be subject to the same transfers, travel, and hardships as the male reporters. They were, and they survived

The traditional path, beginning at graduation and progressing through the ranks, was followed by less than 20 percent of the women managers interviewed. Eliminating the women who were under forty years old brought this number down to 10 percent of the women whose careers proceeded in a direct straight-line path (see Table 6.1).

The largest number of women with traditional career paths were products

Table 6.1 Paths to Power

Route	Percent
Direct, traditional	14
Over 40	10
Under 40	18
Indirect, nontraditional	86
Over 40	90
Under 40	82

of government ministries. Women managers over forty who followed the "appropriate" career path were concentrated in government bureaucracies, where entry criteria by examination and a defined upward path are public knowledge available to all, women and men. Established criteria, known by and transparent to all, made management more accessible to women, but even women following traditional paths in government were not free from obstacles, having to prove they belonged by serving tea for several years, by transferring to remote posts, or, as one said, by "working harder" and "being smarter" than the men.

The two women, mentioned previously, who became managing directors of Seibu and Suntory followed traditional career paths in the Ministry of International Trade and Industry, including *amakudari*, the "descent from heaven," by which retired bureaucrats find and are found for senior management and advisory positions in private enterprises. These two were pioneers for women.

The Ministry of Labor provides a shining example of developing women managers. Alumnae or current managers who have gone through the ministry's traditional career path include Ambassador Ryoko Akamatsu, former ambassador to Uruguay, former minister of education, and director of the Japan Institute of Women's Employment; Ginko Sato, former ambassador to Kenya and Uganda; Kyoko Fujii, first woman director of the International Labour Office (ILO) in Tokyo: and Mitsuko Horiuchi, councilor in the Prime Minister's Office, ambassador to the United Nations, and Asia Pacific ILO director. Its history of incubating women's talents goes back to the creation of the Women's Bureau in 1946.

The hierarchy of elite ministries would probably place the Ministry of Finance at the top, followed by the Ministry of International Trade and Industry, (MITI) Construction, the Ministry of Foreign Affairs, and then the Ministry of Labor. Labor is viewed as less glamorous, less often in the news, but it has a large responsibility for the welfare of workers and has developed enviable career paths for women.

Other Paths

Listen to how women managers who did not take the traditional route described their career paths:

> I just happened to be in the right place at the right time, when they needed to have women advisers for women consumers.
>
> > Electronic executive, 58

> The company was expanding rapidly, and they couldn't find men with my skills, so they put me in charge of the group.
>
> > Pharmaceutical executive, 39

> I was willing to wait and continue to work while they tested me out. There were times when I was ready to quit, but I wouldn't let them "win."
>
> > Manufacturing executive, 45

The paths that did not follow the direct traditional route were referred to as "broken" paths by both men and women, a strong indication of perceived incorrectness. The circuitous, seemingly indirect, route, with sideways movement, appeared as detours in the male model. Women stymied in one company went to another company, others changed professions, went to graduate school, took time off to care for children, had periods of part-time work, or started their own businesses.

The paths they took were often the only ones available to them at the time, and they seized opportunities, but the circuitous path was seen as not quite right, perhaps indicating a lack of commitment or at least not fitting the mold. The so-called broken path reinforces the observation that women do not fit, that they are by definition deviant in the economic world. When the universal is defined as male, successful women are deviant simply because they are successful and not male. All women are outsiders, liminal, on the boundaries, in the anthropological sense of the word.

Manager is not yet a socially validated role for a woman, and women managers must establish two identities, as women and as manager. Those opposed, who cling to rigid models, may attempt to show that women managers do not belong in either category. As outsiders to corporate culture and industry, women require extra energy for success. Unambiguous belonging is very important in Japan, with its strong ideology of social and cultural homogeneity. Women managers threaten both premises, homogeneity and unambiguous belonging. Japanese women are supposed to wield power indirectly, not directly. The most comfortable place to find women leaders is behind the scenes, wielding power manipulatively.

It is accepted practice for wives in the large corporate families to be instrumental in decisions affecting leadership and succession, as they arrange marriages, influence which son will become president, and often through their own family bring greater wealth and power into the company. Matthew Hammabata's description of this exercise of family power by women and the role of corporate wives provides a fascinating insight into the behind-the-scenes maneuvering.[3] Japanese society does not reward the direct use of power by women. Japanese women, even more than men, have been socialized from a very young age to achieve goals indirectly, not by speaking out or confronting, and women have grown expert at such indirect uses of power. As managers, they may be required to wield power directly, but so far they have been quite successful at remaining invisible. As a person at the margins, a woman manager truly straddles two worlds and must find behavior appropriate in both for herself. Those who spent early years without a male sibling in first place felt less trepidation in seeking expanded opportunities and trying out new behaviors.

The Ascribed Status Route

Ascribed status refers to the privileges and responsibilities accruing because of family origins or birth circumstances. It has different meanings in every culture, ranging from class to inherited wealth. Japan officially abolished the class system with its postwar constitution of 1946. However, the strength of the family, blood, and kinship relationships has perpetuated the special place elite families have in Japanese society.[4] Even the younger generation knows which are the elite families. Prime Minister Hosokawa's family heritage, descending from an old *daimyo* ruling family, was mentioned frequently in news reports.

While 90 percent of Japanese people judge themselves as middle-class, in the middle, and only 1 percent consider themselves upper-class, the elite is a subtle but still discernible group. Members of this group maintain ideals of education for service and family responsibility to a high degree, and many of the nation's leaders are from this group, with members of Parliament often following a family tradition from father to son. Tanaka is one woman who followed her father's path.

It appears easier for men to understand and accept the route of ascribed status for women than to accept a woman for whom leadership roles and success have been a choice. That helps to explain why men are so eager to say of a woman company head, "Oh, it's a family business," the implication being, "She did not choose the role. It was chosen for her because of her family."

Korea, where women managers have been even less encouraged than in Japan, provides a good example of this attitude. One of the largest department stores is headed by a woman whose family has owned successful international businesses for several generations. She is the youngest of thirteen children, and all the sons were expected to join the family business. Her older sisters followed a traditional feminine path and married well, providing grandchildren and traditional lifestyles that pleased her parents, but she knew since childhood that she wanted to be in business like her father and her grandfather, whose interesting lives they allowed her to share as the "baby." Even though her family had told her not to bother with the difficult tasks of business, she started with a souvenir business at the airport and built a successful business, including the Korean Duty-Free Shopping empire, Lotte department stores, and hotels. As her business expanded, she asked her husband to leave his government post to work for her, and he is now president of the company. Korean men who have told me there are no women managers in Korea respond uniformly to her name by saying, "It's her husband's company," even though her husband was not involved in the business until she hired him, illustrating how we see what we believe. Their belief that women cannot be successful managers leads to their inability to see women managers.

Many women managers embarked on their path to management naively, almost innocently. Others began with specific goals and, when thwarted, used other avenues. Career planning has not been a common part of women's repertoire. Until recently, women's career was considered to be eventually and inevitably, *shufu,* full-time housewife, toward which education was aimed. Career planning was not actually necessary for men either, since once they navigated the proper education, usually arranged by family, and were hired, the corporation did the rest.

Ironically, a circuitous route may be the career path of the future for both men and women as the demands of new technologies create requirements for new products, new and updated skills, diverse experience, and continuing education, and as industries constantly seek innovative solutions, new markets, and perhaps new people. Career counselors have recently emerged to help both men and women cope with the changing society and economy, with examples like Naoko Doi Banno's Career Strategies, described in chapter 8. Consultants are advising both young and old to make themselves "employable," which seems to mean developing flexibility and skills that are adaptable in a variety of company settings.

Benchmarks

Benchmarks are those points at which important decisions or events were formative and significant for the path taken, in this case, for becoming a manager. The first benchmark for most women managers was a glimmer, an awareness, that they could achieve and didn't have to follow rigidly the rules for women. This knowledge of alternatives came through different avenues and in different forms. Children of fathers, or in one case a mother, who worked in creative occupations, arts and crafts, had not been subject to the rigid rules of behavior as those whose parents worked in more traditional occupations. For some, the awareness of alternatives came through their family's chosen religion. Since Christianity is a minority religion and had been officially banned in the Tokugawa era, those whose parents were Christian were outsiders, and thus not as bound by prevailing societal rules. For others, awareness of alternatives came later through travel, living, or education in other countries.

Travel was cited as an important method of expanding horizons and an eye-opener to alternative ways of viewing the world. In Victorian England, it was considered a necessary part of young men's education, whereas in Japan the country was sealed from contact with other cultures during the 250 years of the Tokugawa era, consolidating and narrowing cultural norms. The opening of the country during the Meiji period began a rediscovery of alternative worldviews. The first Japanese expedition to the United States in the 1870s included five young girls who were to be educated abroad. That early expedition was the forerunner for their present-day compatriots who work, travel, visit, and live outside of Japan, discovering new alternatives and potentials for themselves. Seventy percent of the women managers I interviewed went to school or lived abroad at some time in their lives. Many had gone abroad as children with their families when their fathers worked or served in the military in another country.

Many women managers credited their ability to succeed to their education. For the older women, their education had not followed the same paths as those of their male peers and had encouraged them to achieve and become leaders. Attending schools slightly outside the traditional Japanese model was more possible for girls than for boys, whose whole future career was defined by attendance and a good record in traditional high schools for successful entry into the right university, the University of Tokyo for government, Keio University and Waseda University for business and academia. Women were not accepted in these prestigious universities until 1946.

Conversely, they were also not restricted by the rigid educational guidelines for males. Their schools often developed innovative and international viewpoints, skills the nation needs now as it aims for creativity and innovation and moves to internationalize and globalize. Women managers mentioned Tsuda College, Juko Gakuen, Sacred Heart, the Peeress school, Women's Christian University, Sophia University, and International Christian University as providing alternative models for them.

A few of the older managers and a number of the younger women used education and the specific university attended in a fashion similar to their male colleagues. Allowed to matriculate at the national universities by the 1946 constitution, some immediately took advantage of the opportunities, and that proved a passport to major corporations and government bureaucracies.

Another route to the awareness of alternative cultures is language. Women said they seemed to learn second languages more easily than their brothers, and research substantiates this tendency for girls.[5] The learning of a second language is related to expanding thought patterns, creativity, and innovation. The threads leading to this conclusion indicate that one develops new pathways in the brain and breaks up old patterns when one learns a new language.[6] For women this has been the route not only to expanded awareness and creativity but also to new jobs as their abilities with other languages, particularly English, opened career possibilities in international companies, as interpreters, or in translation and data services. Speaking another language served multiple purposes, breaking rigid socialization and thought patterns and literally opening new career fields. Early years without a male sibling in first place prepared women to more assertively take advantage of expanded opportunities when they appeared.

Benchmarks at Work

Other benchmarks were more directly linked to the workplace, summarized and grouped under categories of entry, membership, recognition, influence and leadership, and quality of life.

Entry

Entry into a system is the first essential hurdle on the path to becoming a manager. Women who aspire to management must make their way into an organization as members, or employees or, in other words, "You have to get past the gatekeeper and into the castle." The first milestone in many cases was the most difficult. Several successful managers told of many frustrating job interviews, with offers limited to "office lady" positions, before either giving up and going to work for a small company, starting their own business, or finally taking a secretarial or clerical job. Even though equal opportunity legislation "encouraged" companies not to discriminate, help wanted ads specified gender and maximum age of twenty-five as late as 1994. For only a few of the women was entry a planned and expected step following from the choice of a prestigious university, where, upon graduation, they had been recruited and hired.

Miyoko Machida graduated from college in 1968 and assumed that she, like her male colleagues, would receive job offers. She said of the employment discrimination she faced, "It was mortifying." Fortunately, Keiso Shobu, a publishing house, was recruiting for the first time in many years in 1968, and she was hired as an editor. Her experiences became the driving force for her editing and publishing over seventy books on feminist issues—issues that concern women and their place in the world. Books with seemingly innocent-sounding titles like *Women's Studies and Its Surroundings* were alien and radical concepts for Japan in 1980, she says, and in the 1990s feminist issues still are definitely not top market items nor mainstream publishing, but she has defined a market niche.

Women, as outsiders to the corporate world, may need more than one entry strategy. They described both traditional and more unusual ones, such as having a name that is usually a boy's and being hired without a personal interview, much to the surprise of the employer. Mentors, sponsors, family members who worked for a company, or support from a professor were all used by women managers to make their initial entry. In periods of economic recession, the entry process becomes more difficult, and a number of women chose to continue on to graduate school when they were unsuccessful in their job search. With a graduate degree, they were generally more successful in less traditional companies. Entry by examination with known criteria continues to be the surest path for women, as evidenced by the numbers in government bureaucracies.

Membership

Once in the door, the next difficult milestone is assimilation, establishing membership in the organizational culture, which is especially difficult for the first women to enter. Having gained entry, they often found themselves serving tea, the cliché used to define noncareer women, or doing "office lady" work, even though they had been hired for a career path. This was true in government bureaucracies as well as in companies.

The strategies used by women in this situation varied from serving tea for two years, even to the "new-hire" men in their department, before convincing their bosses that it was uneconomic to use them for this function, to the younger women who refused to serve tea even initially. They successfully developed a convincing rationale for their refusal, supported by a greater awareness of discrimination. Tea service is only a symbol, the tip of the iceberg, of barriers to assimilation, but it illustrates how difficult assimilation can be. Persons who are not truly insiders must always be alert against the dangers of exclusion, invisibility, and discounting by members of the majority. All said they required individual creativity, perseverance, and the support of external norms to become a real part of the organization.

Some commonly used strategies for membership by "marginal" people are adopting, adapting, and transforming.[7] "Adopting" refers to behaving as if they were members of the dominant group in order "to pass." One pretends to be or actually becomes like the dominant group, which in the case of Japanese managers is male. Women who choose this mode will act as much like men as possible. If successful, they are taken as pseudo-men, as members of the group, with the male's highest compliment being, "You think like a man" or "I forgot you were a woman."

A good example of "passing" could be found in the American South during the period of extreme segregation and discrimination. Many Americans of mixed African American and white blood, who were white skinned disavowed their black heritage and family and "passed" as white in order to succeed in the dominant white culture. The stresses of that way of life and the fear of being discovered have been described vividly, with cases of descendants only now, a hundred years later, realizing the deception and the loss of their nonwhite heritage and family members. The constant alertness to make sure no stated or unstated norms are being violated as one pretends to be something other than oneself creates a highly stressful life. None of the women managers interviewed used a pure form of "adopting," but they described contemporaries whom they thought had tried to act like men or instances where men had complimented them by saying they were like a man.

Adapting

The title of Ichiko Ishihara's book *Think Like a Man, Work Like a Dog, and Act Like a Lady,* summarizes the strains of adapting for Japanese women managers.[8] People outside the mainstream who take this mode become somewhat like the dominant culture, while maintaining a unique identity. In support of the unique identity, many also develop support groups of people like themselves. Professional and business organizations generally are formed for like-minded people to support and inform each other. The emergence of many such support groups for people outside the dominant business and professional groups is a new phenomenon, ranging from established groups like the College Women's Association of Japan (CWAJ) to the Association of Female Executives (JAFE), the Foreign Executive Women, to the Osaka Lady's Hello Work to support women seeking jobs, to women's consumer groups, which out of their communal buying projects have evolved into political voices. In this mode, marginal people form support groups as they enter the dominant culture and adapt to some of the rules, but not the identity. The groups sometimes become influential voices inside and outside the dominant group. Enterprise unions are a hybrid form of adapting to the insider culture of management. They represent workers but only workers in one company, without contact with workers in other companies; they are closer to management of their own company.

The groups of similar people may also take the form of businesses. Women have formed companies employing only or mainly women. One of the most successful moving businesses in Japan is ART Moving Company, which employs housewives as packers and movers. Friends in the foreign community in Tokyo have given the company unqualified recommendations, reporting that a move had never been treated so thoughtfully or carefully. Housewives, knowing the intricacies of the homes they are moving and the emotional meaning attached to household items, are able to manage the moves sensitively. This company provides a successful example of building on the nature of being outside the norm and having unique qualities of this outside group to bring to bear. In this case a woman entrepreneur uses other housewives who are also not members of the mainstream moving profession, turning their unique outsider characteristics into a marketable asset and success. Most of the women managers told of employing some "adapting" in their route upward.

Transforming

Yet another strategy of marginal groups is to enter while only slightly disguising their differentness, as opposed to "passing." They then work secretly from within to move upward, to change the organization and the definition of manager. This form of guerrilla warfare has high risks, and it requires being always alert. As one woman who had successfully climbed to *kacho* said:

> Make sure your accomplishments are public. Don't let your male peers take credit for your accomplishments. Tell people what you are doing. Keep coming back when doors are shut. Go to every training program offered. Volunteer for every assignment that has a possibility of making you visible. Be a vacuum for information. Visit the secretaries and office ladies, so that you learn what's going on. If you feel you have to serve tea, listen to the conversations when you serve. Never reveal your tactics.

These are all guerrilla warfare tactics for the executive suite. This woman emphasized the importance of making oneself visible but not revealing one's tactics. Now that she has "made it," she speaks more openly about tactics, as a spokesperson for less powerful women, but not too openly.

Companies had no experience to guide them in including women in the common, ever-present jockeying for membership and position in the organization. Building trust and finding a comfortable place are parts of the membership process that are puzzling and unfamiliar for many women. Orientation to the company for new male hires was traditionally an intense, lengthy immersion in corporate culture, as described in the earlier chapter on organizational culture, and had not been offered to women. A few corporations are now including career track women in this orientation or immersion, but it is controversial, and attitudes toward women remain difficult to examine and change. Training and development are crucial to success for all managers, especially women, but the inclusion of women has not been automatic.

Because of explicit stated policies and criteria, government agencies have tended to encourage women's development more than many companies. In other companies, the stereotyped belief that women leave careers for marriage and childbirth was a barrier to entry, but it was even more of a barrier to opportunities for education, training, and development. In addition, reluctance to send women on overnight training programs or business trips came from employers, as well as from some male managers' wives. One woman reported being asked if she had her husband's permission to be gone overnight. Overseas assignments, which serve as important training opportunities, have only very recently become an option for career women.

Recognition and Rewards

Having gained a degree of membership, managers face the next important milestones of recognition, rewards for achievement, and promotions. Given the lifetime employment system and seniority-based rewards for male managers that prevail in many corporations, promotions for men were routine, based on years of service.

In this seniority system, *nenko-joretsu,* a salaryman's position rises in direct proportion to his age. The system survives largely with the support of labor unions and the belief that it is an effective method to establish company loyalty. For the salary*men* who cannot be promoted, the company prepares a range of vague titles, which are now sometimes awarded to women as well.

Women managers reported being left behind by the men with whom they entered, getting lateral rather than upward transfers, and generally finding the career ladder not designed for them. Rewards linked to seniority in Japanese organizations usually exclude many of the women, not in theory but in practice. In organizations with a practice of performance appraisals, women's experiences were more positive, mostly in foreign or joint venture companies, but also in the increasing number of Japanese companies that are espousing merit-based pay.

Influence and Leadership

Along with membership and recognition, women managers must be able to influence and lead. Research has substantiated that when women reach posi-

tions of leadership, they may wield power differently.[9] Whether the difference is due to innate differences, socialization, or being a minority with less
power is disputed hotly. The reasons are interesting, but the reality is a tendency toward a different spectrum of management styles by women and
men. Some characteristics identified with women leaders are those that are in
great demand in the changing business world, such as sensitivity, lateral thinking, inclusiveness, and skill in interpersonal relations. A hopeful trend for the
future would be for both male and female managers to be able to choose,
within the parameters of their own personality and the culture of the society
and organization, the best style of management, rather than being restricted
by gender.

> Some say women are born to nurture; others insist we're better leaders
> than men ever dreamed of being. The truth lies somewhere in between,
> where people are individuals and gender, like race and ethnicity, is a highly
> unreliable guide to real-world behavior.[10]

While so-called feminine characteristics are valuable for organizations,
they must be accepted by subordinates and superiors. Women reported that
feeling accepted was difficult for them, with no role models or female mentors from whom to learn. The hardest part of managing for a number of the
women was telling men what to do, for which they had little preparation, especially giving criticism and negative feedback to men they supervised. They
agonized over how to phrase their statements, consulted with women in
other organizations, and tried to avoid meetings. One woman described
practicing in front of the mirror at home and then with her children, preparing how to tell one of her subordinates his performance on a project had not
been satisfactory. She accomplished it successfully, although she had to do it
twice; the first time she was too indirect and the man didn't understand her
meaning. But she said it became easier, since she realized the criticism didn't
destroy him and he was able to improve. All eventually learned to give cri-
tiques in their own way in order to be good managers.

Although difficult, the path up the corporate ranks has not been completely closed to women. Some women *are* found in management in the traditional companies. In compliance with the equal employment legislation,
each company hired women in the career track, but few have been promoted. While many companies see themselves as progressive and innovative,
their operating cultures do not encourage entry of people who are different
than the founding fathers.

Not finding acceptance, many leave. Some stay, modifying their goals,
finding avenues outside work to use their creativity and ideas. On her fifty-
fifth birthday, Ryo, an experienced Sony manager of almost thirty years, was

assigned a two-year stint in an economic organization so that she could broaden her horizons, increase her international expertise, and learn public relations. The president of the company had instructed the vice president of personnel to find the best place for her to develop, and she went unquestioningly to the assignment because she believes the company will do what is best for her.

Norio Ohga, then the president of Sony, had no hesitation in saying publicly that there will be no women presidents of Sony, even though the company is considered progressive and government policy calls for equity. While Ryo might like to be more successful and influential in her company, maybe even president, that possibility is beyond imagination at this time. A strong, assertive women, she is also a realist, so has invested her energy in projects outside the company, such as participating in a government commission, writing for a business journal, supporting the arts, and working to have a Japanese opera composer, known and admired in the West, heard in Japan. In spite of lifetime employment, not all men on the career track can reach the top either. It behooves them to learn from the examples of women how to adapt and create new options for themselves as well. Adapting, making do with what seems possible, is a phenomenon familiar to all women as we are silenced by our culture and accept the role of outsider because of long familiarity living with the rules. The contradiction between a progressive company and limited possibilities for women is taken for granted. Foreigners to the culture see the contradictions and comment on the "passivity" of those affected, unaware of similar situations in their own cultural blind spots.

Increasingly dissatisfied with available options, women have been leaving companies and starting their own. Creating a business is an alternative path to management for women that is growing in popularity. Women-owned businesses now number more than fifty thousand in Japan, and a survey in 1997 by the National Foundation of Women Business Owners estimates that 23 percent of Japanese businesses are owned by women. When women choose to leave situations where they are not achieving, the departure is interpreted by male executives as evidence of women's lack of motivation and perseverance, proof that women "can't make it." Far from lacking motivation, women interviewed left because they were motivated and wanted to work hard and succeed. These women-owned business are the subject of chapter 8.

Each of the milestones for women managers is an important stepping-stone. Establishing benchmarks and criteria for one's own success is difficult and socially unfamiliar. At each stage, the women discovered or developed strategies to move forward, with more than one strategy often necessary, either in combination or sequentially. Combining guerrilla warfare, negotiations, and discreet conversations with open campaigning, Ryoko Akamatsu and her colleagues successfully shepherded the original equal employment opportunity legislation to enactment, working behind the scenes to develop support, speaking out in international settings, collaborating, and compromising when necessary.

Quality of Life

An important criteria and benchmark for women is that of quality of life. The process of balancing work and family life is an ongoing challenge for women managers that has traditionally been considered a women's issue. Working women encountered the need for balance and developed unique methods and skills that could be useful to men and society. While many of the older women were encouraged by family support systems, younger women are learning to create their own. Male managers have only very recently acknowledged the necessity to pay attention to balance, to family, and to the quality of their own lives, and national priorities now include quality of life as a major issue.

Marginal people, those outside the dominant organizational culture, have valuable contributions to offer by virtue of being outsiders. Not being enmeshed in the accepted path, they can bring an outside perspective, new and different viewpoints, and creativity. Innovation and creativity are crucial for Japanese industry. In politics, women who have not had access to the fruits of corruption seem a logical choice to "clean up the government." Barred from the inner political circles and therefore from the corruption loop in politics, they are less committed to the status quo and may be more open to change. But before women can contribute, they must gain entry and membership and become leaders. They must break through glass ceilings or emerge from behind the shoji screens of invisibility as described in the next chapter.

7

Glass Ceilings and Shoji Screens

Perception and Reality in the Workplace

In Japan, glass ceilings are barely centimeters off the floor.

It is still difficult for women to find a company in which they can display their abilities with their work.

The areas of responsibility open to me are still very limited. I am irritated with this dilemma. The people above me lack the administrative ability to make use of my capability and talents in full.

Interviews with Japanese female
managers, ages twenty–eight to forty

Women, by way of straight and crooked paths, are making their way into Japanese companies, businesses, and professions and are moving into management positions. Even so, they are rarely found in top management. They are close to top management, see and interact with the top, but an infinitesimally small number make it. The phenomenon of being able to see the top of an organization, to be within sight and reach but not able to make one's way through, has been termed the "glass ceiling," a vivid image of the position of people with top management in sight but unable to break through. Only 1 percent of Japanese working women are managers, and they are concentrated in lower and middle management. This percentage has remained constant over the last two decades, while the percentage of working men in management has decreased slightly in the same period, from 7.8 percent in 1975 to 6.6 percent in 1994.[1]

A woman bank manager in Japan told of years of training new male employees who went on to senior management while she remained a teller until the passage of the equal opportunity legislation. "Assistant to the president," considered a plum position for women, is another example of being within sight and reach of the top. Several of the women interviewed had taken that position as the best one available to them on graduation, but they described it as a secretarial, glorified "office lady" role, which they found a dead end. I observed one such woman, in her late forties, as she reminded her boss where his next meeting was, held his jacket as he went to the door, and ran behind him with his briefcase, telling the driver where to go. She personified nurturing and caretaking. Japanese society and economy are squarely grounded in these serving and subordinate roles of women at work and at home.

Glass Ceilings

Glass ceilings are not limited to women. My American male colleague who sold his company to a Japanese corporation was asked to stay on as general manager. He reported that he finally knew what it felt like for a woman to face a glass ceiling. After six months as general manager, he knew that he would not advance further in the merged company because he was not Japanese. He saw the top management. They came to visit, smiled, wined and dined him, and issued directives, but his opinions were not acknowledged or factored into decisions. He said this experience of frustration made him more sensitive to the issues of minorities and women, since he had never before faced judgments on the basis of a genetic characteristic, his ethnicity, rather than his competence.

The number and percentage of women on company boards are so small that the comparison with men is difficult to present on the same chart (see Figure 7.1). Two hundred women are board members, while almost eighty thousand men serve. The number of women board members has remained unchanged and static over the last decade as the total number of board members rose rapidly until 1993 and then slightly decreased. One cynical woman manager said, "Really there are probably only one-forth the number of women stated, because the same women are chosen over and over. They chose those who have demonstrated that they will behave, not speak up and not make waves." The number of women senior managers has inched up over the decade, but as shown in the figure, is still minuscule, barely registering at all. The situation for top management in the United States is similar to that in Japan in that men far outnumber women. However, the percent of women corporate officers of Fortune 500 companies has risen to more than ten percent (10.6%) in 1997 (Table 7.1). The percent of women board directors of Fortune 500 companies has increased also to more than ten percent (10.6%) (Table 7.2). As in Japan, there is overlap by women holding more than one board seat. Of the 420 board seats held by women in the United

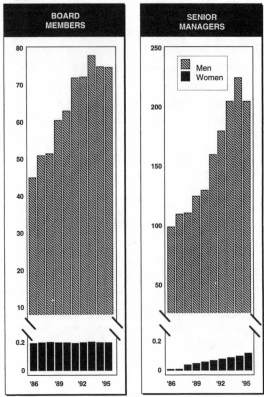

Figure 7.1. The glass ceiling for women in Japanese
organizations is low. While the percentage of women in
management has risen, that of top management and board
members has remained almost static. Teikoko Data Bank,
Tokyo, Japan, 1997. Graphics by Blair Renshaw.

Table 7.1 Women Senior Managers of Fortune 500 Companies

	Women		Men	
	Number	%	Number	%
1995	979	8.7	10,262	91.3
1996	1302	10.0	11,711	90.0
1997	1173	10.6	11,101	89.4

Table 7.2 Women Board Directors of Fortune 500 Companies

	Women		Men	
	Number	%	Number	%
1993		8.3		91.7
1994	545	8.7	5,731	91.3
1995	600	9.5	5,674	90.5
1996	626	10.2	5,497	89.8
1997		10.6		89.4

Source: Catalyst 1996 *Census of Women Board Directors of the Fortune 500,* New York.

States, 115 women are on more than one board. Twenty-three women hold four or more seats. Women are making progress into senior management and corporate boards of directors in the United States. But when it comes to income, women constitute less than three percent (2.5%) of the top corporate earners (see Table 7.3). It is, however, possible to portray them on the same chart (see Figure 7.2).

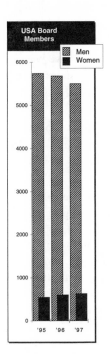
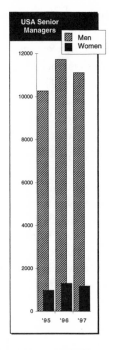
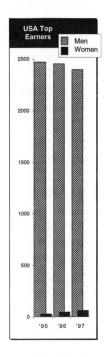

Figure 7.2. The glass ceiling for women in top management in the United States is also low, even though women are 46% of managers at all levels. *Catalyst,* New York, 1998. Graphics by Blair Renshaw.

Table 7.3 Women Top Earners in Fortune 500 Companies

	Women		Men	
	Number	%	Number	%
1995	29	1.2	2,471	
98.8				
1996	47	1.9	2,453	
98.1				
1997	61	2.5	2,397	
97.5				

Source: Catayst 1996 Census of Women Corporate Officers and Top Earners, New York.

In the United States, as a response to the dearth of women in top management in spite of Equal Opportunity laws and affirmative action, the Department of Labor undertook a Glass Ceiling Initiative in 1991 to examine the reasons, to define the problem, to determine the causes, and to see how the situation could be fixed. The Department defined a glass ceiling as "artificial barriers based on attitudinal or organizational bias that prevent qualified individuals from advancing upward in their organization into senior management–level position." It said that "qualified minorities and women are all too often on the outside looking into the executive suite."[2] This initiative was not undertaken for altruistic reasons but because the competitive status of the American economy needs to utilize all its resources, including those of talented women and minorities.

The following passage from Joyce Miller, then director of the Glass Ceiling Commission, makes a strong statement about the wastefulness of barring competent people from using their productive energies:

> The public perception of the glass ceiling is that it is a barrier to the advancement of women to upper levels of white-collar corporate positions. The problem is much broader than that. It concerns those at all levels of the work force—from the executive suite to the shop floor—who find their career growth limited by policies and practices that hamper their *productive energies*. Arbitrary floors and ceilings on opportunity have no moral or practical justification; *they stunt economic growth, retard national productivity, perpetuate exclusionary practices and inflict lasting financial and psychological injury.*[3]

Compliance reviews of companies with federal contracts have contributed to changes in recruiting, hiring, and training practices that are detrimental to the promotion and success of women and minorities in some companies. Although women have moved into more visible management positions and corporate boards, data from a 1996 Catalyst survey found that one hundred Fortune 500 companies still have no women corporate officers. Men hold the top jobs and have the fattest paychecks, with women accounting for only 1.9 percent of the five top-earning officers in Fortune 500 companies. The glass ceiling is alive and well. As one American women manager said, "Glass ceilings are just plain old-fashioned discrimination at the top level." The director of the Catalyst survey tracking women's success, Sheila Wellington said, "The numbers are pathetic."[4]

Japanese Women in the Workplace

A workplace is an environment, a culture, and a mind-set more than it is a physical location, and all have traditionally been male defined. Today women are in the workforce in numbers almost comparable to men in both Japan and the United States. In Japan they are educated as well as, or better than, men and go to the same prestigious schools, yet they are not represented equally in management or decision-making positions in any sector, industry, profession, media, nonprofit organization, or government. Japanese women managers are concentrated in entry-level management, with *kakaricho*, or first-line supervisors, accounting for 62 percent of all women managers (see Table 7.4)[5].

Even when women become managers, their salaries are not comparable with men's. Women managers earn[6] only 65 percent of men's salaries. In companies with more than one thousand employees, women earn 66 percent of what men earn, an improvement over the national average, where women's earnings are a little over 50 percent of men's, having declined from a 1987 high of 52 percent. One rationale often put forth to explain such a discrepancy is that women haven't been working long enough to earn as much as men. The assertion is that the ratio will change now that entry-level salaries of university male and female graduates are almost comparable at 95

Table 7.4 Japanese Women in Management

Management level	Percent of all managers
Bucho General manager	1.2
Kacho Middle management	2.3
Kakaricho First-line supervisor	5.4
Total	8.9

percent. But in 1975, entering female graduate salaries were 94 percent of male salaries, and now, over twenty years later, women managers still earn only 65 percent of what men earn. Women have not kept pace with men over this period even though they entered at a comparable wage.

Sticky Floors

What bothers me is the sexual difference that is shown in the pregraduation employment agreements. Some companies are explaining it saying that the graduating males are specially bright this year. Things such as this make me wonder what the passage of the EEO law has to do with real life experience. Whenever the economy begins to worsen, the first to suffer are women and older people.

Japanese female middle manager
with American graduate degree

This woman's frustration was directed at the entry process, but her later remarks indicated it was related to her own inability to go beyond the lower level of management, where she felt "stuck." Glass ceilings are evident in almost all organizations in Japan with few women in top management. A majority of companies surveyed by the Prime Minister's Office don't anticipate hiring more women managers in the future. Male executives say with impunity, "I can't hire women managers in my company because they leave to have babies." I've never heard a chief executive officer of a company say, "I can't hire men because they may have a heart attack due to overwork." Conversely, I've never heard, "Women have babies, so I'm going to hire them as managers because their listening, caretaking, and management skills practiced as mother and homemaker make them better managers."

The length of time women work for one company now approaches the length of time men work. The reliability of working women as measured by absenteeism is equal to that of men, and their performance is often superior, but statistical data have little impact on beliefs about women's behavior and proper role. Division of labor and roles associated with production and reproduction are culturally defined, with social decisions about appropriate conduct coloring evaluations of women's work and their ability to advance.

Women's ability to bear children is biologically female, just as men's ability to father children is biologically defined, but gendered divisions of labor into manufacturing, policy making, agriculture, food production, social service, child rearing, nurturing, and homemaking are social, not biological, decisions. When prescribed gender roles are the primary rationale for not hiring and promoting women, the risk of waste and dissatisfaction is high.

Shoji Screens

The doors to Japanese-style rooms are of the sliding type and consist of a light wooden frame covered with *semi-transparent* paper on one side only(*shoji*). The doors are rather low, so it is advisable to mind your head when entering or leaving.[7]

Shoji screens are beautiful and functional parts of a Japanese home. They screen the interior from view. They allow light to come into a room but provide privacy from the outside. Images may be seen in hazy outline through the screens when they are lighted from behind. The images are often flowing and beautiful, but unclear and unidentifiable. This describes the image of successful women in top management in Japan.

Along with glass ceilings, Japanese women have shoji screens. When women make it through the barriers into positions of leadership, they are hidden behind these screens. The few women who break into top management are invisible. Few others even realize that they're there. General opinion holds that there are no women managers. Shoji screens serve to maintain a collective denial of Japanese women in positions of power. When women's presence is brought to people's attention, the response is often surprise and disbelief. The next stage of the conversation usually finds reasons that "prove" the woman or women mentioned are not really managers.

Even the smallest shoji was big as the moon.[8]

In an interview with a senior male executive of a large, influential Japanese business publishing company, I asked about women executives. He replied, "No women in management in Japan." When I mentioned women who were members of the prestigious *Keizai Doyukai*, he said with disdain, "They are just flowers—decorations." The shoji screens are so effective that both men and women believe there are no women managers. They have been assigned a place below or behind conscious awareness.

When women become managers, it is in and of itself a social transformation, requiring a redefinition of basic premises. Cultural norms stipulate that men are managers. Women managers are anomalies, requiring shifts in thinking and attitudes by individuals, as well as in the structure and process of organizations. Women in management are difficult to integrate with traditional beliefs about women's role, and therefore must be kept hidden and invisible. When events do not fit existing beliefs, a psychological term for the phenomenon is "cognitive dissonance." A common response to cognitive dissonance is to deny that the unfamiliar exists.

For women managers, the screens also serve as protection from open attack, and so many welcome the invisibility.

> It's better to be invisible than to be pushed down. You learn to disregard your feelings to survive. Korean women are more overtly assertive and are pushed down harder.
>
> Japanese female university professor

Behind the Scenes

Bunraku is a wonderful Japanese theater art form, the most elegant puppet theater imaginable. When I went to my first Bunraku performance, I had been briefed about the form and had read about the play I was to see. The puppeteers, *kuroku*, in Bunraku theater, are draped in black cloth. Three *kuroku* are required for the *ningyo*, the large puppets, one for the right side, one for the left side, and the master puppeteer for the head and main frame. The puppeteers manipulate and move with their puppets. They are always on the stage and visible throughout the play.

My friends had said I wouldn't even notice the puppeteers because they are so expert. As the play began I thought, "Isn't this ridiculous. Grown people pretending they don't see the black-robed puppeteers moving around the stage with their puppets." The costumes of the puppets were beautiful and shining, the play absorbing, and when the intermission arrived, I laughed as I realized that I had forgotten that puppeteers in their black robes were still on stage manipulating the puppets and creating the action (see Figure 7.3)[9].

The puppeteers provide a wonderful analogy to the position of women in many industrial societies, where they perform important work, both in the home and in the public arena, and a collective, unconscious agreement overlooks their contribution and gives men the credit. On stage, in the public arena, in gross national product, and in roles considered masculine, women's presence will not be seen. This social agreement to pretend they are not there is successful. Women are honored as wives and mothers, but their collective presence is not acknowledged in other domains of society. Individual women are acknowledged, but not women as a group. This means women aren't seen as leaders or key actors, even as they continue to perform leadership roles and important work uncounted and unseen.

> I haven't been able to find a role model as a woman. There are no top women, and there's a shortage of information about working women and their environment. Japanese young people have little chance to consider

Figure 7.3. Famous puppeteers designated "National Treasures" are shown as they manipulate the elaborate puppets. National Theatre of Japan, 1998.

their future visions due to lack of knowledge of the business and professional world.

Japanese woman, university senior

In a parallel fashion, early research in 1979 by Rosabeth Moss Kantor on women in corporations in the United States found women placed in the most peripheral and least visible jobs.[10] These jobs were not the routes to leadership or top management, and the positions were almost invisible. Women's career paths were blocked, and new roles for women were hidden.

In Japan the shoji screens that hide women managers act as barriers to their advancement, but women also stay behind the screen because they have learned to get what they want from behind the screens. *Kuromaki* refers to the power behind the screen, with the *kagemusha*, or dummy general, out front being manipulated. This image comes to mind when one considers the invisible nature of Japanese women managers.

The Power of Cultural Imprinting

How are glass ceilings and shoji screens maintained? Closely guarded, shared perceptions about the world, repeatedly reinforced in statements and actions, serve to maintain the status quo. This status quo is reinforced by male executives who say women are not really managers, only decorations in top management. Shoji screens are reinforced by the Japanese mother who told me her daughter, with a Ph.D. and a successful management position, is working only until marriage, in contradiction to what the daughter had said.

Former Prime Minister Hashimoto maintains them when, as finance minister, he remarked to the cabinet that the falling fertility rate was a result of the higher education level of Japanese women, who were being distracted from their duties in the home. The principal of a prestigious preparatory school is maintaining blind spots when he asserts women's entry into the top schools will change the very nature of the school and excellence will deteriorate. These and countless other public and private shared perceptions form the dynamics of glass ceilings and shoji screens embodied in cultural norms. How we perceive events and situations determines our interpretations and evaluation of people, and consequently our behavior. The power of perception is not limited to gender issues; it influences every aspect of our lives.

> If countries in Europe and North America come to believe that full access to Japan's markets is being denied—*and here what people perceive and believe counts as much as the realities*—then inevitably foreign markets will become more closed to Japan.
>
> Ken Courtis, Senior economist,
> Deutsche Bank Capital Markets Asia

The quotation by Courtis, a well-known economist in Japan, not a psychologist, reveals an awareness of the power of perceptions and beliefs on events and outcomes. When we observe an event or see a person or situation,

Figure 7.4. Do you see pillars or profiles?

it seems as if we are seeing what is actually there. What we really are seeing is the event or person as organized and interpreted by our previous experiences and knowledge.

It is possible to see more than one picture, but we usually only "see" one picture at a time. Our brain interprets the stimuli from our eyes, and we "see" the picture with elements most familiar to us. In Figure 7.4, "seeing" one of the images is possible because your brain organizes the stimuli into configurations or networks with meaning for you and discounts other information that seems irrelevant or doesn't match your experience. Once one of the images is seen, it becomes harder to see the other because the brain has organized the stimuli into that particular pattern and afterward resists change. The pattern becomes part of our "map of consciousness," and the brain automatically selects what seems to be relevant information to fit that "map." Perceptions are an approximation of reality, and we choose in each situation, often unconsciously, the approximation that seems most useful.

Eyes are receptors of light waves, but these light waves, as stimuli, are organized by our brain into patterns that have meaning based on previous experiences and knowledge. The brain organizes these messages so quickly that we aren't aware of the process. Performing magicians use this phenomenon to create the perceptual illusions that entertain us. The interminable arguments about "facts," which most of us have engaged in at one time or another are often a result of differing perceptions.

Humans have a small but distinct blind spot in each eye, an area where the optic nerve enters the retina. The spot is not directly observable, but instead of seeing nothing at the left and right of the visual field, the blind spot is filled in with what we think should be there, and we do not know that there are actually blind spots in our vision.

Stereotypes work in a similar way. Patterns are formed, and the brain automatically fills in the blanks and interprets a new situation on the basis of what seems similar to situations in the past. These stereotypes can be useful, allowing us to save time and not have to analyze each new situation. They also can be extremely dysfunctional and harmful, however, when the patterns do not fit the external stimuli, with conclusions and actions based on patterns that do not fit the present reality, and it is not easy to change the patterns we automatically recognize.

In Japan and the United States, most of us were born into and reared in a world in which traditional sex-role stereotypes prevailed and were assumed to be accurate. Women are to be loved and protected as wives, mothers, and sweethearts, and outside the home they function in subordinate roles and traditional nurturing occupations, such as nurse or teacher. It was assumed with little question that women were inherently different than men in abilities, interests, and mentality. Men were objective, rational, independent, ambitious, responsible, and strong. Women were subjective, intuitive, emotional, dependent, and accommodating. Authority roles required men, and women were helpmates. Gender differences were believed to be innate and biological as well as factual and desirable, and some form of these beliefs prevails throughout the world. Most of us tried to live up to our culture's ideals for men and women. Changing circumstances have revealed gender role stereotypes to be just that, and research has substantiated that they are not immutable or innate, as women move into positions of authority and leadership in the worlds of business, government, and education, but the stereotypes persist.

The association of authority with men but not with women is learned early and reinforced daily for most of us. It has the same effect on our perception as the interpretations of the pillars or posts earlier in the chapter. Seeing an image in terms of one set of meanings makes it harder to see the same image with a different set of meanings. When men are "seen" in terms of competence and expertise, and women are "seen" in terms of appearance, nurturing, support, and subordination, these stereotypes supply the tacit or unconscious knowledge our brain uses to make automatic selections for where to place women and men. Beliefs about the proper relationship between men and women are reinforced by the actuality of roles in most organizations. The highest management positions are held by men, while women are often invisible. A spiral of self-fulfilling prophecy reinforces the stereotype of men at the highest levels of leadership and authority.

Research experiments confirm the influence of stereotypes on the evaluation of information. Judges were asked to evaluate essays attributed to male and female authors, which were actually all written by the same sex. The judges consistently evaluated those attributed to male authors as superior to those attributed to females. The judges were not discriminating intentionally. On the contrary, they were sincerely "seeing" the contents as more important, authoritative and convincing when they believed the authors were male. In another experiment, participants judged paintings for an art contest, and the same results were found. Those attributed to men were seen as stronger and more vibrant, even though all had been painted by one sex.

Thus, our perception of situations and information is shaped by unaware beliefs about women and men. We "see" what our cultural conditioning, previous experience, and history have taught us to see. In the workplace, managers' perceptions lead them to discriminate unconsciously, even though the intent may be complete fairness. Since all information is inherently ambiguous, ingrained beliefs about women and men influence perceptions, even though gender may be irrelevant to the situation at hand. A male executive with unusual insight recently said, "All people have strengths and weaknesses. When a man's weakness are identified, we say he needs to be developed. If it's a women, they're seen as something uniquely female and as a reason not to develop or promote the woman." Unless stereotypes are brought to awareness, they continue to influence decisions without our intent and knowledge.

Unconscious stereotypes are a key ingredient in subtle discrimination. Experimental situations in the examples described earlier compared matched performances, and the bias became obvious when the products were revealed to be from the same sex. In the "real world" such behavior is unchallenged because there is no outside control to reveal that the samples are actually all from the same source. As in the experiments, the resulting discrimination is unintentional, but there is no outside judge to reveal the disparity.

Discrimination builds up through many incidental impressions in daily interactions preceding a judgment while the specific incidents have been forgotten. We tend to notice those details that confirm our stereotypes and ignore or reinterpret the discrepancies. Because the individual incidents seem trivial, and often occur while we are focusing attention on something else— getting the product out, staff meetings, sales talks—specific incidents are seldom questioned. Judgments are made from the accumulated information filtered by cultural biases and influenced by unconscious stereotypes. So at the end of a project we may say about a female participant, "She didn't carry her weight," not remembering or maybe even not aware that her ideas had been ignored by the group and remembered and repeated later by one of the men who took ownership of the ideas. A Japanese colleague described her intense frustration at having worked for seven years to have an innovative project accepted and funded. Finally, one of the men who had originally scoffed at her ideas saw its merit and proposed the project as his own. It was lauded as a great idea and given funding with no recollection of her key role.

> In our company, we always treat everyone equally. It doesn't matter whether the person is male or female.

The preceding statement is probably familiar. You may have said it yourself. Japanese male executives I interviewed often said this or something similar. We generally try to behave with equity to others, and most of us believe that we usually do. But the way in which we see people, evaluate them, and behave toward them involves interpretation, a lot of which is unconscious. The reality is that we don't treat people equally, not because of malicious intent or lack of intelligence but because our experience and evaluation are based on our own perceptions and interpretations.

Discrimination is invisible or hidden because our stereotypes influence our perception of the criteria or rules for judging, just as they influence the information received. The problem is not that women are officially held to different rules than men but that the rules are unconsciously reinterpreted for men and women. When a Japanese woman arrived at work in the morning looking tired, her manager asked if she had been out partying or if her family responsibilities were interfering with work. For a male manager with the same look, the boss assumed he had been entertaining a client or had worked too late.

Perceptual distortions are especially difficult when a person is the only one of a certain category in a group. When one of the majority members misses a meeting or fails to contribute, no one notices, but when the group's only woman, or only black, or only man does the same thing, everyone notices. Women's actions are often attributed to their gender. When a woman speaks angrily, the response may be "Women are too emotional." In the same situation a man may be seen as speaking vehemently because the situation was important and he felt strongly about it. Women are supposed to be gentle. Ironically, women may finally speak vehemently because they are ignored when they speak calmly, a difficult dilemma.

Believing Is Seeing

"Seeing is believing" is a cliché that is considered "common sense" in the United States, but let's reverse the saying and suggest that "believing is seeing." It is more likely that we will see what we already believe and may fail to see what we do not expect. This is especially true in any encounter with a cross-cultural or strange situation. The culture of gender contains the most powerful, deeply held, emotional, and unconscious stereotypes, creating potentially difficult cross-cultural situations. In order to recognize stereotypes and move beyond them, a first step is to acknowledge that we may, in fact, be "seeing what we believe."

For example, data do not substantiate the widely held belief that young Japanese women are not serious about careers, but the belief influences the way they are treated and leads to criticisms about frequent job changes. It is "common sense" that women leave when they get married, but only 33 percent of the Japanese female workforce is single. Dissatisfactions about job conditions and lack of advancement expressed by women are dismissed as whining and evidence of a lack of commitment instead of investigated as legitimate problems. Belief that women should be limited to the home musters evidence to support this belief, which can be particularly deadly when coming from "experts." Examples abound in the literature telling women they "can't have it all"—all being career *and* family—while men are never told that.

The preponderance of males in top positions is taken to be the natural order of things and seems to prove that women are not suited for top positions. Men who are on top tend to believe they are there because of their superiority. Women at the top attribute their success to "luck," and women who are not at the top tend to conclude they didn't measure up. If this continues over time, men continue to strive and aspire, and women lower their sights to accommodate to reality, or they gradually tire and give up, finding the requirements for their advancement too great, further confirming the stereotypes.

The Gender of Language

The different forms of language spoken by Japanese women and men help maintain gender stereotypes. Men of all ages told me they don't know how to talk to women in business. This sentiment was expressed not by sexist men but by well-meaning men who said they wanted to support women in the workplace, but whose histories have not included women as working peers. Even though there are innumerable books available on how to work with and talk to women at work, men still find it difficult. Women said impatiently that men aren't reading the books, aren't understanding, or don't want to change. The books are available, but rules for working with women in the office on a daily basis have not been codified, have not become a part of organizational culture. The differences are so embedded that they seem natural and change seems unnatural.

The difficulty of male and female language patterns is very real and obvious in Japan because women and men actually have different forms of address, different verb forms, different noun forms, and a different tone of voice. Everyone knows and accepts this, but it can be a problem when men and women are interacting in new and different arenas at work. The dilemma for men has been whether they should talk to women colleagues in the brusque manner they have always used with men at work, or should they use the gentler form reserved for women. Women struggle with whether to use "women's language," which is more deferential and self-effacing, when their jobs call for expertise and sureness.

So far, no consensus has emerged. Most women in top positions use a gentler manner than the men, and many foreign words and mannerisms have infiltrated business language, making it easier for both women and men to assume a neutral form. In formal business negotiations, language is still a problem for women. If a woman is the boss, subordinate, self-effacing forms of the language are inappropriate to her role, but to older men, her use of a more brusque form would be offensive. Most women have worked out compromises to fit a situation, but language is just one more factor that contributes to both women and men's hesitation in mixed-sex working groups.

In the United States, men and women believe they speak the same lan-

guage, so difficulties in communication are seen as individual rather than social problems, but men and women have different language forms in the
United States also. Witness the spate of books documenting the differences in
meaning between male and female speech, such as those that say women are
from Venus, men from Mars.[11] Research has documented the different language and play styles of young boys and girls. Boys tend to use assertions like
"Get up" and "Give me," and they will do anything to attract and maintain an
audience. Girls more often use "Let's" and "Why don't we?" and may criticize
other girls for being bossy.[12]

The Language of Candor

A once commonly held Western stereotype portrayed Japanese people as
enigmatic and wily. The Japanese words *honne* and *tatemae* are well known
and often used in orientations preparing foreigners for Japan.

> Heavy emphasis on group harmony, traditionally essential for community
> survival, has resulted in the polarizing of form and substance in Japan more
> than in other cultures. In the business world unless you are very familiar
> with a Japanese person, he or she will more likely feed you the official line,
> *tatemae,* than tell you what individuals are really thinking, *honne.*[13]

The message is that Japanese tell you only what they want you to hear, how
they wish to be seen, and what they want known about themselves, *tatemae*, and
that *honne*, or real thoughts and feelings, are rarely revealed, certainly not to
outsiders. This separation of public and private, or revealed and unrevealed is
not so unusual. Each culture and each individual has areas of life that are public, that are known to those around them, and areas that are private.

The private self contains data known to the person, and public areas contain
data revealed to others. Areas we may think are private may actually be known
to others, and therefore are blind spots. Revealing these "blind" spots can be
helpful to a person's own growth and development and to resolving problems.
An example is the boss who pounds on the table and later says, "I wasn't angry,"
truly believing that he was not angry or at least was not revealing it, although
his anger is obvious to everyone else. Recognizing what others see may help
communication. As a consultant called to help with problems in organizations,
I find that communication is always a key issue. Communication and information flow are essential to productivity and problem solving, with a variety of
techniques developed to identify barriers to communication and bring forth
relevant hidden information to facilitate communication.

Whereas in the United States boundaries between public and private are

personal, idiosyncratic, and often unexamined, in Japan they are formal, ritualized, and defined by the rules and norms of the society. Maintaining the
boundaries between public and private is raised to an art in Japan. The for-
malities of social interaction prescribe appropriate times for *honne* and
tatemae. Shadings of public and private such as *uchi-* (in the family), *ura-* (hidden), and *omote-* (formal) are an important part of the culture and non-verbal
cues convey subtle meanings.

For an outsider it is almost impossible to distinguish whether one is being
told what the speaker thinks you want to hear, what he wants you to believe,
or what is actually the case. Testing often leads to a dead end as well. When
the custom of *honne* and *tatemae* and the rules of social interaction are combined with the reluctance to respond with a clear negative, communication
across cultures becomes complex. Some Japanese sociologists maintain that
this distinction between public and private in Japan is so unique that it cannot be understood by anyone outside the culture.[14] Others[15] question this as
another version of the Japanese myth of "uniqueness and homogeneity."[16]
Christopher Wood goes so far as to say that "Japan is far more like the West
than many Japan experts, with their huge vested professional interest in making the place seem more weird and different than it really is, are usually prepared to acknowledge."[17]

Revealing Blind Spots

Whatever the degree of privateness, deep beneath the private areas are the
unconscious, those things that are not known publicly or privately but are
deeply buried in the person. Attitudes and beliefs about gender identity, roles,
and relations seem to be held deepest in the unconscious areas. The beliefs
about proper gender roles and behavior are socialized so early that they seem
to be universal truths rather than culture-related behaviors, and they are integral to self-identity. Changing these beliefs is difficult, with the potential of
disturbing a comfortable status quo. The "glass ceiling" is a reflection of such
deeply held stereotypes, illustrating the difficulty of counteracting beliefs
about appropriate roles for women and men.

A variety of screens are erected to prevent discussions about intractable,
uncomfortable topics, not all of which are conscious. In Japan one such
screen calls on tradition and uniqueness to assert that the present situation is
correct. It may seem easier for both men and women to collude in the belief
that there is no problem, or that "there are more important issues to be
faced," while continuing traditional policies and actions.

> Traditions are generally regarded as unproblematic artifacts of social life,
> the comforting residue of the past carried gently into the present. Particu-

larly in a society such as Japan where the contrast between tradition and modernity has been drawn so forcefully and repeatedly, traditions have a reassuring ring of historical authenticity about them. My research in a Tokyo neighborhood found on closer inspection the apparent retention of traditional patterns is at best an historical illusion, that owes little to historical antecedent but much to the interplay of contemporary political, economic, social and cultural forces.[18]

Clues to blind spots may be revealed through observations by outsiders. When I attended an elaborate dinner reception outside Tokyo with a newly arrived American colleague, interesting cultural blind spots anchored in traditions of American and Japanese cultures were revealed. My colleague had lectured earlier in the day at a conference attended by women and men, and she was puzzled by the exclusively male dinner participants. When she asked through a translator "Where are all the women?" the nonverbal response indicated surprise at the question, with the answer obvious to the men: "The women are at home. They are taking care of the house."

Since we had established earlier that there were no young children in the families in question and that robbery of homes was not a problem in this area, she innocently asked again, "Why are they at home?" There was laughter and no verbally translated response. It was laughable to the men that one should ask why the women were at home. It was common knowledge in this circle that "women stay at home and men go to official dinners." The American blind side assumed that husbands and wives attend functions together, and the Japanese blind side did not question the long-standing norms of women inside the house, responding with disbelief and laughter when the norm was questioned.

Women in management are a blind spot in Japan. Shoji screens hide them and serve to maintain these blind spots. Their presence is obvious to those who seek them, but it is unknown to most inside and outside the culture. The experiences of women managers in Japan and the United States yield clues to blind spots in both cultures that mask problem areas, barriers, and resistance to change. Some people who say there are no women in management truly believe that is true, and furthermore often believe that is the natural order. Discrepancies between publicly observable women managers and statements denying their existence reveal the gap between what is observed and beliefs about how things should be.

Denial takes many forms. The one encountered most frequently was found in the disbelief in women managers' existence, with assertions that "there are no women managers." This view blots out the whole idea of women in management. Denial in another form maintained that women managers were not really managers, only tokens, flowers, decorations. Denial in a third form, equally damaging to women, maintained that the woman manager is not truly a woman, not able to get married or, more kindly, having chosen career over marriage and family. A litany of responses to protect blind spots includes avoidance, ignoring, reconstructing, underestimating, visible signs of boredom with the topic, open or subtle derision, and benevolent condescension. All such denials lack credence in actuality but have a wide circulation in society and are often effective at limiting women's participation. At best they are disruptive and disturbing for women in transition.

As a result, women have to credential themselves at each step of the way, continuously proving their competency. Once men are brought into a company, they are assumed to be competent, and they can count on regular promotions. While lifetime employment is not as secure as it once was, the concept still prevails for men in Japanese corporations. Even with objective criteria, women must still prove they are as committed as men and will not leave on a whim, or when they get married or have children.

Japanese companies have not abandoned a separate sheet on application forms that asks women about their marital status, their plans for children, and if they are unmarried, whether they live with their parents. While this practice is rationalized in Japan as part of the concern for employees and is certainly consistent with the paternalistic culture, it is illegal in the United States. American women given the form by Japanese companies in the United States were shocked. The applicants stated they couldn't decide if the companies did not realize such questions were not allowed in the United States, or if they considered themselves immune from the cultural standards enacted into laws, creating legal problems for Japanese companies in the United States, Canada, and the United Kingdom. When the Mitsubishi Corporation was faced with legal action for sex discrimination, the first response was to mobilize women employees for a demonstration to establish they were good employers, perhaps a clue to a blind spot. Only later did the company acknowledge the possibility of discrimination and hire a prominent American woman to head an investigative task force.

Every culture has screens to mask situations for which solutions are not easy or immediately evident. Pearl Buck, the American chronicler of Chinese culture, was denigrated by the American male literary establishment as a simple storyteller of everyday life. When she was awarded the Nobel Prize, those same critics asserted that it demonstrated the degeneration of the award.[19] Redefining the award was easier than admitting they may have been wrong. Susan Faludi's book *Backlash*[20] identifies "blind spots" in American life about women that affect behavior and social and national policies. She cites the use of emotionally laden words to erect barriers preventing clear assessment of actual events. "Radical feminism" is one such term whose emotional content diverts thinking from the issues by putting forth a distasteful stereotype. The notes section of Faludi's book contains eighty pages of references to the many situations and areas of public life she attributes to "blind spots" in national culture.

A clue to the discomfort and backlash associated with revealing blind spots may be found in the popularity of Michael Crichton's book *Disclosure*,[21] about the statistically rare experience of a man who was sexually harassed and discriminated against. Although Crichton insisted that he wished to communicate the dysfunctional nature of discrimination and sexual harassment against anyone, a sampling of male readers found in his book a relief from the discomfort of seeing men as perpetrators of sexual discrimination and harassment.

In the United States, the paucity of women in leadership and top management is screened out by asserting there is no longer a problem, that the issues have been resolved. Obviously that is not the case as statistics from the United Nations Human Development Index indicate that when gender-related development is taken into account, Japan moves from third place among industrial nations to eighth place, and the United States moves from second to fifth. The increasing feminization of poverty also cannot be ignored. Recent events in the United States, such as the disclosures of sexual harassment in the military, and several large judgements for sexual discrimination in industry, have illustrated the endemic nature of sexual discrimination and harassment and the multiple screens erected to prevent disclosure and public discussion.

Breaking through a glass ceiling may require assertiveness and brute force, with consequent injury and pain for the woman or person breaking through and for those around her from the "broken glass." An American middle manager said her mentor was helping her to use a glass cutter rather than a sledgehammer to cut through the transparent barrier. The shoji screen, on the other hand, may allow Japanese women to move up, sheltered by the screen of invisibility. Protected from criticism and other signs of displeasure, they may be quietly and powerfully forging ahead behind the screen. A Japanese senior executive woman may still function in the serving role, may pour tea for her board of directors and at the same time function in her role as manager. The screen serves as both limitation and protection. It helps to explain the man who said of his wife, the president of a company, "She's not a manager. She's my wife." Thinking of her only in terms of wife as she moved upward in the company protected both of them from acknowledging her power and protected her from resistance.

Women in the United States have their own form of screen and punishment for those who do not comply:

Up front, in-your-face women are more vulnerable in our society because we're applying a lot of old images to the modern women. As long as she stays behind the scenes to do what she does and does it the feminine way, it's okay. Eleanor Roosevelt was even more pilloried than Hillary Rodham Clinton. There's no general acceptance yet of a strong woman standing toe-to-toe.[22]

In spite of programs, legislation, and women's own efforts, women have not yet penetrated the inner circles of power. Japanese women blame lifetime employment and male dominance and attitudes. Japanese corporations blame women's absence in top management on women's lack of commitment and the priority of family responsibilities. American women have not made it to the innermost core either. They blame the old boy networks and vested interests. Whatever the reasons, women managers are not adequately represented. They battle attitudes, structures, and traditions and must try harder and be better even to remain in second place.

A few Japanese women are emerging from behind the shoji screen of discreet invisibility. Their visible presence will make a difference, may change the way boys and girls view the world, and may serve to influence the promotion of other women managers. Both male and female children face potential psychological confusion from mixed and conflicting messages in a society where women's work and feminine capabilities are undervalued. The devaluing may be subtle or not so subtle. The exclusion from gross national product of the work primarily done by women—homemaking, nurturing, dependent care, and family support—is a worldwide devaluing of women's work.

The reasons for the devaluing are complex and systemic. When half a nation's productive resources are not being effectively used, it poses a major challenge, and reasons must be sought at all levels in the system. With awareness and motivation, steps can be taken to change stereotypes, reveal blind spots, and penetrate screens. Stereotypes are created by cultural conditioning and social structure, and they are maintained through individual perceptions, decisions, and actions. For change to occur, the process must involve the social structure in which the beliefs have become embedded as well as individual perceptions, and then adapt social structures to support new ways of behaving, interacting, working, and rewarding individuals.

Individual Japanese women and some men are examining stereotypes, talking together, and encouraging other women to speak out. What happens to Japanese women when they do emerge and make their voices heard? The next chapter reveals women who are taking risks, inserting themselves in public roles, and, in that process, redefining organizations.

Part 3

PAWAA

A Redefinition of Power and Leadership

Samurai and Women Warriors

Creating Businesses, Reinventing Systems

I hope we don't buy into this system. I hope we get a new one.
Japanese career woman,
twenty-five

Warlords and samurai provided the models for current management in Japanese male-defined corporations. When women don't find the models working for them, they are faced with choices described earlier of adapting, adopting, transforming, or leaving. An increasing number of women are choosing to leave and start their own businesses, creating organizations and adapting systems to fit their own visions of the world, and they are succeeding. They are evolving models of management and organization out of their own history and life experiences. This chapter describes the overall situation for Japanese women entrepreneurs, the paths taken by women business owners, and their successes and challenges,[1] then compares their situation with that of American women entrepreneurs.[2]

Starting a new business is not an easy task for anyone, man or woman, and women face unique challenges. They must find credit without the usual networks, and must convince customers and clients that they offer value and will be there when needed. At the same time they are defining roles that fit them. While the role must be feminine, the economic battles require the talents of a warrior. Women warriors have been a part of Japanese history from its beginnings, and the current era requires them anew.

Recognizing that corporate cultures are not welcoming, women in Japan and the United States have set out on their own in increasing numbers to create their own businesses with their own organizational cultures. More than fifty thousand Japanese women have taken the challenge and currently head their own businesses. According to a 1994 survey,[3] this number is eleven thousand more than in 1990. A 1997 survey by the National Foundation of Women Business Owners found that 23 percent of Japanese businesses were owned by women.[4]

Many of these women began their careers in corporations and existing companies, where they found themselves stymied or frustrated. Unlike Japanese men, who tolerate the frustrations of their early careers with the assurance and trust that they will be promoted later, Japanese women do not have that certainty. Not only are they not guaranteed long-term success, they are given fewer opportunities and treated with less respect. It is not surprising that they seek opportunity wherever they can find it.

> When I realized after the first week at work that there were no women above me, I knew that I had to look around for alternatives. It took two years, but I then left to start my own business.
>
> Female executive, late thirties

Types of Women-Owned Businesses

According to Teikoku Databank,[5] nearly 70 percent of companies started by women are in the service sector. Since service-sector businesses usually require a smaller initial capitalization, they provide a logical beginning. Many of the women said they started companies to provide services they themselves missed or would like to have. As users of services, they are well aware of gaps and flaws, with niches they can fill.

Nikkei Woman magazine found that 27 percent of women-owned businesses were in research and planning, 13 percent in computer software, 7 percent in child care, and 7 percent in financial planning.[6] The women-owned businesses range from one-woman home care service for the elderly, child care, or bookkeeping services, to large trading companies, research organizations, executive search firms, and information management and technology services.

Average annual sales of the women-owned companies surveyed were 71 million yen (about $700,000). Women's businesses are found at each end of the sales continuum. Six percent had annual sales of 3 billion yen or more, and 21 percent had annual sales under 50 million yen.

The women-owned business are not newcomers to the business world. Twenty-one percent of the companies had been in business for twenty years or more. Only 11 percent had been in business for less than three years. Forty-five percent of the women had started their business when they were in their thirties, with the next largest group, 31 percent, starting their business when they were in their twenties. But age was no limit. Five percent had started their business when they were in their fifties.

Teikoku DataBank, the business research group, periodically surveys the largest women-owned businesses. Among the total surveyed, the largest number were in clothing (2,715), followed by real estate (2,347) and then construction (1,346). Lodging, restaurants, beauty salons, general retail, kimono and futon stores, and construction were among the top categories.

The ten largest women-owned businesses are listed in Table 8.1.

Types of Women Warriors

Women business owners took different routes to head successful businesses. On each path, they had to work hard and fight to prove that a woman could be a legitimate economic actor, could be on top, with the power to determine the fate of a company. In effect they had to be warriors to succeed.

I have identified four different types of warriors: family business warriors, warrior entrepreneurs, warriors breaking out, and warriors taking over. While there were commonalities in their experiences, there were also unique aspects because each type came to the top by a slightly different route.

Family Business Warriors

Kodansha Publishing Company is one of the top three hundred companies in Japan on a list published each year by *Business Tokyo,* similar to the Fortune 500 in the United States. Kodansha has reported annual sales of more than $2 billion dollars and publishes four books each day, as well as popular monthly magazines and weeklies. The publishing industry in Japan is very competitive, consisting of over four thousand well-run companies. Kodansha is the

Table 8.1 Top Ten Women-Owned Businesses in Japan

Business	Type	President
Kodansha	Publishing	Chiekako Noma
Josen Denko	Discount electronics	Jogu Mitsuko
Akiyama Aisekan	Pharmaceutical	Akiyama
Ikko	Petroleum	Yano Keiko
Otake Boeki	Trading company	Otake
Suzuroya	Kimonos	Koizumi
Iida	Sake	Iida
Yanagen	Department store	Asano
Midori Anzen	Security protection	Matsumura
Yamaichi Kosan	Concrete	Yamaguchi

largest. Chikako Noma became president of Kodansha in June 1987, on the death of her husband, Koremichi Noma.

Chikako's father, Seiichi Noma, had been the previous president, the fourth since the company was founded in 1909. As the oldest child and heir, Chikako spent time with her father, and in later years when he was not well, she was a trusted assistant caring for him. Her husband, in the Japanese tradition of families with no male heirs, was adopted by the Noma family at marriage, took her name, and became president of the company at her father's death. While he managed the company, Chikako Noma was a homemaker with five children. His death at forty-seven was unexpected and shocking. When Chikako took over as president, commentators and analysts made much of her being simply a loyal wife and mother forced to go into the business world.

In our interview, Mrs. Noma said several times that she was "just a housewife," but the reality is that she was and is knowledgeable about the business through her close association with her father and her relationship with her husband. Her protestations underscore the fact that, in Japan, denial of women's power is not limited to men. Women themselves deny and hide their power. It is true that Mrs. Noma had not planned to be president, but she is not simply a housewife and has carried on her husband and father's visions, expanding internationally and into other media, and also imprinting the company with her own vision of world peace and protection of the environment. Mrs. Noma introduces the multivolume *Kodansha Encyclopedia of Japan* by saying, "My father often said books are silent ambassadors. With their ability to transmit thought and culture with precision and accuracy, they are one of the most powerful vehicles for international communication and ultimately world peace and global development. I hope this encyclopedia will serve as a silent ambassador from Japan to the peoples of the world." The New York Public Library, which has been a beneficiary of her wish to be a good corporate citizen in the international community through a bequest of $1.3 million dollars, has renamed a reading room in honor of her father.

As president of Kodansha, Mrs. Noma heads the largest woman-owned business in the country. When her name was mentioned to males who found it difficult to think of any women managers, their response invariably was, "It's a family business. She's only a figurehead until her son is old enough to take over." She had been president for ten years, and none of those using that rationale had any idea whether her son, then in high school, had any ambitions for the presidency. Her management has led the company into a new electronic era in publishing and multimedia and has made it even more profitable. That same rationale of dismissing managers of "family businesses" as figureheads is never heard for the large number of Japanese corporations headed by male family members, which include such world-renowned companies as Toyota, Nissan, Mitsubishi, Matsushita, Kikkoman, Daimaru, and Idemitsu. Seventy-eight major Japanese companies headed by male family members were named by the journal *Tokyo Business Today* in 1992.[7]

Having inherited her company, Mrs. Noma is in the company of the majority (80 percent) of presidents of the top one hundred women-owned companies whose presidency came through family succession or inheritance: 65 percent from the husband and 15 percent from family. Fifteen percent of the women started their own companies, and 5 percent were promoted from within a company for which they worked (see Table 8.2).

These data are for the largest one hundred businesses only and do not apply to the remaining fifty thousand women-owned businesses. In comparison, among the top fifty-two women-owned businesses in the United States, 43 percent were inherited from family or husband, 46 percent of the owners founded their own companies, and 12 percent bought existing companies, one from her boss.

Another Japanese woman heading a family business is Miyoko Sakaguchi, president of Sakaguchi Electric Heaters Company. Miyoko is the eldest of three daughters of the company founder. With a patent on an industrial electric iron, her father founded the company in Asakusa, Tokyo, in 1923. During the war she studied at Nippon College of Physical Education, majoring in home economics, but she also had to work at her father's company. She said he was very strict with her, giving her a spartan education, while he was lenient with her younger sisters.

Miyoko became company president at the age of thirty-three. She successfully led the business, with a majority male workforce, through some difficult times to become an international company with seven subsidiaries and over three hundred employees. She hired her husband away from a civil service job to assist her, and he is now vice president. In her early years as president, employees changed her name in the pamphlets so it was not apparent whether she was a man or a woman. Although she still surprises people, she no longer has to hide her gender, as she led a forty-person trade mission to

Table 8.2 Routes to Success of Top 100 Women-Owned Businesses in Japan

Route to the top	Percent
Succession from husband	65
Husband's death	50
Other	15
Succession from family	15
Death of family member	9
Started company	15
Promoted from within firm	5

Europe in 1990 for the Kanto Employers' Association, the first woman to head such a mission.

Women with brothers are not as likely to head their family businesses. Two women interviewed had wanted to become president but were passed over for brothers. One of the women now has a successful trading company, restaurants, and a food service company. When she was young, she loved spending time with her father as he managed his successful publishing company. After her university education abroad, she returned to Japan and worked for his company. Her brother was much more interested in cars, mechanics, and partying, but she enjoyed the excitement and challenge of the business, as well as the people and travel involved. She and everyone else expected that she would inherit the business and become president. However, when it came time for her father to turn over the business, it was to her brother. He said a woman should not be bothered with business and she should pay attention to her husband and daughter. Overcoming her hurt and anger, she started her own business, first in the import-export business and then expanding into other arenas. She was determined to succeed and show her father, which she did. But she still spoke sadly of being rejected by her father and of her enjoyment working for his business, which had eventually been sold when her brother's management led to losses.

On the other hand, one younger woman, age thirty-five, is the chief operating officer of her family's business, which manufactures superhard alloy for high-technology ceramics. She is the designated next president even though she has an older brother. He wants to follow his creative bent into the music world, and she likes the business, so the family has blessed each to follow his or her own talents. Her husband is a lawyer whose office is in Tokyo. This has resulted in a commuter marriage alternating between Osaka and Tokyo on the weekends and holidays, an unusual arrangement for Japan today but one that may well be a harbinger of things to come. When asked what they would do when they have children, she smiled shyly and said they would have to negotiate that.

Another daughter who started her own company when her brother took over the family business is Merle Aiko Okawara, president and chief executive officer of J. C. Foods Company. Merle was born in Hawaii of Nissei, or second-generation, parents. Her father took his family back to Japan after the war to help in the nation's rebuilding and developed a successful food business. Merle worked for her father but did not expect to inherit the business, knowing it would probably go to her brother. She launched her own business in 1984 as a pioneer in the frozen pizza business. The start-up was hard for a young, ethnically Japanese but foreign woman who spoke little Japanese. Nothing was easy—finance, location, marketing a new product—and she did all the jobs, rolling pizzas, fixing malfunctioning freezers, marketing, trying to train and keep young workers. The company now makes home deliveries and guarantees that customers will receive their orders in thirty minutes or there is no charge, not an easy task in Tokyo's traffic. The business has over 10 billion yen ($100 million dollars) in annual sales. Merle attributes her success to a can-do spirit inherited from her parents.

Warrior Entrepreneurs: Company Founders

Unlike the top hundred women-owned businesses, most of the women entrepreneurs interviewed for this research did not head family businesses but instead started their own businesses. Kaori Sasaki's father was an entrepreneur whom she described as making and losing several fortunes in the course of her lifetime. When she was fifteen, he had lost one and was driving a taxi, so she began work and, as she says, has been working ever since. She sold tickets at a theater, put out an entertainment newspaper, and was generally a go-getter. Then she became a full-time television reporter for The News Station, one of the most popular news programs in Japan.

At the same time, she was working as a freelance interpreter and started her company, UNICUL International. Her initial motivation for starting her company was to improve working conditions for other freelance interpreters and translators, who were often exploited, underpaid, and working erratically. She also wanted to give them better training so that the translations would be better. Since her television programs added to the time she was putting in to develop her business left her only a few hours for sleep, she became a freelance reporter and eventually devoted full time to her company, which now includes one thousand registered interpreters and can handle more than sixty languages. Kaori also began the Network for Aspiring Professional Women, an organization for women entrepreneurs that has over three hundred members. She is working with Japanese banks to create a start-up fund for women-owned businesses, holds classes for would-be entrepreneurs, and traveled to the United States last year to talk with women's groups about affiliations, as part of her vision to expand the influence of women and women's organizations. She and two other women also constitute 10 percent of the members of the new Japanese Young Entrepreneurs Organization (YEO), an affiliate of the international Young Presidents Organization (YPO).

When I interviewed her, Kaori was nine months pregnant and had designed her own maternity clothes because she found none she deemed appropriate for professional women. At the time she was planning to bring her daughter to work with her, and she has since done so, creating a child care area within the office for all employees who wish to use it. One of her most difficult challenges is finding and keeping qualified employees. She expressed concerns about Japanese young women who are not serious about work, who don't understand what is required and leave too easily. It would be hard to match her energy. Having started her consulting company at age twenty-eight with 3 million yen in capital, she is an inspiration for younger women. Her vision is an economy where companies are more valuable for offering a favorable working environment rather than because of their size, market share, or type of business. She believes that Japanese men and society will change when the number of women presidents increases. It is necessary for women to lead the way and change first because they're stronger, she said.

Chiyona Terada founded ART Moving Center in 1977 when her husband's trucking company was threatened by the petroleum crisis in the first year of their marriage. Idle trucks and drivers were mobilized as movers. She was the accountant and manager; her husband supervised trucking arrangements and the moving work. As a woman, she gave the business a whole new slant. The company's name, ART, gives it first place in the phone book and the phone number for its thirty-five offices nationwide ends in 0123, making it easy to remember. The business has expanded to include a recycling center, nonprofit shops for furniture and appliances left behind in moves, house cleaning, trunk storage, and catalog sales. In 1986 the first overseas branches opened in the United States, and the business now has offices in Singapore and Hong Kong.

Chiyona's reputation is built on the quality of the moving experience her company provides. She has found favor with Japanese and the diplomatic community, using housewives to pack and move. The moves are handled carefully and sensitively by women who understand the importance of the home. Her "apron service" does all the packing before and the cleaning up afterward, and the shipment is disinfected en route free of charge. A "dream saloon," a cross between a moving van and a camper, can be hired to carry a family and belongings to the new home together.

A diplomatic friend told me that a move handled by Chiyona's company was the most effortless move of the many she has made. She was able to entertain guests the day after she moved because ART movers had put all her things away, and flowers and basic foods were waiting in her new home. With headquarters in Osaka, Chiyona is a member of the Kansai Keizai Doyukai, for which she chaired a committee on small and medium-sized enterprises whose report echoed her creative philosophy of success. She believes smaller businesses must rid themselves of rigidity to succeed and that managers must have minds that toy with facts, quickly perceiving the new tide of the times and exercising leadership—not bad advice for businesses of any size.

Another television personality who is now a successful entrepreneur is Noriko Nakamura. Her company, Poppins Service, is a child care support service that grew out of her own difficulties and frustrations at finding reliable child care when her daughter was small. The service is a membership system. Members can hire reliable professional nannies who have been screened by Poppins, by the hour or by the month. Noriko herself has a commuter family. Her architect husband's office is in Osaka, her company is in Tokyo, and her daughter attends school in England. Statistics are not available on such commuter marriages, but my interviews uncovered at least five. Noriko treasures weekends as opportunities to spend time with her husband.

After returning to Japan from studying in the United States, she founded the Japan Association of Female Executives (JAFE), affiliated with an international organization called in each country the National Association of Female Executives. She wanted Japanese women to have the kind of information and service networks that she had observed for professional women in the United States. The network, which has more than three hundred members, provides seminars, information, and services. In the "vertical" Japanese society with its firmly established hierarchies, horizontal networking is an alien concept. While women's networks are a relatively new phenomenon for Japanese women, they are growing rapidly. Mariko Tamura's recent book on women entrepreneurs, which is an excellent reference source in Japanese, lists twenty networks for women in Japan.[8]

Another group of women entrepreneurs interviewed were also members of a group affiliated with a network in the United States called The Executive Committee, or TEC, a prestigious group of company presidents with a minimum capitalization in the million-dollar range. In Japan the network was originally an all-male organization of company presidents, called Venture Link. When qualified Japanese women wanted to join the network, they formed a women's group called LBA, rather than admitting them to the men's network. Monthly meetings provide seminars and lecturers as well as problem solving to meet expressed needs. The women have businesses that include a gourmet natural health food restaurant, management consulting and counseling, the manufacture of soy sauce, civil engineering, real estate, and law.

Warriors Taking Over the Company

Yaeko Sagawa is president of Sakura Golf Company, a unique type of company in Japan that brokers golf club memberships, highly prized and very expensive in a land known for its addiction to golf. Yaeko started as a secretary after graduation from a fashion college but after two years asked to be transferred to the business side, where she was the only woman among ten brokers. The industry was new. Its members and potential members were the most affluent in society, but brokers were viewed with suspicion, since some had been unscrupulous. Being a woman was an advantage for her because women, who were seen as more trustworthy, allayed fears. Another successful woman business owner interviewed felt that being a woman was an advantage because, as the only woman in meetings, she stands out and potential clients remember her when they need help. Yaeko became president of Sakura Golf in 1970, instituted clear-cut practices, and insisted on polite, low-key service. Under her administration the company has had steady earnings growth. Women have to work three times as hard as men, she observed, yet at the same time appear modest about competency and success.

Kumi Sato took over an existing firm. After graduation from Wellesley College in the United States, she joined an international management consulting firm, McKinsey & Company. Two years later she formed her own public relations firm. In 1987 she and her husband financed a buyout of Cosmo Public Relations, which had been started and headed by her father from 1960 until his death in 1980. It was a cultural shock for many of the company's employees to have a young, American-educated woman in charge. Feeling that no one was following her, she consulted with other Japanese corporate executives and adopted some Japanese management methods along with her own style developed in the United States and with McKinsey & Company. The Japanese way involves consensus building, socializing with employees, and selling employees on your business philosophy and vision of the company, she said. After five years, instead of thinking of her as a woman, employees now think of her as the boss. It helps that, under her leadership, the company has prospered, doubling revenues from $6 million to $13 million in five years, during which time she also gave birth to three children.

Warriors Breaking Out

Graduating from the university in 1975, the only job offered me at Sony was a secretary. Even though it was for Mr. Morita, there was no place to go from there, so as soon as I found an opening in an international company, I took it.

Female business owner, forties

Many women business owners began their careers in the corporate world and left because they saw no future for themselves. As reported earlier, 87 percent of woman entrepreneurs had worked for a company before starting their own business. Several were secretary to the president, which gave them good experience but little chance for advancement. Several went to international companies but then returned to Japan to start their own successful companies.

Naoko Doi Banno broke out of Fuji Television Network. Her role as a television news announcer, which she attained after graduation from International Christian University in Tokyo, was a high-profile job that was considered very desirable. The network later sent her to New York City for three years. While there, she decided to leave the company and enroll in an American M.B.A. program at Columbia University, so she could "write her own script." She had a long-range strategic plan that included gaining management experience with an international management-consulting company and saving money to found her own company, Career Strategies, in 1993. The company focuses on career design, development, and counseling, management consulting, and market research. With insight into what busy young career women need, Naoko also founded NailQuick in 1996, a nail-care salon with relaxation therapy for busy career women, which gives a fast manicure and massage by the minute. She is planning to build her companies into a franchise network that will eventually be taken public.

In a different mode, Michiko Miyasu, the president of Denno Company, worked for several companies after graduation from a prestigious girls' school. First she worked at the company where her father worked, then moved to Marubeni Corporation, where she studied silk and rayon prices in the textile industry, learning about futures, commercial instruments, and profit making. From there she opened a baby goods store in Osaka that prospered, but soon she wanted more challenge, which the newly opening field of computers offered. She established the Osaka Electronic Brain Center in 1967 on Buddha's birthday by design, consistent with her belief that a computer is a mandala[9] that cannot really be explained. The company soon outgrew its space, and she moved to Tokyo, taking the name Denno, which comes from the Chinese word for computer, two characters denoting electronic brain. Her company develops and markets computer software, including the standardized psychological tests taken by all applicants for a Japanese driver's license. Her successful business career is a good example of the "broken" career path leading to her own business as described in chapter 6.

Two very successful Japanese businesses were started by women who wanted more challenge and stimulation after marriage. Reiko Lyster, president of Elle International Company, a distributor of prestige cosmetics, had a leisurely life as a full-time housewife, but she was not satisfied. As she said, she wanted to do something productive that would contribute to society. Her career started casually when she answered an ad for a translator's job at Max Factor, but she quickly worked into a managerial job, then became the general manager of the French cosmetics company Orlane in Japan. She quit, she said, because instead of doing the job as a hired executive, she wanted to do it for herself. She now does it for herself very successfully.

Hanae Mori, three months after her marriage, was already tired of being a full-time housewife, so she started her own business in 1951. She opened a fashion studio in Shinjuku and almost immediately had a thriving business making costumes for the burgeoning new Japanese movie industry. From there to her present imminence as a world-renowned designer and leader in the apparel industry was a long route filled with hard work and a lot of satisfaction. Her favorite motif, butterflies, gave her the nickname of Madame Butterfly, but when she first saw the opera by that name in New York, she wanted to change their flighty, unstable image. She feels that her designs have made butterflies a symbol of beauty and elegance.

Sources of Money

As stated earlier, the majority of women-owned businesses are service businesses, usually requiring the least amount of money to start. While women often start a business with minimum capitalization, even that amount must be found somehow. Sources of capital for Japanese women have been severely limited. It is not surprising that 83 percent of women surveyed said they began business with their own savings. This situation is almost universal because credit and loans are difficult for women to obtain. Many American women began businesses with their credit cards. Some Japanese women said they had private loans from relatives and supporters. Only 19 percent received loans from private or public financial institutions.

Recent developments have found organizations teaching women how to apply for loans, and they work with banks to facilitate the process. The Women's World Bank is an international institution that works to make small loans and credit available to women starting businesses. A branch of the Women's World Bank in Tokyo conducts training for aspiring women entrepreneurs and helps them find credit.

Education

It is pertinent to ask if any particular educational experiences were especially conducive to the evolution of women entrepreneurs. Of the women-owned businesses surveyed, 25 percent of the owners were high school graduates, 16 percent were vocational school graduates, 15 percent were junior college graduates, and 38 percent were college graduates, with almost 5 percent of the college graduates having advanced degrees. Japanese women business owners are well educated. They have more education than male entrepreneurs, since most male college graduates have traditionally gone to corporations or government. Young women college graduates, increasingly aware of their talents being wasted in office lady or dead-end jobs have become entrepreneurs.

The largest number of university graduates had attended women's universities such as Nihon Women's University, Aoyama Gakuin, Kyoritsu Women's University. Some graduated from Nihon University, while others came from Keio, Waseda, and Meiji Universities. Some research in the United States indicates the advantage of women's colleges in developing leadership for women. Further research would be necessary to determine if that were true in Japan, and whether the education of a women's college made them more willing to speak up, take risks, and become entrepreneurs. It is also not known if a women's college was their own choice or the only one possible.

At least one-third of the women business owners responding to the question of birthplace were born in Tokyo, consistent with the concentration of the population, corporate headquarters, and businesses in greater Tokyo, making business practices more accessible to locals. People who live and work in Tokyo consider it the trendsetter, the center and heart of the nation, and they view the provinces with slight condescension. The next-largest number of women business owners were born in Osaka, which considers itself on a par with Tokyo, followed by Hokkaido and Fukuoka, the major cities of northern and southern Japan.

Motivation of Women Warriors

Given the obstacles to success for women-owned businesses, there must be strong motivation to "stay the course." The usual assumption is that women want to make more money or gain greater prestige. In fact, these two reasons were almost last on the list of women business owners' answers to the question of why they started their own business.

The most important reason, given by 60 percent of the women, was to do work of their own choice, second was to contribute to society and work for social justice. The next three motivations were related. They were to bring to fruition their own ideas, to make the most of their own skills and knowledge, and to feel challenged. Sixth was that opportunity came their way, and seventh was the desire to be a leader. Last on the list was the desire to earn more money. The reasons they started their own business would be useful to keep in mind as we examine what companies might do to attract and effectively utilize women.

Comparison with United States

The fastest-growing business segment in the United States is women-owned and minority-owned businesses. In 1995 women owned almost 8 million businesses (7,700,000), or 36 percent of total businesses in the United States.

Fifty-two percent of the women-owned business are in the service sector, retail trade, finance, insurance, and real estate, but they cover all industrial categories. They generated annual sales in excess of $2.3 trillion, and employed 18.5 million people. Women-owned businesses employed more people than the Fortune 500 companies. Corporate layoffs contributed to this changed ratio, but the real driving force has been the rapid growth of women-owned businesses.

Some estimates predict that one-half of the businesses in the United States will be woman-owned by the year 2005.[10] Factors fueling the movement of American women to their own businesses are similar to those in Japan: frustration with lack of opportunity, the existence of the glass ceiling, and the desire of many to have more control over their own lives and fortunes. In parallel fashion, the same organization estimated that Japanese women-owned businesses, currently estimated at 23 percent of businesses, are the fastest-growing sector of Japanese business.

Sales by the top fifty Japanese women-owned businesses totaled $17 billion, compared with the top fifty United States businesses, which earned $18 billion (see Table 8.3). The largest Japanese woman-owned business, Kodansha, had annual sales of $1.9 billion. Little Caesar Enterprises, the largest American woman-owned business in 1992, the year that data are available from Japan, had $2.3 billion in annual sales. The largest American woman-owned business in 1996, Ingram Industries, had $11 billion in sales. All the women presidents listed are indisputably successful, and their success demonstrates what one successful Japanese woman business owner said: "*Results* come first. *Results* are the important thing. If you have results they have to accept you."

Successful American women entrepreneurs also need talents of the warrior. The challenges also are similar in the two countries. Japanese women business owners ranked the number one challenge as male attitudes and women not being taken seriously, and number two as financial barriers. American women rank financial barriers as number one and being out of the information loop as number two, which has some relation to male stereotypes and attitudes, ranked number three.

Women entrepreneurs, like women managers, have followed different routes than men. Women often start small, find a niche, surmount barriers in each country, and stay the course to make their businesses successful. Apart from the hundred largest companies, woman-owned businesses in Japan are mainly medium and small enterprises, where they have searched for and found niches for themselves. No matter which field they chose, women found themselves carving unique routes and requiring warrior skills as they fought the sometimes lonely business wars. The development of support networks has been one answer to feelings of isolation for many women entrepreneurs in both countries.

Table 8.3 Summary Comparison: Women-Owned Businesses in Japan and the United States

	Japan	United States
Number	57,000	7,800,000
Percentage of total businesses	5.7% of 1.01 million businesses listed in Teikoku Data Bank. Doubled since 1985	Estimate: 50% of total in 2010
Employees		18,500,000 in women-owned businesses; 11,500,000 in Fortune 500 companies worldwide
Average age of owner	57 for the top 100 women-owned business	40s for all women-owned businesses
Size of firms' sales	Top 50: $17 billion	Top 50: >$18 billion; total women-owned business: $2.8 trillion annually
Largest firm	Kodansha: $1.9 billion sales (International publishing co.)	Little Caeser Enterprises: $2.3 billion sales
Plans	Highest % will expand domestically; next expand internationally	37% are or expect to do business internationally
Industries ranked	1. Retail 2. Real estate 3. Construction 4. Kimono and futon 5. Hotels, inns 6. Restaurant	1. Service 2. Retail
Challenges as ranked by the women	1. Male attitudes not being taken seriously 2. Financial barriers	1. Financial barriers, credit 2. Not in the information network

Japanese women are learning to find and use support networks of women, rather than relying on their earlier dependence on men. Many Japanese women tell me that for now, until corporate Japan is willing to change, women-owned businesses are the best place for women to use their talents and find commensurate rewards for their work. This is true not only for the women owners, but their businesses tend to hire more women and provide more family benefits.[11]

This chapter has explored the world of Japanese women business owners, their paths, their challenges, and their success. Not all Japanese women have given up on the corporate culture. Some are warriors inside corporations. The next chapter looks at women who have become managers in spite of the masculine corporate culture and asks how they did it. On the corporate side, the chapter explores the factors that make companies woman-friendly and person-friendly.

9

Moving Shoji Screens to Include Women

The Evolution of Women and Companies

The highly flexible structure of the Japanese screen with its inconspicuous hinge system is integral to its beauty. Folding screens were readily portable and relatively compact to store. Their flexible format allowed for formal presentation aligned in parts with very even spacing of their zigzag folds or informal placement in irregular configurations.[1]

That the nature of screens is to be easily folded, readily portable, and relatively compact makes them just what a woman would need to screen her upward movement into management and to carry the screen upward with her. While a few women have come out to speak up against unfair practices, many women have found it easier and more effective to use or ignore cultural blind spots and continue upward behind the screen of invisibility rather than trying to change corporate attitudes and practices directly. Both men and women have an investment in women's power remaining invisible. For men, it sustains the illusion of power and seems to maintain the status quo, while for women it provides protection as they chip away at the bottom.

Women are making changes in their daily lives and at work to accommodate family, and they are speaking up about sexual harassment. But the difficulty of speaking up while striving to succeed means the majority of women who stay in corporations take advantage of shoji screens and seem to maintain the status quo, even though their very presence is a breach of the status quo.

Mito Nomura, a successful litigant for damages from salary and job discrimination, is one woman who did speak up, saying: "Unless women voice what they think is unfair, companies will not change." But she waited until six months after her retirement and then asked for and was awarded 4.7 million yen in back wages by a court of law, the difference between her wages and those of men with equal qualifications and assignments in the company during her thirty-five-year employment.

This chapter looks at the organizational side of women's success as managers, explores what companies have done and need to do to use women's talents effectively, finds organizational cultures that are friendly or adverse to women, and examines how women have succeeded within existing systems. The intertwined nature of organization culture and the behavior of individual members is less clear while one is immersed in a situation, but it is always important. As one woman said, "I can't tell you I haven't been patronized or discriminated against, but I don't focus on that. Nothing is gained by looking at the negative. I can't help how other people feel." Her screen shields her, at least partially, from the negative behaviors.

The slightly shielded route was taken by Ichiko Ishikawa, president of Takashimaya, described in Chapter 6. She entered the company on graduation and, through a combination of ignoring and pushing through barriers, worked her way from buyer to manager to president. Another such woman is Yukako Uchinaga, the first female board member at a major computer firm in Japan. She is director of software development for the Asia Pacific region of IBM Japan, which she joined in 1971 on graduation from the University of Tokyo. She attributes her success to two things—having specific goals for her career and being lucky to have people around who were not too prejudiced against women working with them. She recalled, however, that each time she was transferred to a new section she had a hard time breaking in. Her statements encompass two elements of the corporate system that are relevant to the success of women managers—the individual and the organization. Women must speak up, but at the same time corporations must listen if changes are to be made.

Woman managers, by their very presence, constitute change for corporations, so an important characteristic of companies to be explored is their openness to change. Uchinaga's company, IBM Japan, is considered one of the best companies for Japanese women, as ranked by an annual survey.[2] In this survey of the best ten companies, Seibu ranks first, with Recruit and Sony tied for second place. These three are followed by IBM Japan, with Daimaru and NTT tied for fifth place, followed by Credit Saison. Isetan and Seiyu tied for eighth place, and then Odakyu.

The survey results offer a first step in examining companies with cultures supportive of women. The criteria for choosing the best companies included many of the things women interviewed said they would like from corporations, ranked by their importance:

1. Long-term perspective
2. Women can be and are managers
3. Equality of opportunity in training
4. *Yutori* (working hours, holidays, less overtime)
5. *Iyohashi* (salary) and
6. Work after having a baby with family leave provided

The ranking of criteria confound the expectations of many male managers, who expect women to rank family leave and child care first. The criteria used by women to rank the best companies are consistent with the motivations of women business owners in the previous chapter. Women want companies that judge them with a long-term perspective rather than as temporary workers and companies that provide training and development opportunities. It is also important that companies already have women in management. This is akin to Joseph Heller's novel *Catch-22*. Women stand a much better chance of getting promoted into executive positions when the company already has women at the executive level. When men exclusively hold those slots, it is more difficult for women to make inroads. The obvious dilemma is how to get women there in the first place. Some experts have suggested that if we want women as well as men to be managers, outside intervention is needed to get the process started.[3]

The importance of training and development opportunities has been amply demonstrated and appears self-evident, but apparently not to systems entrenched in separate and unequal training for women. Criterion 4, *yutori,* or working hours, asked if employees took holidays and vacations and were not pressured by peers or bosses to forgo legitimate time off. The criterion did not indicate an unwillingness to work hard but asked only if there was pressure for longer hours than necessary. Salary was important, both as an indication of value to the company and as an economic necessity for women as well as men. Family leave was important in determining whether a guarantee of their job on return to the company was an integral part of leave policies.

Four of the companies on the list are also among the top one hundred companies in Japan as ranked by *Tokyo Business Today*.[4] These "women-friendly" companies are profitable and effective, not only suffering no loss of productivity but perhaps even gaining enhanced productivity. IBM Japan has a publicly stated and written policy of supporting women managers. Senior managers' rewards are linked to support of competent women in their division, and all training and development programs are published and open to both men and women. Programs are also offered and supported to help men and women work together. So Yukako Uchinaga was correct in saying she was lucky in the people she worked with and, one would add, in the company she chose to work for.

As can be seen from the survey results, six of the ten best companies for women are in the retail industry. Worldwide, department stores have used women as salespeople, but the advancement of women into management in the industry is a more recent development in the United States, and even more recent in Japan. The majority of department store customers are women, with their tastes determining sales and consequently profits. Organizational cultures in the retail industry have evolved over time to acknowledge this customer base and meet changing circumstances, and in the process they have become more supportive of women managers.

Among the top-ranked companies in this listing of best companies for women are Seibu, Credit Saison, and Seiyu, all members of the Saison group, which operates stores across Japan, and has expanded internationally with offices in Singapore and Hong Kong and with the purchase of the Intercontinental Hotel chain. The Saison group has been in the forefront of employer assistance for child care. In 1993 Harumi Sakamoto was appointed a senior managing director of Seiyu, number eight on the list of best companies and a member of the Seibu group. She is one of the few top female executives in the industry, and was the first woman to preside at a directors' annual meeting. Her position fulfills one criteria for best companies, that of already having women in management. Having come from a senior management position at (MITI) the Ministry of International Trade and Industry, she has a broader perspective than many executives, and as the mother of three children, she has an understanding of work-family dynamics. Ms. Sakamoto is an articulate spokeswoman for the rights of women workers, and she has courageously chided industry for its condescending attitudes to women and its callous treatment of both men and women, disregarding family life, requiring night work and long overtime, and offering limited family leave.

Department stores primarily serve a female market and have long needed the perspective of women. Until recently, a man was often at the top, but the culture within the companies has tended to be less male-defined, since a majority of salespeople and first-line supervisors have been women. The necessity to be on the cutting edge of women's preferences has led to the development of department store cultures supportive of women, as evidenced by the six businesses listed as best companies.

The remaining four companies on the list are service industries and postwar technology industries, the latter a category that includes information systems and telecommunications. Recruit, Sony, IBM Japan, and Nippon Telegraph and Telephone Corporation (NTT), *Nippon Denshin Denwa* are communication, information, electronics, and service companies.

Continuum of Organizational Culture

Organizations clearly vary in the degree to which they welcome and support women. Based on interviews with women managers, literature, and experience within organizations, I developed a continuum of organizational culture to describe the characteristics of organizations that contribute to women's success as managers (see Table 9.1). The continuum moves from the

Table 9.1 Continuum of Organizational Cultures*

Traditional-Feudal	Transitional	Evolving	Open	Visions for the Future
■ Managers require lifetime employment			■ Long-term perspective includes women	■ Includes characteristics of "Open" plus
■ Male graduates recruited			■ Flatter, less rigid hierarchy	■ Sustainable productivity
■ Rigid hierarchies			■ Permeable boundaries	■ Inclusive
■ Defined for men			■ Performance-based rewards, merit	■ Women-friendly
■ Criteria of employment and rewards closely held, secret	■ Retains traditional character but hires some career women with clear distinction between career and clerical tracks	■ Includes more of the practices of open companies but retains tradition and usually has third track for women without travel	■ Criteria public and clearly stated	■ Career-positive
■ Reward seniority-based	■ Recruits limited number of female graduates	■ Recruits specified number of female graduates	■ Women found in management	■ Open boundaries
■ Closed boundaries			■ Flexible rules	■ Women help define performance measures
■ Women subordinate			■ Clear guidelines for family leave	■ Value diversity
■ Long-term perspective excludes women			■ Available to both men and women	■ Adaptable
			■ International	■ Flexible
■ Only information specific to each task shared			■ Ecological awareness	■ Citizen of community and world
			■ Information flow encouraged	■ Ecological awareness practiced

*Characteristics associated with each category from interview data and literature search

left, with traditional cultures less friendly for women, to the right, with companies that are most "women-friendly."

The continuum maps in a nonformal way characteristics of companies described by women managers. It depicts factors relative to women's success as
managers in organizations in a variety of industries. Industries whose major
clients are women and which cater to women tended to develop cultures generally more supportive of women managers, as do the newer service and technology industries, government bureaucracies with formal entry and promotion criteria, and some companies headed by women. In their interviews,
women managers talked about the characteristics that made companies
woman-friendly. They were later asked to rank their own and other companies
with which they were familiar on the scale calibrated from least open to most
open for women. The labels for the waystations, or benchmarks, on the continuum grew out of their descriptions from traditional to open, with transitional
and evolving categories positioned between. The final column, "open," contains an amalgam of characteristics on the women's wish lists.

The organizations near the left-hand end of the continuum have the most
traditional values and assumptions. By definition, a continuum is a continuous line, and any point on the line is flowing. Placing real companies on the
continuum provides a snapshot in time and a subjective evaluation. A few
women were uncomfortable in placing Japanese companies on the scale, but
others gleefully spotted where they thought companies belonged.

Originally the continuum began with "feudal," a word often used by
women to describe corporate culture, moving to traditional. No one was
willing to locate her own company on the "feudal" spectrum, even when descriptions matched the characteristics of feudal. The word was apparently too
emotionally loaded and judgmental. Women would, however, give examples
of "other companies" that fit the category. Conversely, their company might
have been defined by someone else as feudal, but they exhibited a general reluctance to have their company, even anonymously, identified as feudal. In
addition, the tendency to be in the middle of a scale, even more pronounced
in Japan than in the United States, seemed to preclude evaluating their own
company as feudal. The continuum was shortened to conform to the Likert
Scale,[5] and still few defined their companies in the "traditional-feudal" category. Most chose the category "transitional," with a rare company defined as
"open."

Companies on the Open Side

Companies in the communications industry fell somewhere in the middle of
the continuum between traditional and open corporations, but usually they

were closer to open. The technologies of the industry are more recent, and the companies are relatively new, so their cultures are less traditional and established. As businesses that began with hardware and electronics gradually become complete communications companies, spanning a spectrum from hardware to content and circling the globe, their cultures have inevitably changed, evolving toward more open.

IBM Japan, with its roots in IBM USA but proud of being a completely Japanese company, has a top-level manager responsible for the effective recruiting, hiring, and promotion of women. Reward systems have been amended to include an evaluation of the success of managers in utilizing and developing women employees. The company was rated open on the continuum by several women. Information services, database management, publishing, journalism, and data research organizations have required new and scarce skills. Women with these skills found entry easier, with opportunities to move quickly up the promotions ladder as their skills and experience are needed. Several of the newer communications, software, and telecommunications companies were founded and are headed by women.

Fuji Xerox, a company in the information hardware, software, and photographic industry, has an innovation support program that fosters new ideas among employees and helps bring them to fruition. One of the winners of the innovation award with start-up money to apply her ideas was Reiko Etoh, who became president of Ariadne Language Link, whose product is *Nihon-go*, a Japanese language program incorporating computer software and training to individualize the learning of Japanese. Reiko was a secretary at Fuji when she submitted her proposal for the company, and now, at twenty-eight, is a young president who hopes that her company will make a good profit before the three-year sponsorship by Fuji Xerox ends. Reiko, the only woman recipient of this grant to date, feels she must justify the confidence shown her.

Sony Corporation is unique in the evolution of its culture. As a postwar corporation in Japan, its culture has been greatly influenced by its large international market. Even before its acquisitions and mergers in the entertainment industry in the United States, it had achieved a reputation throughout the world for innovation. Honorary Chairman Akio Morita is known internationally for his philosophy, his articulate statements, and his books *Made in Japan* and the controversial *The Japan That Can Say No*. His successor, Norio Ohga, has expanded into all phases of the communication business, from hardware to software and the entertainment industry. Since its beginnings after the war in Masaru Ibuka's garage, adapting Japanese radios with transistors to receive the shortwave reception that had been prohibited during the war, Sony has used creativity, innovation, and risk taking to become a powerful player on the world stage.

Sony's most famous product may be the Walkman, the music machine worn by young and old around the world. One of the women managers interviewed, Ryo Ochiai, was part of the market research team that brought the Walkman to market. She developed the methodology and tested the market on sample populations from teenagers to seniors. She is now at the *jicho* level of management,[6] one of four senior women managers in Sony Corporation. Although the former president said in a newspaper interview that a woman cannot be president, a women manager now heads the marketing division, the first woman in line management. When I asked Ryo about her career goals, she replied that that would be up to the president, which seemed surprising given her independent thought patterns. Her response is realistic, however, for the roles of both women and men in Japanese corporations at higher levels are so obvious, particularly for women, and must reflect the philosophy of top management.

The KAO Corporation, a pharmaceutical and toilet goods manufacturer, is known for its quality products. Keiko Kumon joined the company on her graduation from Keio University only after researching its corporate policies and operations, the number of women employees and managers, and then comparing it with other corporations. She found the environment for women at KAO better than at other companies that were offering jobs, so she began her career at KAO, where, when I interviewed her, she was in the Corporate Planning Group in the office of the president.

Her assignments, involving travel to Europe, North America, and Asia with her group, developing strategic plans for the corporation were stimulating and interesting. Keiko is definitely part of the new wave of Japanese professional women, whose presence and visibility may help organizational cultures to evolve. Her mother was in their family business, and both her parents encouraged her, as well as her brother, to discover their talents, to work hard, and to use their talents in whatever ways seemed best. She said she will remain with the company as long as it is mutually satisfactory and will seek a better position when it is not. She intends to marry and have children but is in no hurry to do so, and most likely she will choose a mate as carefully as she did her profession.

CIBA-Geigy is a Swiss pharmaceutical company and therefore not a typical Japanese corporation, but its policy is to have Japanese senior managers in Japan. Junko Mori, a marketing coordinator, chose the company for this reason. Junko received her graduate degree in business, an MBA (Master of Business Administration), from INSEAD, the international management school in France, and had lived in the United States and Europe as a child when her father was abroad on assignment. She speaks four languages and is knowledgeable about international business practices, so she is obviously a valuable resource for any company. When she was promoted to her present position, many of her subordinates were older than she, which is most unusual in Japanese companies. She described this as one of the most difficult parts of her job, to get used to having authority over older men, and for her subordinates to give her their loyalty. She described her management style as participative, moving slowly, and allowing "her people" to test her and learn to trust her, which they gradually have done. She chose the company because of its policies toward women. At twenty-nine, she also intends to marry, and hoped she would find a Japanese man with similar values and attitudes, but she had doubts that this would be easy.

Government bureaucracies have standardized entry and promotion criteria, which places them closer to the open end of the spectrum. Although entry criteria alone do not make organizational cultures open immediately, entry and promotions standards are themselves a change, precipitating other changes. As women have been more and more successful in government agencies, they have begun to influence the organizational culture. Not all ministries were judged equally open to women. The Ministry of Labor has been called the "Queen of Bureaucracies" in the media, referring to the large proportion of women in influential positions. The first career cabinet-level woman was appointed in 1997 as the head of the Women's Bureau was made a vice minister. The Labor Ministry has served as an "incubator" for many of the nation's top women managers in both government and industry. This can be traced to the ministry's opening to women in 1946 and the establishment of a Women's Bureau headed by a woman. All ministries operated under the same guidelines, but the organizational culture developed in the Ministry of Labor continued to support and develop women managers from that time forward, whereas that in other ministries did not.

The Ministry of Foreign Affairs, for instance, hired women in the initial opening year and then did not hire any more in the entry group for the next twenty years. A woman in that first group hired by the Foreign Ministry, Ambassador to Denmark Nobuko Takahashi, became the first Japanese woman ambassador in 1980. Subsequent women ambassadors came from the Ministry of Labor or outside the bureaucracy, since the Foreign Ministry had not developed a cadre of women managers. Organizations that are less bound by tradition and exclusive definitions have more opportunities to be supportive of difference, innovation, and women. The Ministry of Finance, with its rigid hierarchy not open to women managers, was ranked farther toward traditional and away from open on the continuum of organizational culture.

Companies on the Traditional Side

The most traditional companies are generally considered to be the *keiretsu* or conglomerates and the *sogu sosha,* the trading companies. Unlike newer industries, which have had to develop cultures consonant with new technology and a changing workforce and international environment, companies with long successful histories of doing business the old way have not yet felt pressure to change. Companies such as Mitsui, Sumitomo, Matsushita, and Mitsubishi, whose origins go back hundreds of years, have well-entrenched male-defined cultures, with rules of behavior designed for the all-male management world that existed when they were founded. Women have found it difficult to become managers in traditional companies, although all companies have been forced by the equal employment legislation to hire women in the career track. Few of these women, however, have been promoted to senior management, with the companies usually placing the fault for this situation outside the control of the company.

Women *are* found in management in some traditional companies, but they are rare, the exceptions rather than the rule. Auto manufacturing companies are younger and tend to be less traditional than the *keiretsu*. Toyota and Nissan each has a woman manager. Toyota Motor Corporation is number one on the ranking of Japan's largest corporations. Kyoko Otsuka is *jicho*, general manager of Development Department Number 3, in the Human Resources Development Division of Toyota Motor Corporation. She hosted my tour of the robotized Toyota assembly plant in Toyota City just outside Nagoya, Japan. A charming woman in her forties, she is the first and only woman so far to have become a general manager in Toyota Japan, but she insists that other women are close behind her.

She attributes her success, as do many Japanese women, to luck, timing, and good coworkers. When she began to work, her intent was not a career, but as the years went by she found she enjoyed her work. Managerial life and promotions were interesting and rewarding, and eventually she attained a management position that suited her. She and her mother share a house in Nagoya, and she considers her life as satisfying. Her route was not without problems as she described it, but the equal opportunity legislation came at a propitious time in her career, making her gender an advantage rather than a hindrance and allowing her competency to be recognized.

The auto manufacturing culture does not encourage women in management, and those who make it do so because of their own competency, assertiveness, and the support of individuals within the company rather than the company culture. While these companies see themselves as progressive and innovative, their operating cultures do not encourage people who are unlike the founding fathers to become managers. Foreigners and women are generally not found in management. The efforts of individual women and men determine success for women in companies where the culture is not supportive of women. Individual managers and relationships determine how effectively a more traditional culture actually supports women. Women succeed because of individual circumstances and characteristics rather than a supportive organizational culture.

Traditional companies operating internationally, where overt discrimination against women is not allowed, have been forced to develop attributes of more open cultures. Some traditional companies have had difficulty understanding the different values, workplace practices, and discrimination regulations, finding themselves involved in lawsuits over discrimination against non-Japanese and women.

Sumitomo Bank Limited lost a discrimination lawsuit in the United States and subsequently appointed a woman, Nora W. Hughes, as president of its New York–based subsidiary aimed at the American securities market. The vice president, her second in command, is Japanese and reports directly to Japan. His quoted comment about Hughes's role was an interesting example of how individuals define situations to fit their existing models. He said she was a good manager. She was "like a mother" to the organization, taking care of the employees.

Whether the infiltration of women into the overseas subsidiaries will ultimately make a difference in the practices of the home office of corporations remains to be seen. When queried about whether this would make it easier for a woman to be promoted in Japan, the answer was "No. The Japanese company is not ready for foreigners and women in top management. Women are not yet ready to function in the upper management circles of the company." Another top bank, Dai-Ichi Kangyo, named a woman executive vice president of a new financial products group in New York but still has no women in top positions in Japan.

The class action sexual discrimination suit against Mitsubishi in the United States received wide publicity. The company's first response was to try to discredit the claims by mobilizing loyal employees to demonstrate in Washington, trying to erect a screen against criticism. Later a high-profile American woman was hired to head an investigative team. In June 1998 the company settled with a record payment of 34 million dollars before going to trial.

One of the more successful traditional companies, Mitsui, views itself as a progressive corporation in its products, in innovation, and in its personnel policies. It hired women in career tracks immediately after the equal employment law was passed in 1986 but said customers complained to top management that they didn't want women sent to their companies. So Mitsui discontinued women in career sales slots, instead placing them in general administration. Certainly a new technological innovation would not have been sent to customers without preparation. For new products, years of preparation are required for market research, focus groups, marketing, education, and one-on-one preparation of big customers. An innovation in personnel, the introduction of women, was undertaken without such care and preparation. They were "thrown to the wolves" without market research or preparation of fellow employees or customers.

While organizations that are protected by tradition and insularity are the last to develop supports for women's entry into management or a climate for innovation, it would be a mistake to think they are completely closed. It is possible, even if not necessarily probable, for a woman to enter and, by working hard, using skills, initiative, and perseverance with the support and collaboration of male colleagues and supervisors, to make her way into a management role.

When I interviewed several younger women who had left traditional companies, all said that when they realized there were no women managers above them, they began to question their career choice. After retaining, for varying periods of time, the wish or fantasy that they could be the "breakthrough" woman by working harder and being smarter, each eventually decided she must find a more supportive organization in order to succeed. All are indeed succeeding, either in their own companies or in other organizations.

Women's departure after several years is interpreted by male executives as the result of women's lack of motivation and perseverance, proof that women "can't make it." Far from lacking in motivation, the women interviewed left because they were motivated, wanted to work hard, and wanted their work to be productive and recognized. Several executives from such organizations explained the lack of women by saying either that "their companies were not ready" for women in management or that "women were not yet ready." Removing the responsibility a step from themselves, executives in one of the companies assured me they wanted to promote women but their "customers were not ready" for women in management. Those phrases are heard universally when it is feared that change might be disruptive of the status quo.

The most traditional organizations have no women in top management in their operations in Japan. Traditional cultures are committed to the status quo and invest a great deal in harmony and stability. Women in management are disruptive because they are different, and so excuses are found for not bringing women into management roles: "They don't stay" or "They're not committed to a job" or "They don't want the responsibility."

Consequences of Closed Cultures

Not disrupting the status quo has potentially high costs. The quotation from Ichiro Ozawa's book *Blueprint for a New Japan* in chapter 4 described suc-

cinctly the opportunity costs of closed cultures and unquestioned maintenance of the status quo. Ozawa brought into question two icons of the Japanese economy and nation, lifetime employment and close group identity and
cooperation. When carried to an extreme, these characteristics create closed
systems that do not allow new life to enter, with the inevitable consequence
of atrophy and death. Closed organizational cultures with lifetime employment and tight, homogeneous groups run that risk, even though they are sta-
ble in the short term.

Tadashi Matsumoto, who oversees biotech research and development at
Kyowa Kaho, a Japanese chemicals company, captured that risk in discussing
the need for creativity and innovation: "The quality of Japanese scientists is
very good, but it's hard for them to move and change, to innovate. They are
much more staked to their positions than U.S. scientists."[7]

Unexamined and carried to an extreme, any value may become a negative.
On the other side of the continuum, the American ethic of individuality and
mobility, although fostering innovation and creativity, risks loss of loyalty and
group identity, and a lack of long-term perspective and teamwork. America
needs to balance values of individuality with cooperation, and mobility with a
degree of security in employment. Balancing stability and innovation, differ-
entiation and integration is a major challenge for organizations around the
world, and certainly for Japan and the United States. Takeru Ishikawa succinctly defined deficiencies in Japanese corporations needing that balance:
"The changing times demand innovations in corporate management. . . .
Corporations need to be managed with greater emphasis on creativity and
maintaining balance between profitability and social awareness."[8]

In agriculture, biodiversity, or multiple crops, is essential for sustainable
crop production. Without diversity in nature, production declines. Equally in
the economic sphere, sustainability of economic productivity needs cultures
that are open to and supportive of diversity. The narrow paths of closed corporations are not limited to women. Men are also restricted in companies
with closed cultures. The main difference between women and men is that
the original narrow paths were designed by and for men. The rules no longer
fit all men, if they ever did, but at least men have been socialized to fit.

Approaches to Problem Solving

The traditions of lifetime employment and seniority have become synonyms
of rigidity and the status quo. When the myriad issues seem so deeply embedded in the culture, it is easy for a sense of powerlessness to take over.
Women, however, remain hopeful and have made suggestions for simple,
workable, straightforward approaches to greater flexibility and openness to

women. Table 9.2 summarizes some of the most frequently mentioned problem areas and suggested approaches to problem solving.

Lifetime employment and promotion by seniority, which are at the top of
the list of problems for women, are consistently blamed for the lack of
women in management positions. When put forth, it always sounds as if both
features have been foundations of the Japanese economy from the beginning
of time. The words have almost a religious ring. In reality, lifetime employment is a relatively new phenomenon in Japanese industry. While the samurai
world did provide a semblance of lifetime employment as long as the lord
was in power, Japanese industry did not have lifetime employment until the
era of labor unrest in the 1960s.

Nevertheless, the belief in a tradition of lifetime employment and seniority is deeply embedded and is a barrier to women managers in Japan.
Certainly, if a corporation expects to commit to a new employee for life and
employees believe they are making a lifetime commitment, it is a very powerful contract. While this image is the ideal, it is not always the reality in
Japan. The ideal was held up much more strongly before the years of reces-

Table 9.2 Approaches to Problem Solving in Organizational Culture

Problems	Approaches to Problem Solving
Belief in lifetime employment for men only	Recognize women's lifetime work
Seniority the only determinant of rank and rewards	Merit-based rewards and promotions Reward everyone equally for the same work
Recession	Recognize and market women as valuable resources
Exclusive group identity and loyalty	Listen to different voices
Rigid hierarchy	Develop flexibility
Warrior heroes	Become aware of attitudes toward gender Include women warriors
Exclusion from information about training and promotion opportunities	Share relevent information
Women seen as temporary	Examine recruiting and placement practices and policies
Women only in clerical and no-brain work	Listen to women
Belief that long-term perspective and commitment exclude women	Examine personnel practices as distinct from stated policies
Disregard of private lives	Listen to men and women
"What's good for company is good for family"	Realize less-stressed employees are more productive
Japanese career employees do not make a distinction between work and private lives	Become aware of attitudes and examine whether they are effective

sion, but even earlier it was still an espoused value that was not universally true. An employee who becomes redundant, or fired, suffers a terrible shock and struggles with feelings of disgrace. Unfortunately, since the bursting of the "economic bubble," there have been increasing instances of downsizing and "lifetime" employees being declared redundant.

When I asked a group of young male executives if they planned to stay with their company through their working lives, they said no. Now in their late twenties and early thirties, these managers want to have other experiences, and they would move on when an opportunity arose. Men in their late thirties and beyond said they had such "radical" ideas when they were younger, but that one becomes comfortable and family responsibilities change attitudes. Now they planned to spend the rest of their working lives with the company, so employees older than thirty were the believers in lifetime employment. Younger males, crucial to long-term planning and success, are not committed to these ideals. Senior executives in the same company reiterated strongly the company's policy and practice of lifetime employment and their belief that employees are committed to it as well. These varied perceptions suggest that the top and bottom tiers of the hierarchy are not sharing information. As the practice of lifetime employment diminishes, it is time to examine beliefs and attitudes.

Linked to lifetime employment is the issue of seniority-based pay and promotions. Productivity of white-collar workers in Japan lags behind that in other industrialized countries, even though manufacturing productivity is high. It is estimated that 4 million office workers are not really needed; they are the "in-house unemployed." Performance appraisals and merit-based pay might contribute to white-collar productivity and make companies more open to women. Yet change is extremely difficult for Japanese companies to undertake. Even though most companies have espoused merit pay, only 15 percent of 629 major firms surveyed in 1994 had established merit pay, up 2 percent from a 1990 survey.

Coordination and harmony are major concerns of Japanese companies, which fear that a wage system based on job performance would shake up human relations. That fear is reflected in a *Nikkei Weekly* cover story headline from September 5, 1994, that describes the dilemma of corporations wanting to move to more open organizations with merit-based pay: "Necessity Sows Change, but Tradition Deep-rooted: Moves Toward Merit Pay Run into Stonewall of Seniority."

Even companies that want change must face the challenge of deep-rooted practices cloaked in the mantle of tradition. Change is not easy. After voicing the need for changing personnel practices, Harumi Sakamoto, managing director of Seiyu and a Keidanren committee chairperson, said, "Japanese society is in the process of transformation. In this process, tragedy and confusion are inevitable. But only after overcoming them, can we reach the next dimension."9

Bringing women into management is a goal espoused by Japanese government and business, but the gap between espoused goals and behavior is often quite wide. The most frequent advice I heard for male managers was to listen to women and give them a chance. Many women contended that men don't know how to listen. They said, "Men always tell you what to think and define the problem but don't listen to your reply."

This situation is not limited to Japan. During a workshop our consulting company conducted for women and men managers in Hawaii, a senior manager said with exasperation, "What do women want?" and then continued talking about the problems of working with women. When told it's not difficult to learn what women want if one stops talking and instead listens, he was at first miffed. But he later tried a technique of waiting just ten seconds before speaking, and he learned a lot as women talked and he listened.

Women managers said, please share relevant information. A symphony orchestra can pull together a hundred different instruments and voices to create one beautiful sound because the conductor and all the players know the score. When women don't know the score, they can't contribute. With their different voices, women in rigid organizations are shunted to invisible areas where their talents are wasted.

The complex interaction between organizational culture, national culture, environment, and individuals creates the mosaic of a nation's economic and personal life. In the current economy, international trade, domestic consumption, and distribution and quality-of-life issues supplant the previous dominance of market share so that innovation and creativity assume higher priorities and require successful organizations to adapt. To realize Japan's potential in the contemporary and developing international economy, Japanese organizations need to evaluate outmoded personnel practices based on obsolete assumptions from the traditional *otoko shakai*, or "man's world." Policies and practices need to be revised to encourage creativity, innovation, and the participation of women.

Hideyasu Nasu, a senior executive at Sumitomo Corporation, recently said:

> At this point in time, the problems found in the business world must be examined from every angle, including company organization, company consciousness, and the way business is done. And those elements that need to be attacked should be.10

He was referring to corporate scandals, but his comments apply equally well to the need for innovation and effective use of human resources. Women-friendly companies have more open and flexible cultures, and information flows more easily through open boundaries. Innovation and openness to women are both correlated with the availability of different messages and new ideas to influence events. Transparent, accessible paths to promotion and leadership attract diverse talents, and systems with open, permeable boundaries recognize that employees have lives outside work.

Lest women wait too long for corporations to do it all, one successful woman manager in her fifties sent a strong message to women about what to do with their shoji screens: "Poke your finger through the shoji screen. What's on the other side must be wonderful for them to hide it so well. Go over the screen. Do what you need to do. Do what you can do."

As Japanese women poke their fingers through the screens, they are finding the joys of success, and they are also finding some of the dilemmas that the screens were designed to hide. Balancing their roles as women, managers, and parents, they seek a comfortable sense of self in new roles and venues. The next chapter explores the meaning of success to Japanese women and the effect of national ideology on the struggle for equity and quality of life.

10

A Search for Identity

The Many Faces of Women Managers

In the context of Japanese culture, where do women managers fit? Constituting a minority as managers and decision makers in a man's world, how do they feel about their accomplishments? How do they view themselves as Japanese women?

Meanings of Success

Each of the women managers interviewed was asked whether she considered herself successful, the question I have asked women managers around the world. Most were hesitant to respond. The following are some of their answers:

Well, yes . . . because I have come to the highest position as a woman in the company. But it's only in a company. I don't regard myself so successful in society.

Seventy percent. I have a comfortable life, but I could have been better.

Yes, as a wife, mother, daughter-in-law, of course as professional.

Women don't know the sweet taste of success. Only the fear of taking the heavy responsibility is imagined and thus women often run away from the success. We need more models.

The answers followed a consistent pattern. The women generally did not think they were successful. The first answer to "Are you successful? was often "No," sometimes with qualifications but never "yes." When encouraged, one woman said what had been implied in many other answers, "In my own way."

Responding to further questioning, they provided definitions of success that reveal reasons for the hesitation. Success would include such things as creating a balanced lifestyle, preserving and improving the world for their children's future, being a good wife, daughter-in-law, and mother, combined with doing well in their chosen work and gaining respect for their company, service, or product, a hefty list.

On the other hand, men generally thought they were successful and consistently, although perhaps with qualifications, said "yes" to the question. Their responses measured success with financial markers, market share, status, income, and reputation. Issues outside the workplace were rarely mentioned unless the men were asked specific questions about family or work philosophy. These male definitions of success do not fit women's lives. Women consider success in holistic terms, including the meaning and value of their work, family life, the community in which they live, and the environment. The narrower, more specific criteria used by the men made success easier to evaluate.

Success in Japan is measured in comparison with one's peers. The Japanese phrase *yoko narabi shugi* translates as "looking to the side" to convey the way in which individuals and organizations decide how well they're doing. People look to see what other people on the same level are doing and then make sure they do not deviate too much, either by rushing to catch up or by slowing down so they do not get too far ahead. For corporate managers and government bureaucrats, the comparison and criteria for success are relatively simple. Men are traditionally taken into organizations, corporate or government, with a group of peers. This group is now their "class," and progress is measured against the peers with whom they began, a ready measure of success that is consistently used as they proceed up the ladder. Each step serves to reinforce the fact that they are successful.

Women do not have the same internal and external measures of success. Women have only recently held management positions, and traditionally their success has been evaluated on the basis of a good marriage and successful children. Separate criteria for males and females are internalized and deeply held.

Now women participate in the public arena. They work. They are managers. They compete in the economic world and perform essential roles in business, community, and government. However, the old criteria for success are still operative. Women continue to judge and be judged on the basis of marriage and family. Even the more sophisticated younger women are pressured by these criteria. Now they need criteria that are more relevant to professional success, but new criteria are often merely grafted onto the old criteria, so that women find themselves trying to meet multiple criteria simultaneously, an impossible task.

For many of the brighter women, the male criteria of success—progression up the ladder with complete devotion and lifetime commitment to one organization, company, or bureaucracy—do not make sense. So they are forced to create their own definitions. To determine criteria and evaluate achievement individually is strange and unfamiliar in Japan. Group norms and rewards found in the success of the group are usually the ultimate criteria. If one is to *yoko narabi shugi,* look to the side, comparing with peers to determine success and find clues about next steps, to whom do women look? Not to the men whose lives they don't want to emulate. Not to the women who, in their view, have been trapped in the "good wife, wise mother" roles. Successful career women are not visible or readily accessible, since they are often hidden, discounted, and referred to as not real women or not real managers. So women managers are left to judge their success on their own. It is not surprising that they have difficulty saying they are successful, even though they meet external criteria of success. Capable of effectively evaluating the success of their businesses, they often fumble when describing their own accomplishments.

Humility is a highly valued virtue in Japanese society but not one that is shared equally by men and women. Women tend to have more of it than men. Many women attributed their success to luck or circumstances. Men attributed theirs to hard work and talent. A similar dynamic is true in the United States. Different socialization for boys and girls makes it acceptable for men to take credit for success, while women attribute success to outside factors, not wishing to offend, having multiple success criteria, and unaccustomed to claiming credit for themselves. An advantage of such an attitude is that women continue to strive for broader goals, but their feelings of success and achievement are difficult or precluded.

Context for Success

Nobody can tell which way is better for a woman—to continue to be a housekeeper for her entire life, while not being fully satisfied with that lifestyle and not knowing any other options, or to get a divorce after choosing another option existing outside the home.

Harumi Sakamoto, senior managing director, Seiyu

Clearly, there is not just one voice for Japanese women managers. Reflecting the spectrum of society, they are conservative, liberal, international, provincial, frustrated with the status quo, working for change, resisting change. Attempts to define one correct choice for women are rarely success-ful. The Japanese women managers interviewed tend to be less conservative and more open to change than the general population. Having achieved a degree of independence, and personifying changes that men and some women fear, they often speak out with greater confidence about the ills of the present system, which they describe as male-dominant.

Japanese and American women managers strive for similar goals. They want to have their voices heard at home and in social, economic, and political dialogues, to make choices, and control their own lives. They seek empower-ment. They struggle within different national ideologies, so the paths look different and the voices sound different.

A sample of Japanese voices said:

> American women complain about the same things, but as someone who has seen both sides, they have so much privilege in America. The ground zero is different in Japan than in the United States.
>
> > Japanese women manager in Japanese
> > company in the United States

> I saw how happy Japanese families were compared to American families, and I think it has to do with more mothers staying at home to raise the children.
>
> > Japanese woman, recent Keio university graduate

> A friend of mine recently applied for a job at a good Japanese company and was asked whether she had a boyfriend. It's disgusting.
>
> > Japanese woman, university student

> In America, women want it all—work and a family. Maybe in America it can work sometimes. If that's what Japanese women want, then they should go to America. But I don't really think it's possible.
>
> > Japanese woman, recent Keio university graduate

As seen by the sample of opinions, Japanese women have mixed feelings about the accomplishments and roles of American women. For the Japanese who believe the natural order is men working, women at home, the United States exemplifies their fears about changing gender roles. Those who hold this view see successful American career women abandoning the housewife role, and they find America decadent, with its publicized violence, high di-vorce rate, welfare dilemmas, and single-parent families. They attribute such problems to career women "neglecting" their true roles of homemaker and mother, and cite data to justify maintaining the status quo for women and men in Japan. Those who hold the opposite view envy the position of American women and wish to emulate or join them. The proportion of Japanese who believe that men should work and women should stay home has shifted over the last decade. A 1987 survey of Japanese attitudes found 43 percent of the respondents believed in the traditional allocation of gender roles of men working, women at home. In 1995, only 27 percent preferred traditional roles.

Views of the World: Harmony or Equality

Beliefs about appropriate roles grow out of prevailing national ideologies and beliefs. Japanese ideology might be described as harmony, emphasizing balance and homogeneity, while a basic American ideology is equality. The American belief in equality of opportunity and equality under the law is rooted deeply in the laws and psyche of the nation.

On July 4, 1776, the Representatives of the United States of America first proclaimed in the Declaration of Independence: "We hold these Truths to be self-evident, that all Men are created equal, that they are endowed by their Creator with certain unalienable Rights, that among these are Life, Liberty, and the Pursuit of Happiness."

The words remain an enduring guide and the shared ideology of the United States to the present day. The Bill of Rights, which expanded the concepts of rights associated with equality, is quoted by both sides of the political spectrum. The ideology remains powerful and governs laws and practices today. No matter that it took two hundred years for equality to include nonwhites and females. Alexis de Tocqueville, the French observer and chronicler of American life in the eighteenth century, praised the achievement of equality in America and the new doctrine of equal rights without even noticing they were missing.

Japan's historical roots in Buddhism, Taoism, and Confucianism led to a national ideology of harmony, a hierarchy with appropriate roles and a defined place for each person. The reality does not match the ideology in either case. The United States has inequality, and Japan has disharmony, diversity, and conflict. But ideology is powerful. In Japan the myth of harmony and alikeness make it more difficult to speak out against inequities because it disrupts harmony. Diversity is avoided or masked as much as possible.

In the United States women and minorities do not have equal opportunity. Progress has been made since women's rights to equal opportunity were first put on the agenda, but women are not equal in salaries, in opportunities, in education, in career choices, or in family work. Many of the barriers to women's achievement are systemic, but since the national ideology proclaims equality, individual women often blame themselves for not achieving. The reasoning goes something like this: "If the nation is equal, then it must be the individual woman's fault if she is not successful." With equality the ideology, women feel justified in fighting, speaking out, and lobbying for equality. At the same time, they may feel guilty that they are not successful, a damaging psychological consequence of mixed and conflicting messages.

Cultural Roots of Laws Affecting Women

Guiding national metaphors evolve different approaches to providing opportunities to women. This is reflected in the quite different equal employment opportunity laws of Japan and the United States. The United States law was an addendum to the Civil Rights Act of 1964. Gender equity under law is considered a civil right, a human right as a result of citizenship in the nation, growing out of the Constitution's statement that all men are created equal, with certain inalienable rights. Legislation to ensure equality is in harmony with this belief. Equality originally only applied to white male property owners. The history of the United States has been a process of expanding rights to include more of the population. It has taken two hundred years to expand beyond white males to nonwhite males and women, but the ideology has always been equality.

The Civil Rights Act of 1964 was conceived to eliminate discriminatory practices against Negroes, the nomenclature of the time. The evolution from abolishment of slavery to legislated equal opportunity took one hundred years, from 1865 to 1964. Discrimination in government employment had been prohibited since the 1940 wartime years, when the Fair Employment Practices Executive Order was signed by Franklin Roosevelt. The extension of these civil rights to private employment was vehemently resisted. Even in 1964 the fight to pass the Civil Rights Act was bitter. The addition of gender as a nondiscriminatory right was added by southern senators who hoped to defeat the bill.

As in Japan, the American view had been that woman's place is in the home, and that if economic necessity or wartime labor shortages dictated that she enter the economic world, her salary and advancement would be lower than a man's because her tenure would be temporary, lasting only until she could be replaced by a man. Even if she were more qualified than men, she was thought to be working only until she could go back to her proper place in the home. Growing dissatisfaction among working women resulted in a report by a presidential committee on the economic status of women workers in 1963, which eventually led to an equal pay bill. The flavor of those arguments was eerily similar to those still used to discriminate in the United States and around the world, and is reminiscent of statements being made in Japan to justify gender and racial discrimination.

One Congressman who opposed the bill said:

> Imagine the upheaval that would result from adoption of language requiring total equality. Would males be justified in insisting that women share with them the burdens of compulsory military service? What would become of traditional family relationships? You know the biological differences between the sexes. States have laws favorable to women which might be struck down, and besides we are making progress against discrimination of women in employment.[1]

A proponent of the bill, Congresswoman Griffith from Michigan, cited Swedish sociologist Gunnar Myrdal's observation in *The American Dilemma*[2] that white women and Negroes occupied relatively the same position in American society.

After a full week of debate the amendment including sex was passed. The act reads:

> It shall be an unlawful practice for an employer to fail or refuse to hire or to discharge any individual or otherwise to discriminate against any individual with respect to his compensation, terms, conditions, or privileges of employment because of such individual's race, color, religion, *sex* or national origin.

The Equal Employment Opportunity Commission was established to administer the law. The next year, guidelines were issued and procedure established for enforcement of the law, starting with a complaint to the commission and then, if arbitration failed, the initiation of a civil suit.

The equal opportunity law in Japan has a very different tone. Written specifically for women, it is based on harmony, balance, and appropriate roles. It specifically mentions, honors, and protects the role of mother. Article 2 states the basic principles of the law:

> In view of the fact that women workers contribute to the development of the economy and society and at the same time play important roles as a member of the family in raising children who will be a mainstay of the future, the basic objectives of the improvement of the welfare of women workers as set forth in this Law are to enable them to achieve a full work-

ing life by making effective use of their abilities with due respect for their maternity, but with no discriminatory treatment on the basis of sex, and to achieve harmony between their working life and family life.

Article 3 spells out women's responsibilities:

Women workers shall, in awareness that they are members of the working community, endeavor, by their own initiative to develop, improve and make good use of their abilities in working life.

And Article 4 spells out the roles of employers, the state, and local public bodies, "who shall endeavor to promote the welfare of women workers in accordance with the above basic principles."

All are enjoined to endeavor to achieve equality. No recourse or penalties for not endeavoring were specified. The legislation did not include sanctions for failure to comply. The reasons for the exclusion were both political and pragmatic. It was deemed more important to have a law than to have a perfect law, which is understandable. According to its supporters, the law, in and of itself, gave a message that women's rights are recognized. The state has issued administrative guidance to companies not endeavoring, but many Japanese women say the law is toothless. Western women who say the law has no value, as I heard stated by both Western and Asian women, speak from their own cultural orientation. Paradoxically, the law that recognized women's rights to employment diffused the pressure to enact stronger laws.

The original title of the Japanese employment law was *Danjo Koyo Kikai Byodo Ho. Byodo* means "equality." At some time during the debate, *byodo* was replaced by *kinto*, translated as "equalizing" or "progress toward equality."[3] The title, consistent with the words "enjoining" and "endeavoring," implies efforts toward equalizing opportunity instead of a commitment to achieve equality. Japanese are generally uncomfortable with the concepts of equality and rights. An explanation given is that individual rights appear to infringe on other people. If one person has a right, it may take something from other people and will disturb the balance.

Even so, Japanese women continued efforts in the legislature to strengthen the law and have enforcement procedures spelled out. As a result of their efforts, the Diet passed amendments to the law to make it more inclusive in June 1997, with the amendments effective in April 1999. Instead of simply enjoining employers to make efforts to eliminate discriminatory practices, the amendments use the word "ban" discriminatory practices, with a stronger meaning. Recruitment, employment, assignment, education, and on-the-job training and promotion are all included in the amendments. In addition, either party, that is, an employee, may now bring her case to the Ministry of

Labor for arbitration if she does not receive satisfaction from her employer, and the law "bans" dismissal or disadvantageous treatment because of applying for mediation. The original law had required both parties to agree to bring the case to the ministry, which is much more difficult.

Finally the new law allows the Ministry of Labor to announce the names of employers who have violated the law and failed to amend their attitudes even after recommendations from the ministry. While some women consider the penalty still too weak to make a difference, the wording is a major shift in the law because it allows complaints from the aggrieved person and publication of the names of transgressors.

At the same time, Parliament revised the Labor Standards Law to lift restrictions on women's overtime and late-night work, except for pregnant women and those caring for children. Taking away protective legislation was more controversial among Japanese women, as was a similar law in the United States. Those fearing exploitation by employers wanted the new law to limit overtime for both men and women, a provision that was unacceptable to employers. Others, who realized that the "protections" were used to excuse not hiring women in responsible positions, were happier to have the law rescinded.

The Power of Words

When harmony is the ideology, as in Japan, women's role of selflessness and sacrifice is necessary for balance, and therefore harmony, in the group. They are enjoined to make the best of situations and not to speak out for themselves; if they do, they are considered selfish, un-Japanese, inappropriate. Universally, the urge to sweep difficult issues, seen as intractable, *under the rug* or behind the *shoji screen* is strong. The struggle to keep seeking better solutions is not easy.

When I asked a group of Japanese women managers what the future held for women in Japan, the discussion was lively and surprisingly diverse. One woman, who had recently surmounted resistance to obtain credit for an expansion of her business, said with great emphasis, "Japanese women have to be equal if we are ever going to achieve our goals." This clearly disturbed another, who said with uncharacteristic emotion, "Wait. Wait. I don't want to be equal to men." When questioned by the other women, she said she wanted to be "even." For her, equal meant being the same, and she didn't want to be the same as men. She had more difficulty defining what "even" meant to her, but the difference in wording was clearly important for her. In a later private discussion, she said perhaps the word "even" was closer to the idea of harmony. It was important to "feel" feminine, and the word "equal" threatened that feeling for her.

Even women who are committed to greater participation in society disagree about its form. Many women are uncomfortable with the aggressiveness of American women, while others wish to emulate them. These fears and visions are based in deeply embedded social values and beliefs. "Freedom" turned out to be another suspect word in Japanese, implying a danger of hurting others, disturbing the harmony and balance. The open discussion of these differences was at first somewhat threatening for several of the women.

The differing approaches to women's greater participation in society might be characterized in general terms. In Japan women seek complementary, or different but equally valued, roles; in the United States women seek equality. The danger of the complementary view is seen in the United States as leading to separate but equal, which is not really equal. The equality view is seen in Japan as disruptive and laden with conflict. The implications of the different approaches are summarized in Table 10.1.

Assumptions about gender roles rooted in a national ideology lead to strategies that are in line with that ideology, different strategies for women managers dependent on equality or harmony. The early tactics of feminists in

Table 10.1 Beliefs about Appropriate Gender Roles[4]

Beliefs	National Ideology	
	Equality	Harmony
Women and men are	Similar	Different
Contributions	Identical	Complementary
Fairness based on	Equality	Valuing difference
Strategic Goals	Equal access	Recognizing difference
Assessment	Quantitative	Qualitative
Measurement	Statistical	Women's contribution to goals
Method	Counting women and rank	Assessing women's contribution
Effectiveness measures	Identical for women and men	Complementary
Contributions	Same	Complementary
Norms	Same for women and men	Unique for women and men
Based on	Historical norms—"male"	Men's and women's contributions
Referent	Men	Women
Acculturation	Assimilation	Differentiation
Expected behavior	Standardized	Differentiated
Based on	Male norms	Female norms
Dress	Business suit	Elegant, feminine attire
Risks	Rigidity, alienation	Inequity, out of balance
Metaphors	"Color-blind/gender-blind"	*Shogonai* Nothing can be done, "Vive le difference"

the United States demanded attention by their aggressive and public nature in a situation in which they felt desperate to be heard. While "bra-burning" was a strategy limited to one small incident, it was effective at grabbing attention and throughout the world is still associated with the American feminist movement, often by those who are unaware of the multitude of other strategies used by American feminists. The meaning of the term "feminist" itself has become emotionally charged, and many Japanese women avoid participating in feminist activities because of a distorted view of women's collaborative activities. "Feminism," like "empowerment," has become manipulated as politically correct, whereas in its original meaning it referred simply to women seeking to be heard and obtain the vote.

At first glance the harmony model in which roles are seen as complementary would seem to offer greater flexibility and diversity to women. Each model has advantages and disadvantages. It is true that Japanese women like the option to work or not work, which is not available to Japanese men. The reality of economics and lifestyle means that that option is increasingly less available, and the ideology is a barrier to taking career women seriously. The complementary model encourages protective legislation for women for their different needs. Until recently, Japan had an official policy of monthly leave for women's menstrual period and protective legislation limiting hours of women's work. Both policies are controversial. Some think it is important to have protection against the extreme pressures of Japanese working life so that they are not exposed to *karoshi* like men. In the view of one woman bank employee, "If the regulations are eased, we will definitely have to work until late at night. The efficiency of work will decline and I might damage my health."

Others see the protective legislation as a barrier, another excuse for companies not to place women in management. The original law excluded professional positions and management, but companies still use it to excuse the paucity of women managers. As one young women from Mitsubishi said, "I don't feel I am protected by the law. Because of the regulations, I have to report shorter overtime hours than I really did. I want to be paid for what I have worked."[5] Another said she and her colleagues were told not to answer the phone after 7:45 p.m. because they were not supposed to be working that late.

On the negative side, the harmony model discourages speaking out to correct perceived injustices. The dilemma is exemplified by the woman who said, "Women have little say in most matters at work. Management qualifies workers only by their sex and educational background." Another problem inherent in a complementary model is assessing performance when measures for men and women are different and equity is subjective. It is extremely difficult to come up with measures that satisfactorily assess contribution to goals. In the United States, the struggle to adequately assess the "equal worth" of jobs with different job descriptions for male and female, such as nurse and carpenter, is a challenge similar to that of the complementary model, and it has been going on for decades.

The commitment to complementary gender roles may have incongruous outcomes. One woman manager interviewed had been working for twenty-two years. Her husband contracted tuberculosis shortly after their marriage and has not returned to work. She insists she is working temporarily until her husband can take his rightful place as wage earner and she can take her appropriate role as housewife. After twenty years she still maintains that position because her beliefs about her appropriate role preclude a career.

The equality model has the advantage of direct action and women speaking out to correct perceived injustices without feelings of shame. The disadvantages include the one referred to earlier of guilt for not achieving when equality is espoused. Measures of equality are easier to justify than measures of complementary contribution, but strategies to achieve equality are controversial. Production quotas are considered good management, but quotas for personnel are anathema to most Americans.

Affirmative action, the strategies designed to provide more equal opportunity, are often difficult to define and defend. In fact, affirmative action was translated into Japanese as *gyaku sabetsu*, meaning reverse discrimination, which it is not. Glen Fukushima suggested a better Japanese term, *shinki sannyusha yugu saku,*[6] meaning policies, measures, plans, or steps to promote, favor, prefer, welcome or warmly receive newcomers, which is much closer to the original intended meaning. There is always the danger of backlash and conflict in seeking equality for one group as other interest groups feel threatened.

With Japan's official doctrine of complementary roles, discrimination in the workplace may be more open and blatant. Until recently, sexual harassment, *sekuhara*, has been just another barrier for women, which they learned to avoid or go around. As a few women have risked exposure to the press and public and been successful in legal action, there is increasing recognition of the damage of such acts and attitudes for women and companies. In an early public incident, a woman parliamentarian accused a fellow member of grabbing her breasts at a cocktail party. He was eventually censured but excused because he had had too much to drink, and therefore the damage was "not intentional." Another highly publicized case was brought against a respected and popular professor who had been sexually harassing students. Amid great disbelief, he retreated to a monastery for a year.

Some American women say that blatant discrimination is easier to deal with than subtle barriers and ceilings in the United States. At least you know what you're up against, they said. Surveys of Japanese women find that they evaluate their situation relative to men as better than women in the United

States evaluate theirs. Compared with data on Japanese women's status, something appears awry. When the status of women is included in the human development index, Japan ranks seventeenth, after most industrialized nations.[7] Either the measures do not accurately portray the situation of women relative to men in Japan, or the perceptions of Japanese women take other factors into account.

The satisfactions and security of the role of wife and mother with a "lofty" position in society can dim the necessity to seek equity in other areas of life, and many women have become expert at achieving their goals indirectly behind the shoji screen. They have seen their situation in the world change a great deal in the last decades, in their own lifetimes, whereas American women have worked very hard and many feel stuck on a plateau, with little visible improvement. Awareness of discrimination in the United States developed over decades, and it is a relatively new phenomenon in Japan. Japanese women do not blame themselves for their lack of success but feel free to blame men.

Legitimate theoretical differences exist on the question of whether there are inherent differences in thinking, feeling, and modes of performance between men and women, as well as on the question of what constitutes equity. Whether there are innate differences and what those differences might be are not the issue in discussions of equity. The manner in which these differences are evaluated is the issue. Negative evaluation of a characteristic, simply because of its association with a particular group, is discrimination, often harmful and wasteful.

Japanese women find themselves limited by rigid, narrowly prescribed roles, but a complementary model does not require unchanging roles. One said, if the system is complementary, "Why can't men want to make dinner and draw the bath for me too?" Figure 10.1 illustrates complementary roles that are not locked in tradition.

Discussions about gender roles need not take either-or positions, which often lead to dire predictions about what will happen to the family if women become more active in society. Conversely, fears are revealed that women will become masculinized and unattractive, or that men will become wimps. Either-or choices need to be reframed. Men as well as women need new choices and options. The choices need not be between lifetime employment *or* mediocre employment, nor between long workdays with mandatory entertainment in the evening *or* no employment, nor between a good income *or* family time. Approaches that combine productive work with creative solutions to business and social problems can be developed for women and men. A complementary model that includes expanded roles for both women and men would please many of the Japanese women interviewed.

American women feel they cannot complain unless they have a solution.

Good Wife, Wise Mother
Ryosei kenbo
Career Woman

Good Husband, Wise Father
Ryofu Kenfu
Salaryman

Figure 10.1. Depictions of expanded lifestyle options in Japan for both women and men.

Japanese women don't complain because it doesn't fit with the ideology of harmony. Working women may find it worth the discomfort to announce dissatisfaction without rancor or blame. American women deal with backlash and subtle barriers, and Japanese women deal with rigidity and invisibility. The equality model will benefit from the inclusion of balance and harmony to allow balanced lives for men and women, as the complementary model will benefit from redefinition and women speaking up. Shidzue Kato, the pioneer feminist and birth control advocate, said on her hundredth birthday: "Japanese women are now among the best educated and the richest in the world, but we need to push ourselves forward more, to elbow our way into more decision-making jobs. . . . Men's attitudes will not change unbludgeoned."[8]

"Bludgeon" is a strong word, but it is justified by her lifetime experiences working for better lives for women. Reframing the dialogue about gender to include the demands and visions of a global world requires women to speak up, so that the voices of both men and women are heard. Parenting, the nurturing of future generations, nurturing the planet, and ecological strategies all require the talents and skills of men as well as women. Creativity, adaptability, and leadership are needed wherever they are found.

And what about the men whose attitudes are often cited as major barriers? Husbands were listed as both positive and negative factors for women managers—not usually the same husband. Some seemed to be hindrances to progress, and some were key supporters. What are male attitudes, and how can they change? How are men feeling as women find new roles and seek change and more active public lives? The next chapter will look at the men's lives for clues to next steps.

11

The Men in Their Lives
at Work and Home

Finding Rewards in Uncharted Roles

On the surface, it would appear that Japanese men had achieved the best of the modern world. Personal incomes are at an all-time high. Men seem firmly in charge of the economy and government; 99 percent of boards of directors and 91 percent of corporate managers are male. Former Prime Minister Hashimoto's 1997 cabinet was 99 percent male. Japan's per person gross domestic product is at an all-time high, higher than that of the United States, and Japanese stores are still filled with luxury goods from all over the world. And yet, all is not well. There are cracks beneath the surface. The recession just won't go away in spite of all the usual stimuli. The security of life-time employment is wavering. Young men are having difficulty getting married, and the number of divorces for those over fifty-five has increased often initiated by the wife. Many wives, daughters, and even mothers are questioning the established order at home and work. Men are also increasingly aware of and uneasy and dissatisfied with, the incongruities of assigned gender roles, as is apparent from the following comments:

> There is no such thing as lovers in Japan. There are only women and over-size (male) babies.
>
> Juzo Itami, film director

> I am the king in my family.
>
> Fifty-five-year-old Japanese man

204

I would like to take family leave when we have our first baby if I can.

Japanese male Manager/engineer at major trading
company, recently married to an engineer in another division

These quotations represent vividly the inner and outer conflicts for Japanese men in the 1990s. The dependency observed by Itami and the desire to retain the perceived power and role of king are in direct conflict with the wish and demands to share in nurturing and building family relations. The realities of economic, political, and social life and customs reflect these dilemmas and are acted out in daily life. Younger men, especially, find themselves in the middle of contradictions that are becoming more transparent. Male and female gender roles are defined as mutually complementary, so that changes in one require examination and changes for both. While this chapter focuses on the struggles and dilemmas of Japanese men, a few examples from other countries also indicate the universality of male dominance, with changes in the hierarchy fermenting throughout the world.

Sources of Gender Identity

Chapter 2 described ways in which gender socialization starts at birth for women. The same is true for men, or actually sometimes at conception because it is now possible to determine sex in utero. Each culture surrounds families and children with the cues of the role to be played. When I was pregnant in Iran, the common first greeting was *"Enshallah* a boy" (May god give you a boy). Different celebrations are given for boy and girl babies, different colors are worn to alert people whether to treat a baby as a boy or a girl. Early messages in a patriarchal society establish the hierarchy of male status. In the United States, a Joseph Kennedy could say to his bright, assertive daughter, "It's too bad you're not a boy." Encouraging his sons to become president of the United States, he could only commiserate with his daughter that she was not a boy.

A grandfather and other relatives often said to one little Japanese girl who was not judged pretty by Japanese standards, "It's too bad you weren't the boy." Brothers on both sides of her in age were sickly, while she was healthy, strong, and assertive. That the strong, healthy one should be a girl and the boys sickly, gentle, and dainty was a "reversal" of nature. Fortunately, in both cases the women were spurred to work to prove them wrong and were able to achieve competency and success, but not without difficulty and rebellion, and perhaps not to the degree their intelligence and potentials warranted, nor as high as if they had been boys. Powerful early immersion makes it difficult to think of one's identity outside the defining gender envelope.

Dilemmas of Male Identity

The power and restrictiveness of male gender socialization is not so immediately evident, since it seems to place boys in preferred positions. In reality, both men and women are prisoners of their culture. *Karoshi*, death from overwork, is a manifestation of the chronic overwork of many Japanese males. School bullying is a troubling phenomenon that results in an increasing rate of young male high school suicides, with the bullying reportedly continuing into the corporate suites. Having made it past all the early hurdles, many Japanese men experience a true tragedy of modern life when they retire at the age of sixty or before. At the height of their achievements, they are forced to step down, diving from the heights of samurai warrior, king of the mountain, salaryman, to the everyday plane of unemployed dependents without a real place of their own.

Having devoted their total energies and lives to their job, to the neglect of family and personal life, many men are left with nothing when their company identity is taken away. Common phrases used to describe retired husbands at this stage of their life are "big garbage, oversized garbage" (*sodai gomi*) or "wet leaves" (because they're hard to sweep out of the house). And retired husbands are reputed to ask, "What about me?" (*Watashi-wa*) as a wife leaves for her busy, interesting day. But not to worry; a male's life expectancy is not as long as a female's, so he won't have to suffer long. Male life expectancy is seventy-seven years, and that of females is eighty-four years.

A man's wife, along with taking care of the house and children while he was occupied with company business, has usually established an interesting, independent life, taking classes or engaging in sports. Now that the children have gone out of the house to make their own lives, his wife has more time for ikebana, golf, painting, calligraphy, or a long list of possible interests and occupations to which she has become attached; she doesn't want a condescending husband tagging along or whining when dinner is not ready. No wonder divorce rates within this age group have had the most rapid rise, especially since the law awards half of the husband's lump sum retirement payment to his wife. Some women have the ultimate revenge by refusing to be buried with their husband in the family grave site; such "divorce after death," or *shigo rikkon*, defies hundreds of years of tradition

Lee Kuan Yew, the former prime minister of Singapore, now senior minister, founded modern Singapore with strict ground rules for social behavior. He recently expressed his regrets that he had given equal rights to women because the marriage and birth rates have reached alarming lows in Singapore. He attributed part of the problem to Asian men's opposition to marrying women with higher qualifications than theirs. He said such values, while outmoded, still run deep in Singapore and Asian society. "We thought we would open up the whole system, give equal opportunities for education and jobs to women, like the West. But we forgot that culture does not change rapidly. As a man, you want to be the boss in your family. You don't want a wife who is smarter than you and earning more than you." He concluded, "But you can't unscramble the egg. So all you have got to do is re-educate the male." When asked by an audience of female university students what he would do if he were a female undergraduate today, he said, "I would know, reading the statistics, that the Singapore male is a duffer, a fool."[1]

Systems Nature of Gender Roles

Prime Minister Lee was acknowledging the systems nature of gender roles, in which a change in any part of the system requires changes in the rest. Education changed women's role in ways that contributed to the rapid growth of Singapore, but it disrupted the established system of male superiority. The preferred, or higher-status, role of master or male requires the collaboration of those in serving roles with mutually complementary parts, one not possible without the other.

Takie Sugiyama Lebra,[2] in her book on status culture in Japan as embodied in the modern nobility, used the term "vertical symbiosis" to describe the dependency of a superior's status on the complicity of those defined as inferior. Reliance on inferiors is a necessary price paid for status-bound respectability in Japan, she maintains. The subservience and service of the inferiors are necessary to define the status of their masters, but they do not give the superior independence or freedom. On the contrary, superiors are also bound, and often do not realize that superior status does not bestow independence.

The dynamics of class are parallel to the dynamics of gender status roles, with males in the superior status requiring females in nurturing, serving positions. Men's superior position is possible only with the complicity of women in serving roles at home and work. Why else would it be so important that women, and not men, serve tea in the office? That women are defined as nurturers and men as warriors? The dependence of a superior's position on the compliance of inferiors is a universally accepted social logic that is usually ignored in practice and only of interest to outside researchers and analysts trying to understand a system. The identity of the superior is possible only with the participation of the person in the inferior position. This makes the open discussion and mocking of men's helplessness by young Japanese women in recent years a strong threat to men whose status depends upon their cooperation. Women's dissatisfaction and anger at men, expressed in decreasing marriage rates, increasing divorce, and in public surveys such as the prime minister's white papers, must be discounted and explained away.

Diversity of Japanese Males

However, the Japanese male does not have a singular identity. Just as women and women managers in Japan have diverse and varied beliefs, attitudes, and lifestyles, so do the men in their lives. The openness and warmth of some of the men who were interviewed were a pleasant surprise, given the topic, while others were more careful and wary. It often took a long period of their observing interviews and discussions with female colleagues or friends to trust me with their thoughts and dilemmas. The "armor of masculinity" made it difficult to acknowledge any vulnerability. The contrast was striking between the men, who often quietly, shyly approached me, and the women, who eagerly talked about their work and personal lives with very little encouragement and in great detail.

Men told about taking their children to day care on the way to work and having to make elaborate excuses if it was necessary to pick them up before everyone else had left the office at the end of the day. Many said they were often exhausted from trying to meet the conflicting demands of work and home. They expressed confusion about how to relate to women at work, and they asked about gender relations in the United States.

A few younger men actually sought me out, having heard about my research and wanting to talk about dissatisfactions with Japanese social prescriptions for men. One young man who had attended a university abroad was particularly unhappy with the difficulty of having good women friends. At age thirty, he found the women he now meets always thinking of him as a potential marriage partner and either ending the relationship when they find that is not his immediate intent or trying to push him toward marriage. He said yearningly that he missed the long hours of conversation over coffee or dinner that he had experienced with women at the overseas university.

My sympathy for the struggles and ambivalence of Japanese men grew as they talked about attitudes, lifestyles, hopes, and visions. We explored hopes that Japanese men carry for themselves, their families, and their nation, as well as fears about what they see happening to their lives at work and home and to the women in their lives, their country, and the world. When they were asked what excitement and rewards they see for themselves, their work, and their relationships in these changes abroad in the land, their responses revealed a range of attitudes and beliefs. They discussed gender roles and visions of the future. Some responses were directly correlated with age, while others were seemingly idiosyncratic and related to individual life patterns and experiences.

Men in their sixties were often completely convinced of male superiority. Unfortunately, men of this generation are still in charge of the top corporations and companies. Certainly this generalization is not true of all men in this age cohort. Some have been bulwarks of strength for women entering the corporate world.

Generally the comments of older men reflected a benevolent paternalism, whose public tone asserted a concern for women and wonderment that women would want to enter the difficult, ruthless world of the salaryman, not unlike the attitude of a traditional American male lawyer at the end of the nineteenth century who tried to discourage a friend's daughter from entering his profession. "My high regard for your parents forbids encouraging you in so foolish a pursuit (law). You invite nothing but ridicule and contempt. A woman's place is at home." The young woman, Clara Shortridge Foltz, eventually became the first woman attorney in California.

In most countries, the socialization of men in their sixties was clear about the limits and boundaries of each gender role, usually imparting unquestioning acceptance of the distinct spheres and positions of women and men. Generally, Japanese executives of this age have little contact with women managers, only with women in serving roles. If they are still working, they are found within the ranks of top management or boards, where there are few women. They dismissed questions about numbers, insisting that there were many talented women in their companies who are working their way up, but the ones they introduced were translators or support staff. Their wives were generally, but not always, "professional housewives," occupied with the job of taking care of him and rearing children full-time.

At the time these men matured and their values formed, gender roles were very traditional, with segregated education and women's role codified as inside the home: "good wife, wise mother." Some haven't changed their beliefs about gender roles in the intervening years, but their female contemporaries, both wives and coworkers, have changed, as have the generations of women following them. Women no longer accept the same treatment they once did, and they are asserting their rights at home and in the office. Even the wives of some of these men are in the ranks of what they termed *uman ribu,* or women's lib, seeming to mean any behavior that is not acquiescent. A few smiled indulgently about their wives' behavior, almost as if they were little girls testing the limits of acceptable behavior by not being available occasionally when summoned. Since most of the wives of these men had sufficient money and time to develop comfortable lives of their own within the given parameters, they apparently were not openly questioning the system.

Institutionalized Gender Roles

Many corporate policies and practices are based on traditional gender socialization, with office ladies perpetuating the ideals of feminine nurturing and service. Anne Allison,[3] in a recent book about hostess clubs, avers that even the after-hours sessions in hostess establishments serve as a means to construct and reinforce sexual roles with ritualized encounters between the women of *mizu-shobai*, the water trade, and the *sararimen,* middle-class, middle managers. Corporate masculinity is carefully orchestrated in these clubs to perpetuate the gendered nature of work by having it also enshrined in the male-serving institutions of corporate entertainment. In the book, Allison's sympathy is expressed for both the women and the men; she considers the men to be the unwitting victims of the corporate treadmill, which discards men upon their mandatory retirement.

While traditional male attitudes were expressed by most men in their late fifties and early sixties, there are many exceptional men in this age cohort who have worked to support women's achievements and who speak out publicly for women. A prominent Diet member who is known to be supportive of women said he had learned to do housework while he and his wife lived with an American family during his graduate school days; since his wife had also shared this experience, he couldn't regress, he said, laughing.

Yoshiharu Fukuhara, President of Shiseido, represented an example of nontraditional attitudes cited by one of the women managers. In a professional meeting with him, the topic was employer-supported child care, about which she had undertaken research. A man was expounding on the economics and problems of such child care, while the woman manager who was junior to the speaker had been quiet. Mr. Fukuhara interrupted finally to say, "I think we should hear from a woman who has studied this issue and also may be closer to the issues we are discussing." His statement opened the discussion for her to present her findings based on her research. Fukuhara's actions, opening the door and encouraging her to speak, were not typical in such meetings, but they were appreciated and remembered by the interviewee. A more informed discussion ensued, and she was nominated to write the report for the committee.

The exceptional men of this age head major corporations. Shiseido, Fukuhara's company, was founded by his grandfather in 1872 as a pharmacy and is now Japan's largest cosmetics company. One of the so-called feminine industries with women as its major market, it has four women managers in the company headquarters. Shinichiro Torii, president of Suntory, a successful international beverage and restaurant business, said in an interview that the chances of a woman eventually filling his company president's post are quite good.[4] Suntory has ten women managers, and one of the women managers interviewed was on his board of directors.

Exceptional men of this age also supported and voted for equal employment legislation and family leave policies. They are the ones who encouraged, or at least did not discourage, their wives when they chose to follow an independent profession. A few reported sharing in child care, and at least one had learned to cook while pursuing his graduate studies in the United States and living with an American family. Many wanted to keep up with changing practices, but they found it difficult. When queried about how they had gained nontraditional attitudes, many revealed that they came from unusual families, with a mother who worked or parents committed to more egalitarian practices, or that they had lived outside of Japan for periods of time.

Men in their fifties tend to be confused and a little bewildered by the changes, wanting the best for their daughters, often bemused by their wives. They want their wives to behave more traditionally, yet at the same time they wish for their daughters' success. Although they recognized these paradoxes and dilemmas, they were generally unwilling or unable to undertake the massive personal changes necessary to reconcile and understand the complicated changes. They found it easier to maintain the status quo, or "not rock the boat," while trying to provide opportunities for daughters.

"My wife has gained a scholarship to Europe," a fiftyish man told me. "When I asked her if she were going to take me along, she said, 'No. You're no good. You can't cook or keep house and I need to concentrate on my research.'" So she took their adult daughter with her instead. This story was told with amusement, knowing it would entertain me, but there was a wistful note in the man's voice. He said, "I don't understand what's happening in the world." And this was someone who had traveled widely and lived abroad for his own graduate studies and later work.

For those in their forties, experiences are forcing changes in their lives in relationship to their wives and families, but their resistance is often strong. They feel betrayed by a culture that did not prepare them for the changes that are now taking place at home and work. Yet they are also proud of their wives' achievements and sometimes sheepishly told of their beginning efforts at cooking or doing the laundry.

Reflections of Change

A popular video series in 1992 depicted this generation's predicament with humor and sensitivity through the ongoing chronicles of a family in which the wife had a good job and two children in school. The husband was responsible for breakfasts and homework because the wife's job kept her at the office both early and late. His trials, tribulations, and ineptness were made comic, but such a portrayal in the media and popular culture reflects the changes that are taking place in society.

One Japanese television commercial depicts a husband coming home from the office. The wife greets him at the door, asking if he wants dinner or a bath. He smiles broadly with great pleasure, and when he chooses the bath, the next sequence shows him in the bathroom scrubbing the bathtub with the sponsor's cleansing product. When he chooses dinner, the subsequent scene shows him returning with grocery bags to begin cooking dinner with the sponsor's product. While such shifts in gender role are not the norm, the fact that they are being used to sell products and not viewed as completely outlandish is a strong indicator of changing attitudes.

Men in their thirties and younger are the generation caught in the swirling vortex of transition. Their mothers took care of them, expecting only high achievement from them in return. In families with few children, they often received a degree of mothering that some observers now call "smothering," while the accompanying expectations for achievement seemed to grow higher and higher. Most did not learn to do household chores or take care of themselves, but now the women in their lives expect a great deal from them, both in the workplace and in the family.

A national response to limitations in male skills has been to require a home economics course for all secondary school students in a revised course of study that took effect in 1994.[5] Young men and women must take one course, either "General Home Economics," "Home Life Techniques,"or "General Home Life." Young men are especially enjoying the cooking portion of such courses. The reported resistance came from male teachers who felt it was a waste of time, taking attention away from their "important" courses.[6]

The changes can be bewildering to younger men. Bright women are competing with them at work, and it is not clear which behaviors are acceptable with their female colleagues. Looking toward marriage, they encounter the trendy definition of a desirable boyfriend as "three K," or in English the "three highs": *koshincho* (tall), *kogakureki* (well educated), and *koshunu* (high salary). If men don't achieve 3K, they are *oji san,* or middle-aged, with comic book, *manga,* depictions of oafishness, and no one wants to be that. The stress of trying to meet conflicting demands can be very high.

Courtship is one thing, but after marriage women are said to want a "good daddy, hard worker and healthy." The women their age, who usually lived at home with parents, have been able to spend their money on travel, clothes, and entertainment, becoming cosmopolitan and accustomed to lifestyles they want their husbands to maintain after marriage. At the same time, the men were concentrating narrowly on careers and building relations at the office through long hours and company socializing, while saving their money to get married. This combination of differing and unclear expectations holds many risks for successful marriage partnerships, even arranged ones.

More variation in attitudes and behavior was seen among those who are in this age group and younger as pressures increase from women, corporations, and society. Self-examination and questioning are widespread, as many find they prefer not to lead lives like those of the older men at work, whose whole life experience and relationships seem centered on their job. They want to be successful, but they also want free time for themselves, with leisure, travel, and sports depicted enticingly everywhere. Many want to marry a woman who makes a good salary, but they also would like to be taken care of as their fathers were cared for by their mothers.

A group of young Japanese naval officers was queried about whether their marriages were arranged.[7] They smiled shyly, and all said they either had or wanted marriages of the heart. The Japanese word for wife, *okusan*, means literally inside, or in the depths of, and commonly refers to a wife as the "woman in the depths of the house." When it was suggested that perhaps they could change the meaning of *okusan* from "in the depths of the house" to "in the depths of the heart," the men seemed puzzled at first, but then they smiled and nodded affirmation.

Ambivalence, dilemmas, and transitions are probably felt most keenly by this age group. One young woman told about suggesting to her fiancé that they live together while he finished college and she worked, because it would be more efficient and less expensive. She was hurt by his refusal and said, "He was afraid of what his parents would say." When interviewed, he said that he didn't want to cause her shame. Transitional times make rules and norms unclear for both men and women.

The men in their thirties who married working women find themselves spending more time on housework and, when there are children, taking more responsibility than their fathers did for them. They are learning new skills of cooking, cleaning, and child care, which some enjoy and others simply resent. A poignant phrase I heard from younger men and women was "Knowing your father's back," referring to seeing only his back as he left the house for work. Neither men nor women wanted their own children to say that.

Narita divorce (Narita is the Tokyo airport) is attributed to women in this age group who only get to know their husband on the honeymoon and then find him in daily life "selfish, incapable of taking care of himself, and unwilling to change." So when the honeymoon comes to an end at Narita airport, they leave the new husband and file for divorce. The challenges and problems loom large, but this age group probably has the most potential for real change in gender roles and relationships.

According to a periodic survey by the Prime Minister's Office, more men than women still think men should work and women should stay home, but the proportion of men who believe this has declined from 52 percent in 1987 to 33 percent in 1995, while the proportion of women who believe this dropped from 37 percent in 1987 to 22 percent in 1995.[8] Women as well as men (65 percent of women and 69 percent of men) believe "married women should think of the family, primarily their husband and children, before themselves." The comparable question was not even asked about married men.

Examples of changes by young men were numerous, such as the male journalist who longed for female companionship on an expanded plane, not necessarily focused on romance or marriage, but sharing music, ideas, and fun. An engineer said in a focus group that he had assumed his wife would continue to work when they married and that he would like to take a parental leave when he had children. The other men in the focus group squirmed uncomfortably, but when they were asked to talk a little more, they began to acknowledge the difficulties of men's taking parental leave. Finally, they together decided to try to support him in taking parental leave when the time came. Men, like women, are questioning who they are and who they want to be. Men's studies courses are appearing, in which men explore their own identity and study women's issues. One such course was translated into English as "Male Reformation Class," another as "Male Remodeling," perhaps apt titles.

Resistance to Change

Over lunch a Japanese friend and I were discussing, as usual, what is happening to women and men in Japanese society. The friend, an executive in her late forties, was bemoaning the difficulty of teaching her twenty-year-old son, who lives at home while attending the university, to put away his clothes and take responsibility in the house. She said, "How can I get my son to put his clothes away when he sees his father come in and drop his clothes in a trail from the door to his favorite chair? Then my son sees me pick them up and put them away in the morning." In my naive American way, I asked why she didn't just leave them where her husband drops them until he picked them up. She responded to me as if I were somewhat moronic, saying, "They would be there forever."

The message from that interchange was important. I can imagine leaving clothes dropped by a member of the family on the floor, but I wouldn't expect the clothes to remain there for several days. After the first day someone would surely insist that the owner of the clothes, whether it was the father, mother, or child, must pick up the clothes. In my friend's family, she said, the clothes would not even be noticed by the husband, or if he did notice, he would be discreet and not mention that she wasn't doing her duty. The clothes might actually remain on the floor forever, and Gloria Steinem's suggestion to nail them to the floor would have been as alien to her as to some-one from another planet. Her son's future wife may be the one who will reap the rewards of his mother's attempt to change the home system.

In her husband's office it would not occur to him to serve tea himself to a visitor. Given his position in his organization, tea, and a woman to serve it, would immediately appear with the arrival of an important guest. If it did not appear, he would call for it and probably feel aggrieved, with the delay a cause for rebuke. He would also never think of copying papers himself, while many women managers told of copying materials for themselves at the office when their subordinates were busy. One had been told by a male manager that she would lose face by so doing. Another said a male manager had asked her to do his copying when he saw her at the machine. What we see or don't see, how we interpret what we see, and consequently how we behave are based on our perceptions and beliefs about appropriateness in each situation. Discussing women in management with a male official from the Ministry of Finance was confusing until I realized my questions were about women in management and his responses were about "office ladies," the only women in his office, declaiming their satisfaction and disinterest in more responsibility. Perceptions of reality and propriety are not dissimilar at home and work. Not "seeing" clothes dropped on the floor and not seeing women's subordinate roles at work are parallel. The personal becomes political. Whether change is best initiated at home or at work is conjectural, but women sometimes have more leverage at home.

An American male colleague teaching English in Japan decided to leave his homestay family and take a small apartment alone so that he could retreat at night to write and study. His desire to be alone seemed strange to his hosts. At first they were a little offended, but when he explained his needs to their satisfaction, they were very concerned that he would not be able to manage alone. They asked, "Who would cook for him?" He assured them that he had been cooking since he was a small child. "Who would do his laundry?" He also was accustomed to doing that for himself. Most surprising of all to him was the third question, "Who would wake him up in the morning?" He said facetiously, "Seiko," but then he realized that underlying the question was a Japanese lifestyle very different than his own in which the mother always awakened the men and children of the family with tea and had breakfast prepared for them. Apparently both women and men collude in the belief that men are incapable of caring for themselves.

The question is not capability, but is often situational, as illustrated by one woman's story of her marriage. She and her husband met and were married in the United States, where both were working and studying. She said their life had been wonderful overseas. Both worked hard and shared the cleaning and cooking, going out to eat many nights and sharing leisure activities after shopping and cleaning on the weekend. When they returned to Japan she said, "He forgot how to cook or clean." He even began to talk about her leaving her job, because he said his friends thought he could not support his wife. Although they were in their early thirties, traditional values still seemed to prevail in his peer group, refuting the claim that traditional attitudes are simply a generational issue that is automatically resolved with a new generation.

Resistance to changing male sex roles seems even stronger than resistance to changing female sex roles. It is difficult to be a man who wants a more flexible, nurturing partnership role with women, just as it is difficult to be a woman who wants a more active, assertive role that allows her to use her potential. Although it might seem that having a dominant status would make it easier to make changes, that is not the case when it comes to gender roles. A stronger vested interest seems threatened when changes in the male roles are suggested, and strong resistances are mobilized. The vertical symbiosis seems deeply embedded in self-identity and thus difficult to change.

Entrenched Male Roles

The young professional man who wanted friendships with women, as he had in his student days in the United States, without their necessarily being seen as the first step to marriage, apparently lost hope or grew impatient. He managed to secure another scholarship for graduate study in the United States and left Japan. Rationalizing that this would further his career goals, he also hoped to enjoy the companionship of both female and male friends that he missed in Japan.

The strength of entrenched male roles socialized to a position of privilege may make change more difficult for men than for women, who, from positions of less power, seek tangible gains. The difficulty for males who seek change was illustrated in a recent study of former social activists in the United States who had worked for change in the mid-1960s. Surprisingly, the results indicated that the men who had been activists had lower-paying jobs than either nonactivist males or activist females, and that the activist males were the least happy.[9] The women generally had protested for the rights of everyone—women, blacks, the poor, and draft resisters—whereas the men had taken on a personal cause against the Vietnam War and the military draft. Interviewed at age thirty-one and again at forty-one, the women were happier and more successful, even though both males and females had fought against the traditional roles of wife/mother and soldier/provider. Society had changed more to include women's changing roles than to accept nontraditional male views.

By their entrenched nature, practices may be outside conscious awareness.

A successful woman author and consultant answered the question about obstacles to success by saying, "Three hot meals a day." She expanded, explaining that her mother-in-law, whom she liked and respected, had come to live with them and required three hot meals a day. Her husband, a sophisticated manager, assumed that his wife would take on that responsibility, as she herself had also originally assumed. Realizing the extent to which this limited her productivity for other things, she could not communicate directly with her husband, afraid to hurt him or his mother. Her indirect statements to make him aware of the problem were confusing to both of them and usually led to distance and coldness, but no understanding.

Another example of resistance to changing the male images was shown by an Adidas shoes promotional ad, which created a flap recently. The ad featured almost nude males discreetly covered with basketballs, hands, and so forth. *Sports Illustrated* would not carry the ad, even though the magazine's annual swimsuit edition, with its shots of nearly nude women, is highly promoted. The reverse exposure of men was unacceptable to the publishers, and the hypocrisy of their position received much publicity. Adidas was able to sell out the entire edition of the male advertisement as collector posters, while vowing not to advertise again in *Sports Illustrated*. By refusing to change its stance, the magazine communicated that it was happy to expose and exploit women but not men, providing another example of perception blinding people to the incongruities of a decision.

Gendered institutions provide obvious advantages to men, but significant disadvantages hidden within those institutions may not be so obvious. *Karoshi* ("death from overwork"), difficulties with relationships, alienation from families, lack of meaning in life at retirement, and decreased quality of life for both men and women are directly related to some aspects of male-defined and male-dominated institutions seen in Japan.

> I don't think men are happy in this society either. The issues are the way our jobs are structured, the long hours, the poor housing, the imbalances in employer/employee relations. That's what is at stake, not so much women's issues.
>
> Akako Hironaka, female Diet member

A pressure release valve has been seen in popular bars called "Office" in Shinjuku, an entertainment section of Tokyo, where hostesses are dressed as "career women" whom the patrons may harass and touch as they please. The most popular of these establishments have American hostesses, the most untouchable at work, who allow "harassment" and provide an escape from increasing awareness and punishment of sexual harassment in the office.

More recently, manifestations of unhappiness have emerged in stories about "a disturbing new national pastime taking root in Japan: male obsession with schoolgirls dressed in uniforms."[10] Hundreds of "image clubs" have sprung up in Tokyo, where, for $150 an hour, men can live out their fantasies with make-believe schoolgirls in make-believe classrooms, locker rooms, or commuter trains. In a period of shifting gender power relations, some men seek to affirm their superiority with younger and younger girls. Some women in their middle to late twenties dress and act like shy young girls for the men who find schoolgirls sexually alluring.

Masao Miyamoto, a psychiatrist and author of *The Straitjacket Society*,[11] attributes this phenomenon to Japanese men's feeling threatened by adult women. Rika Kayama, a psychiatrist and social commentator, agrees, saying that men want to behave with young girls in an overbearing way to position themselves as superior. She and others believe the increasing sophistication and power of women are difficult for middle-aged men to accept, and so they turn to make-believe schoolgirls, females over whom they can still exert some control. At the same time, some real schoolgirls make pocket money after school by working as prostitutes. The original reaction to this development was to blame the girls and their parents, since men in Tokyo may legally have sex with children over the age of twelve.

In another vein, Japanese newspaper reports about men seeking transvestite bars after work to relax and relieve the cares of the day have been seen as an indication of men's increasing fear of women and the deleterious effects of women moving into more prominent roles in the workplace. Cross-dressing is not a new phenomenon in Japan, contrary to some analysts' protestations. Transvestitism dates at least as far back as the early samurai periods. Noh and Kabuki theater are the epitome of cross-dressing, and the men who play women, *onnagata*, are famous, well paid, and highly sought after by both men and women. They often carried their cross-sex roles from the theater into their personal lives and had admirers in both.

A tradition of cross-dressing is found in all cultures, and in the Japanese tradition it was highly developed in the seventeenth-century theater and entertainment world. It is not surprising, in a male-dominant and male-defined world, that some men prefer the company of men to that of women even in the most intimate relationships. Blaming this on women's changing roles and the pressures on the salaryman, who seeks relief in a female role, may have some validity, but its roots lie deep within the culture and are connected to a long line of respectable tradition.

The fear of women is not new. The prominence of female ghosts who return to haunt their families and former tormentors or lovers is a recurring theme in Kabuki and Noh plays. A fear of women and ambivalence about the feminine become intertwined with fears of change, of disturbing the known by allowing women entry to areas previously defined as male.

In most countries the three last bastions of male dominance are the military, corporations, and government, in that order. As these bastions are threatened, the resistance to change solidifies and accelerates. In the United States women have been legally a part of all three institutions since the 1960s, but the evolutionary process is bumpy as each new pocket of resistance is challenged. A striking example surfaced recently with integration of the remaining male-only military academies, which are state schools. When ordered either to accept women as full cadets or to provide absolutely equal facilities, these academies first chose the latter at a far greater cost but then were ordered by the judicial system to integrate.

A successful woman candidate who had deleted all references to her gender was refused admittance when her sex was discovered and she sought legal redress. The institution fought unsuccessfully to the Supreme Court to maintain a male-only school. A comment by one of the alumni recruited to help finance the fight against women was significant. He said, "It's not that women can't do it. But we should preserve some stuff. If women come here, things will change. I mean, what else, what else do they want? This is like the last thing we have. I would just like to keep it for ourselves." The woman applicant's response was, "Hey, wake up and smell the '90s."[12] As Japanese women are integrated into the "self-defense," police, and naval forces, learning about the experiences of American women may help ease the transitions.

Systems Nature of Change

Many men, as well as women, believe change will be positive, with rewards that include not only a more equitable nation but also increased opportunities at home and work and more productive learning in the schools. Some of the strongest supporters in the fight to bring women into the all-male United States military academies were male students who testified about the previous repressive and "macho" atmosphere, described as a culture of "hog jogs," with intentional debasement and name-calling condoned and preferential treatment for star athletes.

For societies worldwide, changes in any element of the system requires each of the other elements in the system to respond. Institutions and power structures embody traditional definitions of male roles, and organizations have been defined to fit those same socially constructed roles. When women change their roles, the system as a whole must adapt. An elder, the headman in a village in Turkey, provided a vivid example of his realization of this when faced with United Nations representatives who had provided a new well for his village and now wanted to teach the girls in the village to read, where previously only boys had been taught to read. The headman's response was an exaggeration of some of the more universal fears men share about changing gender roles. He asked, "If the girls learn to read, how will I control the village?"[13] For him, order and control in the village were associated with men's superiority and women's cloistering, illiteracy, and lack of knowledge about the world. He knew, intuitively, that girls' literacy would change the village, causing them to question the existing rules, and he wanted to keep control, hold back the world. Analogously, Japanese women managers felt men who were seeking schoolgirl prostitutes and those who said their companies were not yet ready for women managers were trying to "hold back the world."

Collaboration for Change

Japanese men, as well as women, are prisoners of the culture and face contradictions, dilemmas, and choices. Since men have more political and corporate power than women at this moment, they have a greater responsibility for change. As one young man said, there is a window of opportunity for men to be generous, before being forced to change. Younger men feared that change might be forced by circumstances and the rebellion of women because so many older men in power were resistant.

Japan is known as a vertical society, but it is also a lateral society. The custom of "looking to the side" to see what your neighbor is doing so that you will know what to do, could be mobilized to support innovation and new directions. The young man who expressed a desire for more egalitarian relationships with women can contribute to the change process if he returns from the United States. He can add his voice and actions to those already speaking for change. Both lateral and vertical relationships and support need to be mobilized if women and men are truly to live in a society with "joint participation by women and men," as stated in the National Plan of Action Towards the Year 2000.[14] Initiated by men and women in policy-making positions with a will to change, Japan's hierarchical structure encourages change from the top down and is sensitive to external pressure. This could be combined with nemawashi, gathering consensus from the roots. A return to the "good old days" of rigid gender hierarchies and status is hardly possible.

Changing gender roles eventually precipitate and require changes in social structures and institutions. The voices of individual men are being heard in Japan in greater numbers, supporting changes to allow men more freedom. For both men and women the changes they seek have trade-offs. Japanese men with working wives gain greater freedom to choose and define their work, knowing that there is an additional source of income. In return, they must take on a more equitable portion of the responsibility and work of maintaining a family and home and receive rewards that have been reserved to women, the satisfaction of relationships, nurturing, and family building. Women, in sharing the workplace and the home with men, must relinquish some control of the home and children, as well as take on more responsibilities in the workplace.

Surveys reveal and news commentators publicize Japanese women's privately expressed hostility and anger toward Japanese men. The frustrations and dissatisfaction women feel about their role in society are often aimed at individual men, the most logical target. A next level of awareness reveals the social system conditioning of both women and men as the true culprit. Yes, they say, many Japanese men, old and young, are difficult, insensitive, and unaware of women's situation. Men do need education about relationships with women and the problems faced by women as they take on new roles, and both men and women need to recognize that the cultural norms conveyed by home and school about male superiority need examination, awareness, and revision. Both men and women face the dilemma that they must be partners in marriage, in child rearing, and at work, and so cannot be viewed as outsiders. No wonder women managers are confusing to men who are forced to define "inside" and "outside" in new ways and to learn new modes of interaction. Assigning sole responsibility for the home and family to women, and sole responsibility for the economy and government to men, is no longer viable.

Discovering positive changes that can be made to benefit both men and women is a major challenge. Women's visions for a better future for women, men, and the nation are the subject of the next chapter, which explores what is known about factors and strategies that lead to successful transitions.

12

Visions and Strategic Choices

Strengths Women Bring to Leadership

We sincerely hope that efforts made in the remaining years of
this century and at the beginning of the 21st century will
make the movement for a gender-equal society irreversible
and create a new relationship between men and women based
on genuine equality in the 21st century.

> "Vision of Gender Equality—Creating New Values for
> the 21st Century," Council for Gender Equality,
> Office of the Prime Minister, Tokyo, Japan 1996

As Japanese women look toward the twenty-first century, their hopes, wishes,
and dreams will influence choices and actions. This chapter examines visions
that Japanese women managers shared in the course of my research. Even
though they may not always agree on specifics and priorities, most Japanese
women managers concur on the need to improve the quality of life in Japan
for their families, communities, and themselves and to make work more
equitable. Previous chapters have demonstrated the importance of women's
work, ascertained that they are successful managers, and looked at their career
and life paths, the nature of Japanese organizational culture, and the men in
their lives. This chapter looks at their hopes for the future and the strengths
of women leaders, and summarizes the factors that helped them succeed.
From these flow strategies and desired changes that reverberate throughout
society.

Clearly and with little hesitation, women described their visions for themselves, their daughters, and society in the twenty-first century. Their visions
were wide-ranging. Most encompassed a holistic view of the world, wanting
collaborative work and resolution of problems of the environment, human
relations, and the economy. All agreed on the desire for improved quality of
life in Japan. They want to be able to enjoy both work and family and not al-

222

ways be tired achieving it. They want partnerships and joint participation with men.

As managers, they want to help create companies that contribute to society and value people, and they want their voices counted in policies and decisions. They want to make sufficient money to live comfortably. Younger women especially wanted not always to have to fight to be accepted simply because they are women. Women managers did not want to be like men, but they want to use their feminine intelligence, to earn equal salaries for equal work, and not to have to work three times as hard as their male peers to succeed. Chizuko Ueno, a professor of sociology at University of Tokyo, is described as one of Japan's most articulate feminists. Her vision is a world that "values feminine intelligence." She argues for a culturally sensitive feminism for Asian women that is the product of their own context and meaningful to them.[1] Learning what that is requires input from women in all stages and walks of life.

Some women managers wanted a wider scope of responsibility that would more fully engage their abilities, while others wanted more time to share with family and friends and to engage in creative activities. Several women who had achieved success voiced a desire to share what they had learned and "to engage in educating and training younger women in business." Several wanted to start new careers, as a university lecturer, to write a book, to use their knowledge and experience in consulting. Their visions were not limited to their own achievements or even to Japan, as is apparent from the following comments:

> I want always to be a part of active social activities whether in business, company, or free-lancing, to be in an international environment and be able to provide first-class output. I also want to have a partner in life with whom I can share the value of daily happiness and life and be a mother of two children.

> I want to be always honest in myself. I don't want to do what I think and feel questionable even if it is effective for my business.

> I want to put the person in the center of medicine and health care, to move from "patients" to customers and decision makers for their own health.

> I want to help those who will be my followers and set up a nonprofit fellowship foundation.

> Most important, I want to be proud of myself being a woman. To stick to my dreams and continue and endure and be faithful to all the people I contact.

> I want my daughter to be able to do what she does best and have a full life without the conflicts I had.

A recurring theme was a desire for a world in which they can use their talents, participate freely, and influence the direction of society.

Official Visions

For anyone interested in seeking them, publicly stated visions for the future of Japanese women are not in short supply. They are embodied in the "Plan for Gender Equality 2000, the National Plan of Action Towards the Year 2000"; the "Vision of Gender Equality-Creating New Values for the 21st Century" from the Council for Gender Equality; and the themes chosen annually to symbolize Women's Week in Japan. All contain visions for Japanese women.

- 1991 "To build an age in which we can live without sexual stereotypes"
- 1993 "Free Styles of Living for Both Men and Women"
- 1994 Individuals Play the Melody—Men and Women Create the Harmony"
- 1995 Men and Women Building a New Age Together—The Possibilities are Endless"
- 1996 "Improving the Status of Women in the 21st Century"

Women's Week was established in 1949 to celebrate the date Japanese women won the right to vote, April 10, 1946. The celebrations and the visions have both evolved, as shown by the themes for the 1990s.

Perhaps the most significant statement of shared vision can be found in *The Japanese National Plan of Action*, formulated in 1977 after the first International Women's Year Conference and revised periodically. The December 1996 revision, builds on proceedings at the Beijing International Women's Conference. It is a compilation and official statement of visions, strategies, tactics, and specific areas of action, titled *The Plan for Gender Equality 2000*. The preamble sets forth for the first time in Japan a philosophy of the human rights of women:

> The concept of human rights is a universal value shared by the human race and is the basic idea behind a gender-equal society. All measures must serve to achieve fairness by respecting the human rights of men and women equally in all aspects and enable each individual to lead his/her life as comfortably as possible for which an important precondition is world peace.

Recognizing and articulating the wide discrepancy between national espoused values and the reality, it says,

> Gender equality is enshrined in Japan in the constitution and is provided for by various laws and regulations. Nonetheless, it has not yet planted its roots in Japan nor has it brought about equality in reality. Therefore, five

objectives are presented for the solution of problems concerning women and issues relating to men, the other side of the same coin.[2]

The plan is divided into four basic areas, which cover in general terms most issues articulated in the visions of women managers. The first target in the plan is to "build social systems that promote gender equality. Specific measures for this include increasing participation by women in policy decision-making processes, reviewing social systems and practices, and reforming awareness from the perspective of gender equality."

The rationale states that women are, by international standards, represented extremely poorly in the policy decision-making process in Japan, in both public and private sectors. The government should take the lead in promoting efforts to redress this underrepresentation and in studying the feasibility of introducing positive action.

The second target is to "achieve gender equality in the workplace, family and community." The objectives are "Promoting equal opportunity and equal treatment at the workplace, building partnerships in agriculture, forestry and fishing villages, and supporting women and men to harmonize work with family and community life, and develop conditions to enable elderly people and others to live in peace of mind."

The discussion of these points emphasizes that those social systems and practices that do not treat individuals without bias, which still persist in Japan, should be studied and reviewed.

The third target is to "create a society where human rights of women are promoted and defended." The priority objectives are "eliminating all forms of violence against women, respecting the human rights of women in the media, supporting lifelong health for women, and promoting gender equality to open the way for a diversity of choices through enrichment of education and learning."

Enlarging on the target, the plan says that "a wide-ranging response to violence against women is required from a variety of perspectives, from building an environment to prevent such violence to creating measures to care for women who have suffered from violence. In particular, stronger efforts should be made to protect the rights of the child, eliminating child prostitution and preventing sexual harassment."

The plan continues: "Measures to promote respect for the human rights of women in the media should be studied, including moves to distance the media dealing in expressions of sex and violence from minors and others who do not wish to be exposed to them." The phrase "to distance expressions of sex and violence from minors" is an illustration of the difficult task of changing social customs while avoiding the appearance of censorship, a culturally sensitive subject.

"In keeping with international trends, child pornography should be eliminated. The development of rules for new media such as the Internet should be studied. Perspectives such as reproductive health and rights should be incorporated into lifelong measures for women's health management and for maintaining and promoting women's health."

The fourth and last target is to "contribute to the equality, development and peace of the global community." The strategies say that official development assistance should be promoted, seeking to strengthen the status of women and redress gender discrepancies at all stages of women's lives, with particular emphasis on education, health, and participation in social and economic activities.

The Council for Gender Equality has set a goal to implement the measures by the year 2010. This plan is more comprehensive than the previous plan of 1992 and introduces for the first time women's rights as human rights, a major departure from other documents on improving the lot of women. An uneasiness with the concept of rights persists, since there is considerable concern that rights could potentially lead to taking rights from others, and thus could be harmful to society.

The need to review social systems and practices from the perspective of gender equity is another new addition. The latest plan expands the vision of women to include their influence in the total society, in contrast to the greater emphasis on motherhood and child rearing that permeated previous versions, and it specifically targets violence against women and child prostitution, not mentioned in previous official documents. If the plan were implemented totally, the nation and the world would be a very different place.

While the National Plan of Action was dismissed by some as simply a paper document to placate women and impress other countries, it does embody important visions for women and constitutes national policy and thus is an important framework for action. The Office of Gender Equity has disseminated the document widely and is working with local governments, nongovernmental organizations, and private groups to further action toward the objectives. A quarterly update on women's progress is published by the Prime Minister's Office to support continued interest and progress.

Shared Visions

People today have an impatient urge to participate in the events and processes that shape their lives.[3]

The 1995 Fourth World Conference on Women in Beijing, China, which influenced the latest national plan, was an important milestone for Japanese women. Japan had the largest delegation of women attending, six thousand for the entire conference. While several attendees expressed embarrassment that their delegation was headed by a man, Chief Cabinet Secretary and Minister for Women's Affairs Koken Nosaka, when all other delegations were headed by women, they didn't allow that to interfere with networking and learning. The large number of women attending and the international spotlight provided a needed impetus to Japanese women and their organizations.

They led workshops, heard completely different women's perspectives, and interacted with Chinese women who articulated their historic anger at Japan. Their experiences motivated many to speak up, to enlist other Japanese women when they returned home, and to work for change in business, education, family life, and politics.

Follow-up activities were encouraged and planned not only by the participants of the conference but also by Japanese government agencies. The Prime Minister's Office promised to revise the plan of action in line with women's recommendations. The quarterly newsletters from the Office for Gender Equality took on new life as the number of events related to women quadrupled.

One newsletter included a graphic presentation of a vision for Japanese women and men titled, *A Society with Active and Joint Participation of Women and Men*. The woman in the graph says, "The office is better when woman participate," and the man is saying, "Home is better when men participate."

The Prime Minister's 1998 gender equity poster (see Figure 12.1), chosen from nationwide submissions, depicts male and female musicians playing in harmony. The caption says, "Let us weave (create) a great future by joint participation between men and women, both men and women determining their participation by their own desire. Help share love and responsibility. Such love and effort for the future will create happiness."

Advantages Women Bring to Leadership

Human rights and equity are the most commonly used rationale, serving as powerful justification for a more equitable society and joint participation. Convincing a traditional male-dominated power structure of the importance of changes to encourage women in management, however, will require mobilizing all the best strategic arguments in addition to human rights and equity. Articulating the advantages women bring to leadership may help persuade government and corporate leaders of the necessity for change.

Women managers make a difference by their presence, actions, and words, or there wouldn't be so much resistance. In a speech at Harvard University in 1994, Katherine Graham, longtime publisher of the *Washington Post,* said an

Figure 12.1. Winner of the Prime Minister's gender equity poster contest in 1998. The caption says, "Let us weave a great future by joint participation between men and women, both men and women determining their participation by their own desire. Help share love and responsibility. Such love and effort for the future will create happiness." Office for Gender Equality, Prime Minister's Office, Tokyo, 1998.

important benefit of including women is that they bring unheard voices and issues to the table:

> Gender doesn't matter in covering the news. Gender does matter in decid-ing what news is. By raising different issues to the level of national debate, women have changed the agenda of our country. None of these issues are "women's issues." Nor do all women view these issues the same way. What could be more patronizing or stupid than to believe all women think alike. *Rather these are societal issues that most men overlooked, ignored, downplayed, mis-understood, or simply didn't get.*[4]

Women are changing conversations and public discourse, taking so-called women's issues off the society pages and onto the front page. No longer can date rape and sexual harassment be dismissed with a wink and the comment that "boys will be boys." Previously ignored issues and a need for equity are inserted into politics, commerce, entertainment, and sports, mandating changes.

In addition to raising different issues, women bring a variety of other strengths to leadership. Women's life patterns have shaped views of the world with different priorities, different styles of solving problems and reaching ob-jectives, and different approaches to power, decision making, and manage-ment. Traditionally, men's career paths have been linear, in contrast to the paths women trod. Women may marry and follow husbands, have children, and take a week or six months or a year off. Finding they cannot get ahead in one company, they find another. Such varied experiences bring a viewpoint that is not usually found in a rigidly homogeneous management circle. The circuitous routes taken by women managers, described in chapter 6, have generally given them a broader perspective of work and how to manage.

Women have honed skills of negotiation to get what they wanted when they were physically outdistanced or psychologically denigrated. Functioning in both a male world of business and a female world of home, children, and community, women have learned to speak multiple languages, with a differ-ent language for each area of their lives. As outsiders in male institutions, in-siders in family, and a combination of both in national life, women have had to manage multiple roles and tasks, giving them skills of multitasking that are so important to the information age. They have been forced to weave to-gether conflicting demands of family members, negotiate among competing factions, schedule complex family tasks, and mediate conflicts with ingenuity rather than power.

Research by Judy Rosener and Sally Helgesen, among others, indicates that women's styles tend toward openness and inclusion, revealing and using the strengths of others.[5] The photograph of Ambassador Ogata in Bosnia

(Figure 12.2) radiates welcome, warmth, and reassurance in extremely painful circumstances, illustrating an open approach that contrasts sharply with the closed stance of her male colleagues.

Gender differences are also linked to power. An interesting study on gender differences in language at work found that differences between male and female language patterns narrowed when women became boss:

> Some say women are born to nurture; others insist we're better leaders than men ever dreamed of being. The truth lies somewhere in between, where people are individuals and gender, like race and ethnicity, is a highly unreliable guide to real-world behavior.[6]

Classifying certain characteristics as feminine or masculine introduces the danger of creating artificial gender distinctions. Good management is rooted in day-to-day circumstances, the industry, and markets and in appropriate responses to the mix. Neither men nor women have a monopoly on integrity or the ability to inspire a team, develop good personal relationships, and establish a flexible and accountable organization structure—the diverse qualities all executives need to make business thrive in the future. Rather than

Figure 12.2. The many faces of feminine strength. Ambassador Sadako Ogata, United Nations high commissioner for refugees, stands on the Fraternity Bridge with the UN commander, Sir Michael Rose, during her visit to Sarajevo. *Agence France Presse,* March 1994.

classifying characteristics as masculine or feminine, I have used a situational view that looks at management and leadership styles women have developed in response to culturally ascribed gender roles. Their styles tend to be less hierarchical and more collaborative, and they invite participation, all of which will be essential in the twenty-first century.[7]

Future Corporations and Managers

The changing times demand innovations in corporate management. . . . Corporations need to be managed with greater emphasis on creativity and maintaining balance between profitability and social awareness.[8]

Creativity and innovation are key words as Japan faces the twenty-first century and the accelerated pace of technological and economic change. The Japanese Economic Planning Agency's *White Paper on the Life of the Nation* notes that creativity is as important as productivity.[9] Creativity is defined in various ways to include making or bringing something new into existence, seeing the familiar in new ways, and producing along new or unconventional lines.

Many of the characteristics of creative people apply to women as a consequence of their life patterns. Creativity requires an "insider's" knowledge and an "outsider's" perspective. Creative people usually have lived in more than one culture, and they often speak a second language while also remaining grounded in their own culture. Summarizing from creativity research sources, the characteristics of creative people include the ability to live with complexity, recognize and organize patterns, and value intuition, as well as openness to other views and perspectives, tolerance for ambiguity, self-knowledge and self-confidence, and willingness to act on incomplete information. These characteristics are similar to the success factors of women managers.

It's a new world, in many ways better than the old, in some ways harsher. The largest corporations are finding they must respond to the world as it is—not as it was, or as they would like it to be.[10]

As people face uncertainties of a new world of information, global economy, and shifting expectations, the need for companies to change is recognized, and a variety of strategies and tactics have been tested, some successful in the short term and others less so. Individuals, as well as corporations and governments, are finding their very existence questioned, and a satisfactory response requires articulating new goals and strategies.

While male-defined organizational culture is acknowledged as a major barrier for women managers, it is often viewed as impossible to change. In reality, however, organizations are changing. To gain a competitive advantage, they must quickly and effectively respond to changed circumstances. Successful organizations of the twenty-first century will be able to scan the environment in order to know the world, grasp opportunities, create organizational versatility, and respond rapidly and continuously to opportunities and threats. Above all, they must be able to empower people to carry out these mandates.

Managers will need the skills to carry out new mandates. Scanning the environment requires managers with critical thinking skills and the ability to access, process, select, and prioritize information. To grasp opportunities managers need versatility, adaptability, and the ability to recognize, flow with, and manage with change. Managers need self-knowledge and self-confidence to act, and an ability to create balance in personal and working life. Empowering people requires communication and relationships skills as well as self-knowledge.

Characteristics of Successful Women Managers

Successful Japanese women managers have been able to transcend limitations of gender role expectations that dictate supportive, self effacing, invisible behavior and use their competencies and talents to achieve their goals. Somehow they escaped early imprinting of inferior status and subservience to men. In the process, they seem to have developed many of the characteristics that will be needed in corporations of the future. A common thread running through the lives of all the successful women I interviewed was the presence of one or more factors that propelled them outside the normal rigid socialization for girls. Some avoided the usual gender socialization because there were no older brothers; others had families where profession or inclination put them slightly outside the prescribed norms. For some women, living in a foreign country had introduced alternative possibilities. Major external events or upheavals were the causal factors that allowed others to transcend the boundaries of gender. Factors in the lives of the women managers that contributed to their success, discussed in depth in earlier chapters, are summarized in Table 12.1.

Each woman had developed an inner conviction that she could do what she wanted to do, as well as a belief in her own ability. Doing things that were normally considered out of bounds for women required a knowledge that there were alternatives to the traditional way. The journey to success was set in motion by these factors, evolving from a variety of sources in their life histories. "Can-do" messages were especially important to nurture a self-

Table 12.1 Success Factors: Japanese Women Managers

Preconditions, predispositions	Era	Majority: *Showa* period, 1926 onward
	Family of origin	Grow up without older male siblings, or youngest
	Mother	Role model, encourager, or negative model
Preparation	Socialization	Achievement encouraged, gender socialization weak or absent
	Heroes	Nonsexist, foreign, Sailor Moon cartoon figure
	Education	Higher, often University
	Travel	Outside Japan
	Language	At least one besides Japanese, generally English
	Experiences	Less restricted than average for girls
Opportunity	Economy	Expanding
	Organizations	Increasing numbers and formation of new types
	Organization culture	Opening
	Legislation	Equal employment opportunity
	Societal attitudes	In flux
	Class and social networks	Opening and changing
Achievement	Timing	Postwar, equal employment opportunity
	Training	Increased opportunities
	Hard Work	Habits formed early, home, school, social
	Insert self	Assertion not discouraged
	Mentors	Exposure to success
	Visibility	Early public relations
	Grasp opportunity	Skills—observation and speaking out
	Personal relationships	Diverse
	Family support	Did not discourage achievment

concept, an inner belief that they could achieve. While outside the usual norms for girls, the successful women were a part of social systems that gave them emotional support. Belief in their abilities and the strength to counter prevailing norms of behavior most often were fostered in early life.

Rigid hierarchies that define women as subordinate to men are barriers beginning at birth and continuing through a lifetime. The most consistent factor for successful women was the absence of older brothers. The implications of this absence of brothers in their early lives appear profound, applying across age groups, education level, class, and lifestyle. The absence of an older brother allowed budding Japanese women leaders to expand their visions of the world and themselves. Whether this has a more general effect on women's development is worthy of speculation and further research. The atmosphere and training that came from not having an older brother need to be duplicated for girls who have brothers. The challenge is to develop tools and support similar strategies of success for other women and at any age. As stated by the politician Mariko Mitsui, "We need a new strategy, new priorities, new thinking, new ways of putting issues on the agenda. If you don't raise an issue, it's not an issue."[11] Ability in languages other than Japanese was important to surmount the barriers, and currently a second language is part of the curriculum required for all Japanese students to graduate. Travel outside of Japan, which is common for the current generation, was one of the success factors mentioned by women. A vision of possible alternatives is a prerequisite to being able to evolve to a more equitable distribution of power.

Parents have an important role to play by becoming aware of gender inequities and avoiding rigid gender restrictions for both male and female children. Their encouragement of daughters is important to help them have goals and use their abilities to accomplish them. A Japanese American friend related how she was not encouraged to go to college, while the pressure on her older brother was stifling. He rebelled by dropping out, and she graduated from Harvard Law School.

Women themselves need to become aware of early learned, and now unconscious, limits they place on themselves. The educational establishment has an important role in examining and changing the gendered limits embedded in curriculum and practice. The examination for bias in government policies and practices is spelled out in the National Plan of Action and is essential for the development of women managers.

Networks and Other Workplace Strategies

When women find companies to be demanding, they work as hard as or harder than men; when companies do not offer them the same future prospects as men, they have difficulty putting their work in a long-term perspective. The paucity of women in senior and top management positions becomes a ceiling on other women's aspirations. If they believe change is possible and it can be demonstrated that changes will bring success and contribute to a better quality of life, it is easier to mobilize energy and set change in motion. The image of success creates possibilities, while visions provide a basis for action. Aspiring women managers would like successful women as mentors, coaches, and role models.

Japanese men use their "old boy networks" to get information, projects, and jobs. Male networks often consist of school classmates across company and political borders that connect them with power sources. Within the company, school networks function alongside peer networks of the "class" in which men entered the company, and these contacts serve to smooth their way to success.

> The future of Japanese women lies in getting together.
>
> Young Japanese woman manager

Working together when they are minorities in a male-dominant system not only requires self-confidence but sometimes seems foolhardy. Divide and conquer is a well-known strategy in military operations. Career women, not wishing to be seen as office ladies, often distance themselves from clerical staff. Office ladies, in turn, often are reluctant to work for women managers for a variety of reasons. Male bosses seem more powerful, and some women may want to be associated with that power, or they might feel an element of threat or envy when they realize some women are treated differently. Fragmenting women into separate categories lessens opportunities to share information and makes it more difficult for them to support each other. As long as reasons can be marshaled to show that successful women are exceptional, or "special cases" (*tokubets na keisu*), the need to change attitudes toward women can be brushed aside.

In order to get things done in the home, community, and as parents, women instinctively engage in networking. They have developed their own informal circles for information and support. Consumers' groups and shared baby-sitting are instances that have grown into more formal organizations. Japanese women, like men, have their early school networks, but only rarely are they in the power positions of male networks.

An intentional networking strategy to gain access to information and power in the workplace is a newer, rapidly developing phenomenon for women managers. A recent book on women entrepreneurs lists two pages of women's network addresses and phone numbers. While some women are self-conscious about using networks for business or personal advantage, a few not only are developing women's networks but also are joining male networks like the Young Entrepreneurs Organization and use the contacts effectively and unabashedly.

Given a chance, women are experts at networking. Edward Staiano, President of General Systems, a Motorola division, was asked in an interview to identify determinants of his success in a highly competitive advanced technology industry. He said, "We network a lot. We have learned how from our women managers."

Asking the Unasked Questions

When outsiders observe extremely qualified Japanese women retreating into a shy, self-effacing demeanor, they often wonder why they don't rebel. The women may have complained earlier about unequal treatment, or been ignored or punished, so now they may quietly acquiesce. Wanting to be accepted within the power hierarchy, they ignore or pretend to ignore slights and condescending attitudes toward themselves and toward other women. However, men may not change willingly, Shidzue Kato advised, as she encouraged women to elbow their way in. Madeleine Albright, United States secretary of state, said she taught her women students to interrupt, to insert themselves. It is not easy for Japanese women to elbow their way into power, nor to bring themselves to interrupt at work, but sometimes painful and seemingly awkward strategies are required.

International events and pressures supplement internal arguments for change in economic and political systems. Responding to outside pressures is a familiar change strategy in Japan. Referring to the term used for Admiral Perry's forced entrance into the barricaded nation, one woman executive said there have been three *kurofune* (black ships) for Japanese women. The first, in 1853, gave women the opportunity to go abroad. The second was the new constitution, adopted in 1946 after Japan's defeat in World War II, which gave women the right to vote, and the third was the United Nations International Decade for Women, which exerted pressure on Japan to improve the conditions of women. Collaborating with forces simmering from within, all three *kurofune* have induced major changes.

Without external pressures, bringing about change is often a much more tedious matter. It requires the use of tactics of adaptation and maneuver, much like guerrilla warfare, including manipulation from behind the shoji screen. Direct challenge has been suggested as a strategy by women who are frustrated with the pace of change, but it is seldom used by Japanese women. Professor Chizuko Ueno is an example of working within and outside a traditional system. Her earliest books, quickly labeled "feminist," were written while she was teaching at a small college near Kyoto, outside the mainstream of academia. When her books, which were seen in Japan as radical, acquired an international reputation, the traditional University of Tokyo invited her to join the faculty. She now serves alongside conservative professors who still fight against the inclusion in history texts of stories of the battle of Nanking and comfort women.

Companies give lip service to equity and increasing the number of women in senior management positions. Successful strategies need actions to train the entire organization on the value and rewards of diversity. In our consulting experience, all levels of the organization need to be involved, and a clear public commitment from the top is required. Customers and clients as well as employees need to be "sold" on changes. As discussed previously, the marketing of a new product would be undertaken only after extensive market research and preparation of the market. The same process of creating an awareness of the need for and value of change is important to make the transition from a traditional, exclusively male management structure to a structure that includes women.

Keidanren, the premier economic organization for Japanese companies, has taken on the task of convincing its member companies of the necessity for better utilization of women and distributing materials to do so effectively. It has published the results of a survey of member companies about women managers, as well as a primer on increasing their numbers. The stimulus for this project came during an official visit by Chancellor Helmut Kohl, the head of the German government. During a speech at Keidanren, he observed that in the audience of five hundred people there were no women, and he wondered why. Although this state of affairs had been considered normal by the organization before, Kohl's public question raised awareness, was embarrassing, and required a response.

Women need to ask the unasked questions and make the invisible visible. In a discussion about problems women are encountering at work and home, the wife of the president of Chinese University said, with great insight, "We women must take the responsibility for treating our sons and daughters differently. When we tell our daughters to wash up after dinner and our son to do his homework, we are perpetuating the inequalities." Giving both men and women more flexibility and family time requires questioning the "normal" and making profound changes in attitudes and behavior as well as structures.

Heroes for Women

Older women managers had difficulty remembering heroes or models from childhood. After reflection, the ones they were able to recall usually turned out to be male. One remembered a doctor she had read about in elementary school who went into the villages healing people. Others cited their father's work or their mother as homemaker or uncles who did interesting things. None could remember a female hero from life or literature.

During the period of my research, the *manga* (comic book) and television show *Sailor Moon*[12] were the rage, with many related accessories available in stores, to the tune of over $500 million (see Figure 12.3). Three-year-old girls sang the songs. In the series, which is the creation of Takeuchi Naoko, a cartoonist in her midtwenties, a fourteen-year-old high school girl, Tsukino Usagi, becomes Sailor Moon when needed and rights the wrongs of the world, "fighting for love and justice." She is clearly in charge, calls in her girlfriends, Sailors Jupiter, Mars, and Venus, or occasionally a boyfriend, to save the earth from the villains of the Dark Kingdom. She is a reincarnation of the Fabled Moon Princess, who provides a role model for young girls that is very different from the "good wife, wise mother" helpmate inherent in traditional Japanese education. One six-year-old girl said, "I love them because they are strong, gentle and look great." The potential of the market has spawned a new breed of girls' comics, so that now at least half the stories are about independent girls like Sailor Moon. Nonsexist textbooks and female heroes in children's early years support a vision of equity, accomplishment, and confidence.

Figure 12.3. Tsukini Usage, a fourteen-year-old high school girl, becomes Sailor Moon and rights the wrongs of the world, "fighting for love and justice," calling in her friends when needed. Takeuchi Naoko, cartoonist. Reprinted with permission.

Systems Nature of Change

Looking at men in Japanese society, as in chapter 11, makes it clear that a change in women's social roles eventually reverberates throughout the system. An executive of the Japan Federation of Employers' Association recognized this in his response to demands for shorter working hours for everyone, both men and women: "If we consider companies need to maintain their dynamism, we cannot ask them to reduce the work loads of their male workers. The whole society has to shift in the direction of denying fixed male and female roles."[13]

The visions stated in the National Plan of Action require change and adaptation by men, women, businesses, and government. Recognizing that women are deeply embedded in the complicated social and economic systems of society, each element must be considered.

> The climate for change is propitious. . . . Once ferment begins in one area of national life, it is not easily kept from spilling over into others.[14]

As men, albeit reluctantly, adjust to women managers at work, the need to collaborate at home and work becomes more evident. The challenges and issues for women in management are a manifestation of broader changes in the world. The most deeply held values are being questioned: beliefs about gender roles, the structure of families, religion, government, and society. In Japan the questioning may not be straightforward, instead taking the form of declining birth rates, increased single population, attitudes toward divorce, work, and family, school refusers, bullying, violence, and in the most tragic cases, murder. Strategies for change must evolve from within, but stories of success may aid the process. Many Japanese men, old and young, seem unaware of women's situation and they often respond when they learn about problems faced by women taking on more societal roles. Men's cooperation is more likely when their lives are directly affected, for example, by not finding a marriage partner, by having a female boss, by a daughter's harassment, or by facing the responsibility of caring for elderly, ailing parents alone.

The political system has been written off by some Japanese women as beyond repair. Fortunately, others continue to work to make it more responsive to issues important for women, families, and communities. While the number of women in government at the national and local level is small, it has increased over the last decade. In the national Diet the proportion of women in the House of Representatives is 4.6 percent (it has never returned to the high of 8.4 percent seen following the first election in which women voted in 1946). The upper House of Councillors has 13.5 percent women, close to the highest point of 15.1 percent in 1994.

Women have not fared well even in local government, but more are now attracted as they become concerned about clean water, education, environmental safety, and child care facilities. The proportion of females in local assemblies rose from 1 percent in 1976 to 4.3 percent in 1995. At the prefecture level, Mariko Bando was appointed a vice governor of Saitama. The proportion of women on national advisory councils and committees has risen from 2.4 percent in 1975 to 16.1 percent in 1996, in line with the goal of 15 percent set out in the National Plan of Action. An unfortunate anomaly was the published picture of the headquarters for the Promotion of Gender Equality in 1998 in which there were no women.

Prime Minister Hosokawa appointed three women to his cabinet in 1992, the largest number ever, and more than the United States cabinet at the same time. The news photo of Hosokawa's cabinet is interesting in that, as can be seen in the photo (Figure 12.4), all three women ministers are together on the margins of the group rather than in the middle.

For the first time the Ministry of Labor has promoted a woman from within the organization to the top post of career vice minister. Each ministry has a role to play in supporting the success of women. The Ministry of Education in its curricula and teachers' attitudes toward gender roles; the Ministry of Labor in the collection of data disaggregated by gender, and in writing and enforcement of laws for working women and men; the Ministry of Finance in taxation and budget allocations to give equitable treatment to women working at home and office; the Construction Ministry in encourag-

Figure 12.4. Prime Minister Morihiro Hosokawa and his cabinet in an official portrait on the grounds of the Prime Minister's residence. *Asahi Shimbun,* August 9, 1993.

ing building that takes into account the needs of child care, family, and community; and the Ministry of Foreign Affairs by encouraging women to speak up and carry policy-making roles so that international issues affecting women and families are not forgotten.

Work and Family

Family has always been a central focus of Japanese life. The celebrated strength of group identification begins with the family. At holiday seasons, New Year's, and Golden Week, the highways are jammed with Tokyoites journeying to their ancestral homes. The homing instinct remains intact even for the ultrasophisticated city dwellers. While Japanese family focus is still strong, the traditional extended family is no longer the prevailing model.

> As more women have to work, Japan needs to contemplate preserving the structure of its families. Japan is now debating whether traditional family functions should be kept inside the family or should be socialized in the new age. Throughout history these have been age-old questions. More family or more society? More family or more individualism? Japan is searching for the answers.
>
> Taichi Sakaiya, author, *The Knowledge-Value Revolution,*
> at symposium "Family in Transition Toward the 21st Century,"
> Osaka, Japan, November 16, 1991

The basic functions of reproduction, production, and community are constants for society. To accomplish the economic production tasks, organizations, corporations, and businesses build upon the foundation of the reproductive and community systems for which women carry the major responsibility in Japanese postindustrial society. The basic functions of reproduction and community are often taken for granted, assumed to be personal or private responsibilities done by women. However, work, family, and community are interdependent systems that have essential tasks unique to the total mission. Each requires resources and people transformed into desired outcomes. People are forced to link the two worlds in their own individual lives. As the complexities of modern life place more stresses on each, their interactions need to be balanced.

Paid employment is organized on the unrealistic premise that the normal wage worker is not responsible for other social functions. Postindustrial market economies generally define the gender contract, the roles assigned to each gender, around the labor market structure, and yet all must be combined in individual lives. Events in either work or family make the interplay obvious and point up the attendant stress and conflict. Each day women confront the contradictions between production and reproduction, between work and family. Wartime mobilization was an extreme instance of the work system stressing the family system, as male family members were taken into the military and women were drafted for production tasks. Currently there are less extreme examples, such as the birth of a new baby, or a nanny's illness, or care of elder parents, which occur daily and bring stress. Extended business travel or additional work requirements accentuate interactions that are ongoing and continuous.

Visions of a society with equal and joint participation must embody an awareness that "men have families too." Men, as well as women, are making trade-offs, consciously or unconsciously, between the work and family systems. Does the family want more of a father's time and relationships if it means less success at work? Companies need to ask, "What is a reasonable level of performance, allowing time and energy for family?" The espoused values and actions of family members need to be examined to see where, why, and for whom each is investing time.

So long as gender roles that assign women to serving, sacrificing positions are seen as "natural," change will be difficult. Powerful early immersion makes it difficult to think of one's identity outside the defining gender envelope. Some analysts have said that a critical mass of women, which they define as 20 percent, is needed to make change. Women feel overwhelmed by the enormity of the task of trying to change stifling customs and attitudes embedded in the power structure. They are socialized to endure and persevere, so elbowing their way in to make change seems unnatural. Attitudinal and structural changes are tedious, requiring hard work and time, but change is possible.

Norway provides a striking example when a seven-year-old boy asks if a man can be prime minister, since in his lifetime the prime minister has always been a woman. A single event such as a Japanese woman astronaut in space, Ambassador Ogata's appearance on television and newspapers lauding her accomplishments, a visit to a woman doctor who listens carefully to women's opinions can illuminate women's strengths. The cumulative nature of such events has a ripple effect that expands visions for both women and men.

Organizations need to recognize that it is difficult to be a minority of one or two. Making one's voice heard and making a difference is a heavy load. One manager was the first woman to be invited to attend a workshop to think about the ten-year future of the company. The participants were told to nominate junior employees to contribute ideas about the future of the company. She suggested three women. Fortunately, one woman was invited, making two women of a total of twenty-five participants. The assumption was that they had one young and one older woman to represent women. One or even two women cannot represent womankind, but it's a beginning. This woman's response to the incident was typically resigned and philosophical: "Well that's progress. Next time maybe there will be more." Designating one woman as representative of the entire class of women helps keep women in line.

Paths to Power

> The biggest hurdle that women have yet to overcome is the acceptance of power. . . . Women must increase their self-confidence to embrace power and see it for what it can be—ultimately liberating, not an overdose of testosterone.[15]

Japanese women do not envy men, nor do they want to be like them. Linked to this is a reluctance to wield power directly, which may be one of the biggest hurdles facing women. A fascinating discussion grew out of questioning several successful woman managers about the word "power." Wanting to include the Japanese word as a section heading, I tried two commonly used words, *chikara* and *jitsuryoku*. Neither was appropriate. The women felt both words implied putting someone else down. The word used for political power was completely unacceptable because it implies coercion. After several discussions and a restless night for one, the foreign, *katakana* word, *pawaa*, was deemed acceptable. As a non-Japanese word, it escaped the traditional connotations of coercion, power over, or domination that the Japanese words held for them. It is very important to Japanese women that they not fall into the male model of domination, so they carefully choose their own methods and words.

Those women who are more activist fear that this approach will not prevail against the aggressiveness of male power. Whether an evolution toward women's visions continues or regresses is a crucial issue for Japanese women and Japanese society. No other government has mobilized its populace so successfully behind strategic policies as Japan, from household savings, to mobilization of industry and exports, to private responsibility for the welfare of the elderly. A crucial question for women and Japanese society is whether this vaunted collaboration between government and industry can be used to actualize the official visions of equity and partnership contained in the National Plan for the Year 2000.

If Japan is successful, the United States and other countries may be able to learn from it how to facilitate that collaboration, since most of the critical problems of the day require public and private collaboration with government leadership. Since neither Japan nor the United States has all the answers, it is important to learn from each other's triumphs and mistakes to realize a vision of equity and partnership.

Perhaps we can find antecedents of present visions of partnership and peace in the dim recesses of our remotest past. Archaeologist Marija Gimbuta's research unearthed evidence of nonpatriarchal, peaceful, and more equitable civilizations that flourished between 7000 B.C. and 3000 B.C. that might inspire women and men today:

> Archeologists and historians have assumed that civilization implies hierarchical political and religious organizations, warfare, a class stratification and a complex division of labor, typical of androcratic or male-dominated societies.
>
> This does not apply to the gynocentric, women-centered, cultures that flourished in Old Europe between the seventh and the third millennium B.C., The primordial deity was female, reflecting the sovereignty of motherhood. . . . In spite of the revered status of women in religious life, the evidence does not suggest a subservience of one sex to the other, but instead suggests a condition of mutual respect.
>
> These civilizations enjoyed a long period of uninterrupted peaceful living which produced artistic expressions of graceful beauty and refinement, demonstrating a higher quality of life than many androcratic, hierarchical societies.[16]

The image of a non-patriarchal civilization that enjoyed a long history of peace, artistic expression, and quality of life is consistent with the vision of Japanese pioneer feminists with which this book began. Raicho Hiratsuka's poem exhorts Japanese women to let their energy, their own sun, their authentic vital power shine so that they can "build shiny golden cathedrals at the top of crystal mountains."[17] Surely Japan needs this vision as it confronts ongoing national and regional crises.

Epilogue

A Future for Japanese Women Managers?

Evolution or Retreat

In a global economy, political and economic turmoil in Japan is significant for the region and the world, and crucial for Japanese women managers. My fears that the Asian financial crisis would reverse the gains that Japanese women managers have made in the last decade have been only partially realized. One might expect an economic downturn to be very bad for women, given a personnel practice of "last in, first out." In fact, the signals of the economic crisis' impact on Japanese women managers are a mixed portfolio of positives and negatives. In an article in *Sankei Shimbun*,[1] I asked what the future holds for Japanese women managers. What will happen now that there is no longer a bubble economy? Will the strides that women have made be negated or reversed?

The large and vibrant response to the article was unexpected. Japanese women were eager to talk about what they saw for the future, and they gave both optimistic and pessimistic answers. The energy in the groups of women was exciting and their achievements impressive. Among managers interviewed earlier, four had achieved their objective of writing and publishing a book: one an autobiography;[2] another a book about turning fifty and enjoying it;[3] a third, a book on women entrepreneurs with useful statistics and resources;[4] and another a book with practical advice for working women.[5]

One woman had retired at the age of sixty and was teaching marketing classes at two different colleges. She coordinated leadership courses for younger women, using her own leadership support group as a resource, and was excited about the future. The manager who had doubted she would find a Japanese husband to share her life had married and just had her first child. Another had left the corporation where she had gained valuable experience but realized she could go no higher; after leaving, she started her own consulting business. Those with established companies were doing well, prospering and growing. A newspaper media executive had extended her responsibilities to produce a television program for small children to learn English, partially satisfying her yearning to use her creative talents more fully.

Stimulated by the Beijing International Women's Conference the enthusiasm for getting together with other women to exchange information, learn from and support each other continues. Activism and a multiplicity of women's organizations characterized these women's activities as they looked toward the end of the twentieth century.

On the other hand, a group of younger career women said 1994 had been a watershed year, an "Ice Age," for women, with only slight improvement since. They said there was an abundance of talk about equity, but they often despaired about lack of positive action. Several said they were deeply tired and found the struggle to make it against such odds exhausting. In the reunion of a focus group, a sophisticated manager said her husband and teenage stepson would be waiting for her to cook dinner, and she wondered resignedly how long they would wait before deciding to feed themselves.

The optimists and pessimists still seemed to be divided by age. Older women managers tended toward optimism. They had generally achieved success, but they remembered the cycles of attitudes toward women and recalled other more difficult times. Thus they could see progress for women. The younger women were struggling and did not have that historic view. Several wondered if they should pursue opportunities outside Japan.

There have been many changes on micro and macro levels, including everyday things like expansions of *bento* departments in local markets where people crowd around to buy ready-to-eat food to take home. While Japanese friends said, "That's for working women," there were many male buyers— maybe the working men who hadn't learned to cook. Solitary males with strollers or carrying children are much more in evidence in markets, on the streets, and in the subways.

There had been significant events at the macro level as well. The passage of stronger equal opportunity legislation in 1997 was a major accomplishment. Keidanren, the prestigious economic federation, issued a report on a study to utilize and advance women more effectively, with recommendations for future programs for its members. This constituted an important statement of greater awareness and priority in the corporate world. Harumi Sakamoto, a female director of Seiyu, brilliantly chaired the subcommittee on Woman's Advancement in Society that authored the report and received a standing ovation from the members when she presented it. Ironically, Keidanren itself has yet to place women in top management or committee chairs.

Attitudes are changing. A survey of gender preferences for children found that 75% of those polled preferred to have a girl if they could have only one child. The reasons for such a change are complex, but some suggest it is linked to a better chance of being taken care of in old age by a daughter. Perhaps resistance to a female heir to the crown needs to be reexamined.

Demographics are also changing. A Japanese woman colleague who had expressed pessimism about the future of women in leadership in Japan brightened after hearing that the absence of older brothers was a consistent success factor for women managers. "Given the high proportion of single-child families," she said, "maybe there's hope for Japan after all, since 40% of Japanese households have only female children now."[6] Certainly the desire for daughters and the absence of brothers in 40% of the families will affect the socialization and self-esteem of girls.

The success of the Japanese economic system continues to be dependent on the labor of women in the family and paid workforce. In the workforce they still serve as a buffer against economic fluctuations and as less expensive, expendable labor to supplement those with lifetime employment and seniority. Cracks appeared in this nicely organized economic system when women's aspirations began to interfere with their defined roles. The falling birthrate (down to 1.39), the growing number of women choosing to remain single, the long-term recession, the increasing dissatisfaction with the political system, and corruption in government and industry all point to the need for reexamination of the basic premises on which the industrial structure is built.

Despite enormous obstacles, Japanese women have become successful managers in business, government, and education. They are the best educated women in the world, while they remain the most flagrantly wasted national resource, accounting for less than 10% of managers while providing over 40% of the workforce. Some are breaking their traditional silence to insist their talents be used more effectively. A growing number say they are tired of being exploited as temporary, and therefore less expensive, labor. They are no longer willing to be cast out at "a certain age" for a new, younger crop of women college graduates. Other women are simply tired from the combination of balancing care of small children, demanding careers, and husbands who have difficulty sharing the work.

The fabled foundations of Japanese management—lifetime employment, the seniority system, and the bureaucratic, tightly knit nature of industrial policy—that have served as barriers to women's entry into management are slowly eroding. Institutionalized discrimination against women, while not necessarily written policy, is still widespread and accepted. Help-wanted ads specify age, with companies still setting specific limits on the percent of women college graduates who may be hired in April. Other practices, such as restricting women to staff positions, not including women in informal meetings or off-site training sessions, and limiting transfer and travel, all serve to restrict advancement. Attitudes that assign women decorative and service roles are still the foundations of unwritten but powerful institutional practices.

The buzzwords for the current political climate are reform and creativity. While there is cynicism within Japan and in other parts of the world about the willingness to make real reforms, the need for creativity and new policies and practices is clear and obvious. Creativity requires viewing problems in new ways and using untried, sometimes risky, ideas and processes. Creativity requires new voices that previously have not been heard. Women can provide some of those creative voices by virtue of having been outside the system and having a different perspective.

The call for Japan to become a "normal" nation has been associated with security treaties and its own military defense. But normal for Japan in Ozawa's words "begins with the autonomy of the individual and needs an accountable government as a member of the international community."[7] Becoming a member of the international community requires a reexamination of exclusive and isolationist management practices dominated by "old boy" networks. To support an international vision and a "normal nation," women often have language abilities and relationship skills ideally suited for international operations. The majority of Japanese officials in the United Nations are women, including Ambassador Ogata, who is universally admired. Women bring needed and unique talents for both creativity and internationalization to the table.

Japanese women have the ability, the education, and the desire to lead and contribute to reform. One clue can be found in their large attendance at forums on leadership and empowerment, a phrase they have adopted and adapted. They want their voices to be heard, but many do not want to lead the same old organizations. They want to create organizations and institutions that will contribute to a better quality of life for themselves, their families, their communities, and the nation.

The declining birth rate and aging population present important social challenges. Some analysts maintain that the declining birth rate is a function of a housing shortage, which could be remedied fairly easily. A different message from women is that they are no longer willing to shoulder total responsibility for family, children, and elder care. Young men are also expressing a desire for a life outside of careers.

The exodus of young Japanese women from Japanese corporations to start their own businesses or to go to foreign companies and international organizations also gives an inkling of changing attitudes. Senior male executives tend to interpret their departure as a sign that women don't really want to work. An alternative explanation expressed by many women is that there are too few advancement possibilities for them in Japanese corporations.

On the other hand, major corporations found themselves with a glut of women in their forties: top college graduates hired in their twenties for secretarial positions and expected to retire by age thirty or thirty-five. Many of these women continued to work after thirty and after marriage, limited to clerical work even as their salaries rose with seniority. Relieving the company of these "excess" women who are now over forty is an onerous task that is often delegated to expatriate male managers who are called home for this mission.

Will the desire for reform and the wish to become a "normal nation" be strong enough to encourage the use of women's creativity? Japan's recent history has been one of providing narrow openings for revolutionary ideas and then to regroup, close, and return to traditional power bases and old ways. Waves of reform have been most successful when powerful external forces supported internal movements for change. Western technology and mercantilism were adopted after the forced opening of Japan's borders in the Meiji era. The vote, equal education for women, and changes in inheritance laws were imposed by Japan's wartime defeat. The equal opportunity law was spurred by a desire to become a permanent member of the United Nations and sign the UN Convention on the Elimination of All Forms of Discrimination Against Women, which required such a law.

Attitudes of male dominance embedded in institutions and organizations must be acknowledged and dealt with for real change to occur. As McCorduck and Ramsey said in *The Futures of Women: Scenarios for the 21st Century,* "Future scenarios need to acknowledge and deal with unfinished emotional business."[8] Whether embedded attitudes can be acknowledged and institutional culture can change sufficiently to utilize the creativity of diverse voices is an important question for Japan today. Traditionally, Japan has retreated to old ways in times of crisis, pulling back from real structural change.

Will the momentum of women who have experienced the possibility of influencing their own lives be strong enough to withstand the pressures to retreat?

> I certainly hope management—or at least most of them—will choose evolution rather than retreat. If, for some reason, it chooses to retreat, I think there will be a revolution. But then again, that might be fun too.
>
> Japanese female senior executive

Revolution is not the traditional choice for Japanese women, but younger women's rebellion expressed in dress and behavior now extends beyond adolescence for many. Many see their choices as complying, leaving, quiet anger, and repressed hostility, or fighting the system, with the last the most unlikely. Japanese management is undergoing what seems like a sea change to many older Japanese, with lifetime employment, seniority, and male prerogatives being threatened. The official unemployment rate is at an unprecedented high of 4% with estimates of hidden unemployment ranging as high as 11%. Advertisements for a clerical job often bring hundreds of applicants, including college graduates. The choices the nation will make between evolution or retreat are not clear. A complete evolution is a long-term process that requires changes in societal attitudes; government's role; corporate culture and management with collaboration among corporations, employers, government, education, women, and men. Those with greater power have greater opportunities and responsibility for change.

Resistance to change is normal, and the Japanese, with a surplus of wealth, have been able to resist change more adamantly than most. The election for a new upper house of parliament in July 1998 provided hints of people's willingness to risk change and move away from the rigidities governing their lives as an unexpectedly large number of voters turned against the ruling liberal democratic party. The stunning defeat led to the resignation of a prime minister and an opportunity for change as the troubled economy becomes more visible. Indeed some changes have been made and others are possible at short notice without major upheaval.

More transparent recruitment, promotion, and job allocation processes would open organizations to women. Women themselves can expand and use existing networks, such as consumer action groups, Leadership 111 (an exciting networking group of women leaders in different fields), Young Entrepreneurs Organization (YEO), Young Presidents Organization (YPO), and other professional associations to make contacts, obtain credit, increase technical skills, market themselves, and influence policies. Educators can implement already recommended changes for remedying gender-biased education, and government can reexamine tax, employment, and procurement policies and enforce existing rules prohibiting discrimination on the basis of gender, while awaiting implementation of the new laws.

"We must reject the myth of time. We must come to see that human progress never rolls in on wheels of inevitability."

Martin Luther King, letter from Birmingham Jail

The framework exists for a positive future for both women managers and for Japan. Whether it will be achieved depends on national will and the untiring efforts of women and men. This book has highlighted the experiences of Japanese women managers, but it is about both women and men as they face the questions, struggles, challenges, excitement, and opportunities of change and transition—abrupt transitions as a result of catastrophic events as well as evolution through slow erosions of the status quo. A recognition of the rewards of increased productivity for corporations, and of increased freedom for men in sharing income production and household management, will accelerate the evolution.

A company president commented on marketing in the twenty-first century, "Companies cannot rely on the same old armies of blue-suited, fortyish, workaholic men to reach women customers."[9] Perhaps more important, companies cannot rely on the same old corporate culture and practices to attract and retain the next generation of managers essential for innovation and survival. The government also cannot rely on the same old people and practices to prepare for the twenty-first century. The best and brightest young people are demanding a forward evolution. I am hopeful that the positive forces that have been unleashed, and a more widely shared vision of a better quality of life for both women and men, will keep Japan from retreat. My experience with Japanese women managers makes me believe that evolution toward increased use of their talents will produce a more energetic, rewarding future for Japan.

Glossary

amae.	Desire for dependency; usually mother and child, fusion of identity
amakudari.	Literally, descent from heaven, transfer of government bureaucrats to corporations as management or adviser
bentō.	Box lunch, ready to eat food
buchō.	General manager, head of department
dajö-tennö.	Regent or ruler for minor
en daka.	High yen exchange rate
en yasu.	Low yen exchange rate
fujin.	Lady, woman (considered old-fashioned)
fushō fuzui.	Husband suggests, wife follows, different characters, but sounds the same as wife suggests husband follows
gaiatsu.	External, foreign pressure to do something
honne.	Natural, real, or inner wishes and feelings as opposed to *tatemae* (the persona or appropriate roles)
ie.	Household, family system, patriarchal social organization of the family
ippan shoku.	General or clerical track
jichō.	Deputy director
jinji-bu.	Human resources department

jōmu-torishimari.	Managing director
josei.	Woman
joshidai sei.	Female college students, used in a somewhat derogatory manner in the media to imply interest in fashion and enjoying themselves, killing time until they get married
jūyaku.	Company director
kachō.	Manager
kagemusha.	Puppet general on stage being manipulated
kaisha.	Company
kakarichō.	Section chief
Kanji.	Japanese writing system adopted from the Chinese
karōshi.	Death from overwork
Katakana.	Form of script used for foreign words
Keidanren.	Abbreviation of *Keizai Dantai Rengo-kai*, Federation of Economic Organizations
keiei-sha.	Manager, executive
Keizai Doyukai.	Association of Corporate Executives
kokusai.	International
komon.	Adviser
kuroku.	Black-robed puppeteer
kuromaki.	Power behind the screen
kyaria ūman.	Career women
kyōiku mama.	Education mama
manga.	Comic book, cartoon
meishi.	Business card
Mombushō.	Ministry of Education
nemawashi.	Groundwork necessary to build suport for a course of action or secure informal consensus before a formal decision is made. Literally means "to dig around the root of a tree to prepare it for transplanting"
nenkō-joretsu.	Seniority system
Nikkeiren (Nihon Keiei-sha Dantai Renmei).	Japan Federation of Employers' Associations, composed of regional employer and trade associations, concerned with labor relations
ningyō.	Puppet
ningyō tsukai mawashi.	Puppet master

Nissho (Nihon Shōkō Kaigisho).	Japan Chamber of Commerce and Industry
nyūsha shiki.	Hiring ceremony held each April
okusan.	Wife; literally in the depths, commonly assumed to be in the depths of the house
onna kotoba.	Women's language
onna no jidai.	Era of women
onna rashii.	Feminine speech style
onnagata.	Men who play women
ōrudo misu.	Old maid from English "old miss"
otoko masari.	Superior-to-man, has a lot of vigor, for some implies a lack of femininity, for feminists, a positive meaning
pāto.	Part-time work or worker
ringi.	Process
ringisho.	Documents circulated among relevant managers of all levels for approval and stamping with individual seals, after *nemawashi*
rōjo.	Old woman
ryōfu kenfu.	Good husband, wise father
ryōsai kenbo.	Good wife, wise mother; the appropriate role for women
sankin kotai.	Compulsory alternate-year attendance of feudal lords at the capitol Edo to pay tribute, traveling the old Tokaido road, portrayed in *ukioye* prints
sarariman.	Salaryman, Corporate salaried worker, male
satoba.	Community of wives of monks in a religious order who perform household duties for the monks
sengyō shufu.	Profession of full-time wife
shachō.	President
shaka.	Company song
shakun.	Corporate articles specifying desired mental and spiritual attitudes, recited daily in the morning assembly in some companies
shanai gyomu.	Company rituals
shasho.	Employee badge
shigo rikkon.	Divorce after death
shikata ga nai or *sho ga nai.*	There's nothing to be done about it. Nothing we can do about it. It cannot be helped
shimbun.	Newspaper

shinnenkai.	New Year's party
shokuba no hana.	Office flowers
shufu.	Housewife
shujin.	Husband, derived from feudal term for master in relation to servant. Feminists prefer *paatonaa* from the English partner, or *tsureai,* a mate
shushin-koyō.	Lifetime employment system, literally lifetime devotion
sogo shoku.	Career track for women, as opposed to *ippan shoku* (clerical track)
tanshin funin.	Transfer of employee without spouse, usually wife and children
tatemae.	Persona, appearance, what should be, the person presented publicly
tennö.	Empress, ruler, heavenly king
üman ribu.	Women's lib, a derogatory term generally referring to the strident American version. "Feminist" is a frightening term for Japanese, male and female. It implies changing gender roles, and therefore must be ridiculed by men and avoided by women
ure nokori.	Unsold merchandise, women unmarried past the "marriageble age"
yoko narabi shugi.	To look to the side, to see how well one is doing.
yōshi.	Adopted by the wife's family and takes family name; sometimes *muko yōshi* (adopted groom)
zaibatsu.	Tightly knit interlocking companies

Notes

Introduction

1. UNDP, *Human Development Report 1995,* United Nations Development Programme, Oxford University Press, 1995.

2. Chalmers Johnson, "Japanese-Style Management Revisited," JPRI Working Paper No. 4, Japan Policy Research Institute, Cardiff, CA, November 1994; Chalmers Johnson, "Japanese Capitalism: The Intellectual and Ideological Controversy," speech, Japan Policy Research Conference, JPRI, and Ahlers Center for International Business, University of San Diego, September 15, 1995.

3. *Mainichi Shimbun,* June 4, 1994, reporting Economic Planning Agency head Yoshio Terasawa's statement to the cabinet.

4. UNDP, *Human Development Report 1993,* United Nations Development Programme, Oxford University Press, New York, 1993.

5. Frederick W. Taylor, "Principles of Scientific Management," first published in *American Magazine,* March, April, May 1911. Reissued: Hive Publishing, Easton, PA, 1985.

6. Frank B. Gilbreth, *Primer of Scientific Management,* Van Nostrand, New York, 1914. Reissued: Hive Publishing, Easton, PA, 1985.

7. Lillian M. Gilbreth, *The Psychology of Management.* Reissued: Hive Publishing, Easton, PA, 1973.

8. Peter F. Drucker, *Managing for the Future,* Butterworth Heinemann, Oxford, 1992; Peter F. Drucker, *The Practice of Management,* Harper and Row, New York, 1954.

9. Thomas Peters and Robert Waterman, Jr., *In Search of Excellence: Lessons from America's Best-Run Companies,* Harper and Row, New York, 1982.

10. Peter Senge, *The Fifth Discipline: The Art and Practice of the Learning Organization,* Doubleday Currency, New York, 1990.

11. Michael E. Porter, *Competitive Advantage: Creating and Sustaining Superior Performance,* Free Press, New York, 1985.

12. Lester Thurow, *Head to Head: The Coming Economic Battle Among Japan, Europe and America,* William Morrow, New York, 1992.

13. Kenichi Ohmae, *The Borderless World: Power and Strategy in the Interlinked Economy,* Harper Business, McKinsey and Co., New York, 1990.

14. A limited sample includes Daniel Katz and Robert L. Kahn, *The Social Psychology of Organizations,* Wiley, New York, 1978; Arthur A. Thompson and A. J. Strickland, *Strategic Management Concepts and Cases,* Business Publications, Plano, TX, 1987; James Gleick, *Chaos: Making a New Science,* Penguin Books, New York, 1988; Margaret J. Wheatley, *Leadership and the New Science: Learning About Organization from an Orderly Universe,* Berrett-Koehler, San Francisco, 1994; Alvin Toffler, *Future Shock,* Bantam Books, New York, 1970; Alvin Toffler, *The Third Wave,* William Morrow, New York, 1980; Alvin Toffler, *Creating a New Civilization: The Politics of the Third Wave,* Turner Publishing, Atlanta, GA, 1995; John Naisbitt and Patricia Aburdene, *Megatrends 2000,* William Morrow, New York, 1990.

15. Jean R. Renshaw, "Exploring Pacific Stereotypes: Women in Management in the Pacific Islands," in *Women in Management Worldwide,* ed. Nancy Adler and Dafna Israeli, M. E. Sharpe, pp. 122–140, New York, 1988.

16. Nancy Adler and Dafna N. Israeli, eds., *Competitive Frontiers: Women Managers in a Global Economy,* Blackwell, Oxford, 1994; Judy B. Rosener, *America's Competitive Secret: Women Managers,* Oxford Universtiy Press, Oxford, 1995.

17. Sumiko Iwao, *The Japanese Woman: Traditional Image and Changing Reality,* Free Press, New York, 1993.

18. This poem is often quoted as a women's manifesto. SEITO was founded by Raicho Hiratsuka and its journal published in Tokyo from 1911 to 1916.

Chapter 1

1. "No. 13 Strikes Lucky: The Singular and Satirical Vision of Filmmaker Juzo Itami," *Business Tokyo,* November 1990, 14.

2. Sumiko Iwao, *The Japanese Woman: Traditional Image and Changing Reality,* Free Press, New York, 1993.

3. George Hicks, *The Comfort Women: Japan's Brutal Regime of Enforced Prostitution in the Second World War,* Norton, New York, 1994.

4. International Labor Office, *Yearbook of Labour Statistics,* Geneva, 1995.

5. The number and percentage of women managers varies slightly among sources. The Japanese statistics used in this book are an amalgam of those obtained from the Ministry of Labor, the Bureau of Labor Statistics, the Prime Minister's Office, and the ILO. The ILO data are publicly available comparative data, but where more current in-

formation from ministries was available and at variance, it was used. United States data from the Department of Labor, the Bureau of Labor Statistics, and the ILO.

6. "Why Women Still Don't Hit the Top," *Fortune,* July 30, 1990, 40–62.

7. Catalyst, *Census of Woman Corporate Officers and Top Earners,* A Series on Women in Corporate Leadership, Catalyst, New York, 1996.

8. Dr. Takeo Sumioka, translation from *Bungei Shunju,* September 20, 1993, the Asia Foundation.

9. Personal communication, Leslie R. Patterson, President and Chief Executive Officer, Pfizer Pharmaceuticals Inc., February 1998.

10. Editor, *Japan Weekly Mail,* Yokohama, Japan, January 15, 1910, 75.

11. Women in the Workplace," p. 21, *Women's History,* Cowles Publishing Co. Spring–Summer 1996.

12. *Japan's Working Women Today,* Japan Institue of Women's Employment, Tokyo, 1995.

13. Susan Berfield, "Staying Single: Why So Many Women Won't Settle for Marriage," *ASIAWEEK,* June 21, 1997, 30–37.

14. *United Nations Demographic Yearbook,* New York, 1994.

15. Mary C. Brinton, *Women and the Economic Miracle: Gender and Work in Postwar Japan,* University of California Press, Berkeley, 1993.

16. *The World's Women, 1970–1990 Trends and Statistics,* United Nations, New York, 1991.

17. Asia Foundation translation, Tokyo, 1994.

18. JIJI Press Newswire, March 15, 1997, *Japan: Annual Value of Unpaid Work,* Economic Planning Agency report, Tokyo, 1997.

19. JETRO and Ministry of Labor statistics.

20. Prime Minister's Office, Public Opinion Survey on Women's Lives and Work, June 1992. Employed men spend eight minutes a day in housework, and employed women spend three hours.

Chapter 2

1. A more detailed description of the research model and criteria for sample are found in chapter 5.

2. Ichiko Ishihara, editor and translator, *Think Like a Man, Work Like Dog and Act Like a Lady, Otoko No Yoni Kangae Redi No Yoni Furumai Inu No Gotoku Hatarake,* Sankei Shuppan, 1980.

3. Yuriko Saisho, *Women Executives in Japan: How I Succeeded in Business in a Male-Dominated Society,* Yuri International Incorporated, Tokyo, 1981.

4. James Valentine, "On the Borderlines: The Significance of Marginality in Japanese Society," in *Unwrapping Japan,* ed. E. Ben-Ari, B. Moeran, and J. Valentine, Manchester University Press, Manchester, England, 1990.

5. Takeo Doi, MD, *The Anatomy of Dependence,* Kodansha International, Tokyo, 1971.

6. Frank Sulloway, *Born to Rebel,* Pantheon Books, New York, 1996.

7. Haru Matsukata Reischauer, *Samurai and Silk: A Japanese and American Heritage,* Harvard University Press, Cambridge, MA, 1986.

Chapter 3

1. Emiko Ohnuki-Tierney, *Rice as Self,* Princeton University Press, Princeton, NJ, 1993.

2. Ibid.

3. Mayumi Oda, *Goddesses,* Lancaster-Miller, Berkeley, CA, 1981. Mayumi Oda's wonderful goddess pictures were my introduction to the power and beauty of goddesses in Japan's history.

4. Motoori Norinaga, "The True Tradition of the Sun Goddess," from Motoori Norinaga Zenshu VI 3–6 and V 459–62," in *Sources of Japanese Tradition, Volume II,* Ryasku Tsunoda, Wm. Theodore de Bary, Donald Keene, eds. Columbia University Press, New York, 1958.

5. St. Thomas Aquinas, *Summa Theologica, Question XCII, Article i Reply Obj. i,* Catholic Encyclopaedia XV, Rome, 1890.

6. A. Hyman Charlap, *Sidur Tifereth Jehudah,* Hebrew Publishing Co., New York, 1912, p. 14.

7. Marija Gimbutas, *The Civilization of the Goddess: The World of Old Europe,* HarperCollins, New York, 1991.

8. Matrifocal is used to connote a society in which women are honored leaders and have high positions, not reversing the patriarchal hierarchy, but completely different with more equality of the sexes. See Marija Gimbutas's work on goddess civilizations. Ibid.

9. "As witch-hunting developed into a craze some thousands of women were murdered. No serious estimate is possible; guesses have ranged as high as several hundred thousand—even to nine million." Irene M. Franck and David M. Brownstone, *Women's World: A Timeline of Women in History,* HarperCollins, New York, 1995, pp. 32–33.

10. Nagoyo Homma, "What Does It Mean to Understand America?—A Japanese View" *IHJ Bulletin,* 14, no. 2 (May 1994) p. 2.

11. Gerda Lerner, *The Creation of Patriarchy,* Oxford University Press, New York, 1986.

12. Leonard Shlain, *The Alphabet vs. the Goddess: The Conflict Between Word and Image,* Viking Penguin, New York, 1998.

13. Teiji Itoh and Gregory Clark, *The Dawns of Tradition,* Nissan Motor Co., Tokyo, 1983.

14. Shikibu Murasaki, *The Tale of Genji,* trans. E. Seidensticker, Vintage Books, New York, 1985.

15. E.g., Edwin O. Reischauer, *The Japanese,* Harvard University Press, Cambridge, MA, 1980.

16. Kathleen S. Uno, "Women and Changes in the Household Division of Labor," in *Recreating Japanese Women, 1600–1945,* ed. Gail Lee Bernstein, University of California Press, Berkeley, 1991.

17. E.g., James Fallows, *Looking at the Sun: The Rise of the New East Asian Economic and Political System,* Pantheon Books, New York, 1994.

18. Yoshiko Furuki, *The White Plum: A Biography of Ume Tsuda, Pioneer in the Higher Education of Japanese Women,* Weatherhill, New York, 1991.

19. Akiko Kuno, *Unexpected Destinations: The Poignant Story of Japan's First Vassar Graduate, Oyama,* Kodansha International, Tokyo, 1993.

Chapter 4

1. Lotfi Zadeh, "The Nature of Fuzzy Sets," University of California, Berkeley, paper, 1974; Lotfi Zadeh, Kiga Langari, and John Yen, eds., *Industrial Applications of Fuzzy Logic and Intelligent Systems,* IEEE Press, New York, 1995.

2. Chalmers Johnson, "Wake Up America! Wake Up America! Advice from Dr. Chalmers Johnson," *Critical Intelligence* 2, no. 8, Boardroom Inc., New York, August 1994, pp. 3–13.

3. Shinya Arai, *Shoshaman: A Tale of Corporate Japan,* translated by Chieko Mulhern, University of California Press, Berkeley, 1991.

4. Zoher Abdoolcarim, "How Women Are Winning at Work: Asia's Business Culture as Corporate Women See It," *Asian Business,* November 1993, 24–29.

5. Towers Perrin, "Study of Compensation and Management of Fortune 1000 Companies," New York, 1993.

6. The term originates from gardening, referring to the Japanese method of transplanting trees in which after the tree is dug up from its original location, the roots are bound and the tree is left in place for a week before it is moved to its new location. This metaphor describes the process of getting preliminary consensus in organizations before the actual decision is made.

7. "Roundtable, When Will the Individual Come First? Three Executives Discuss How Organizational Behavior Can Be Changed," *Japan Update,* Keizai Koho Center, Tokyo, February 1992.

8. Thomas P. Rohlen, "The Education of a Japanese Banker," in *Inside the Japanese System, Readings on Contemporary Society and Political Economy,* ed. Daniel I. Okimoto and Thomas P. Rohlen, Stanford University Press, Menlo Park, CA, 1988, 129–139.

9. A haiku is a Japanese verse form becoming popular in the United States as well, which is usually rendered in English as three unrhymed lines of five, seven, and five syllables whose subject is most often nature.

10. Ichiro Ozawa, *Blueprint for a New Japan,* Kodansha, Tokyo, 1994.

Chapter 5

1. *Japan's Working Women Today,* Japan Institute of Workers' Evolution, Tokyo, 1995.

2. Jean R. Renshaw, "Women in Management in the Pacific Islands: Exploring Pacific Stereotypes," in *Women in Management Worldwide,* ed. Nancy Adler and Dafna N. Israeli, M. E. Sharpe, Armonk, New York, 1988, pp. 122–140.

3. Henry Mintzberg, *The Nature of Managerial Work,* Harper and Row, New York, 1971.

4. A vast literature exists that purports to define each in precise terms, (e.g., Block, Schein, Tichy, Hennig, Mintzberg), but theories and definitions shift as the environment of business changes. Generally "management" has referred to operational management, while "leadership" has referred to the broader terms of vision, motivation, and image creation, but all managers must have leadership skills, and all leaders must have management skills.

5. *Keidanren Review,* no. 150, Tokyo, August 1995, p. 1.

6. Baroness Shidzue Ishimoto, *Facing Two Ways: The Story of My Life,* translated and introduction by Barbara Molony, Stanford University Press, Stanford, CA, 1935, 1963.

Chapter 6

1. "From the Japanese Princess: A Hint the Crown Feels Heavy," *New York Times,* December 10, 1996, A-4.

2. Shinya Arai, "Tale of a Shoshaman," *Japan Update,* April 1992.

3. Matthew Masayuki Hamabata, *Crested Kimono: Power and Love in the Japanese Business Family,* Cornell University Press, Ithaca, NY, 1990.

4. Takie Sugiyama Lebra, *Above the Clouds: Status Culture of the Modern Japanese Nobility,* University of California Press, Berkeley, 1993.

5. John J. Gumperz, ed., *Language and Social Identity,* Cambridge University Press, New York, 1982.

6. Richard M. Restak, M.D., *The Mind,* Bantam Books, New York, 1988; Floyd E. Bloom, Arlyne Lazurus, and Laura Hofstader, *Brain, Mind and Behavior,* Freeman, New York, 1985; Calvin Williams *How Brains Think: Evolving Intelligence Then and Now,* Basic Books, New York, 1996.

7. E. Ben-Ari, B. Moeran, and J. Valentine, eds., *Unwrapping Japan,* University of Hawaii Press, Honolulu, 1990, 44.

8. Ibid.

9. Sally Helgesen, *The Female Advantage: Women's Ways of Leadership,* Doubleday, Currency, New York, 1995; Judy B. Rosener, *America's Competitive Secret: Utilizing Women as a Management Strategy,* Oxford University Press, New York, 1995.

10. Jon Entine and Martha Nichols, "Good Leadership: What's Its Gender?" *Executive Female,* January/February 1997, 50–51.

Chapter 7

1. "Labour Force Survey," Management and Coordination Agency, Tokyo, 1996.

2. U.S. Department of Labor, *A Report on the Glass Ceiling Initiative,* Washington, DC, 1991.

3. Joyce D. Miller, *Report of the US Department of Labor's Glass Ceiling Commission,* Washington, DC, 1995.

4. Reported in Associated Press article, *San Diego Union,* October 18, 1996.

5. "Survey on Women Workers' Employment Management," Ministry of Labor, Tokyo, 1992.

6. Office of Policy Planning and Research, Ministry of Labor, Tokyo, 1994.

7. *Living Japanese Style,* Japan Travel Bureau Inc., Tokyo, 1991.

8. Catalog, "Japanese Traditional Art," Freer Gallery, Washington, DC, 1996.

9. National Theatre of Japan, 1988 Calendar, with permission of the producer, Toshio Abe, National Theatre, Tokyo, February 1998.

10. Rosabeth Moss Kantor, *Men and Women of the Corporation,* Basic Books, New York, 1979.

11. E.g., John Gray, *Men Are from Mars, Women Are from Venus, A Practical Guide for Improving Communication and Getting What You Want in Your Relationships,* Harper-Collins, New York, 1992; Deborah Tannen, *You Just Don't Understand: Women and Men in Conversation,* Ballantine Books, New York, 1990; and Deborah Tannen, *Talking from 9 to 5: Woman and Men in the Workplace: Language, Sex and Power,* Avon Books, New York, 1994.

12. Daniel Maltz and Ruth A. Borker, "A Cultural Approach to Male-Female Miscommunication," in *Language and Social Identity,* ed. John J. Gumperz, Cambridge University Press, New York, 1982, 196–216.

13. *Doing Business in Japan, an ABC,* JETRO, Japan External Trade Relations Office, Tokyo, 1991.

14. E.g., Takie Sugiyama Lebra, *Japanese Patterns of Behavior,* University of Hawaii Press, Honolulu, 1986.

15. Masao Miyamoto, MD. *Straitjacket Society: An Insider's Irreverent View of Bureaucratic Japan,* Kodansha International, Tokyo, 1994.

16. Norma Field, *In the Realm of a Dying Emperor: A Portrait of Japan at Century's End,* Pantheon Books, New York, 1991.

17. Christopher Wood, *The End of Japan Inc. and How the New Japan Will Look,* Simon and Schuster, New York, 1994.

18. Theodore C. Bestor, "Conflict, Legitimacy and Tradition in a Tokyo Neighborhood," *Japanese Social Organization,* ed. T. S. Lebra, University of Hawaii Press, Honolulu, 1992, 23.

19. Peter Conn, *Pearl S. Buck: A Cultural Biography,* Cambridge University Press, Cambridge, 1996.

20. Susan Faludi, *Backlash: The Undeclared War Against American Women,* Crown Publishers, New York, 1991.

21. Michael Crichton, *Disclosure,* A. Knopf, New York, 1993.

22. Helen Thomas, UPI senior White House correspondent, quoted in *Modern Maturity,* October–November 1996.

Chapter 8

1. Major sources of data on Japanese women-owned businesses are Teikoku DataBank Ltd., Tokyo, Japan, 1994; "Fact-finding Survey on Women Entrepreneurs," Nikkei Research Institute of Industry and Markets and *Nikkei Woman* magazine, Tokyo, 1992; Fact-finding Survey on Women Executives," Isaka Prefectural Institute

for Advanced Industry Development, Osaka, Japan, 1992; and "1994 Fact-finding Survey on New Business Start-ups," People's Finance Coroporation Research Institute, Tokyo, 1994.

2. Major sources of data on United States women-owned businesses are National Foundation of Women Business Owners, "Women-Owned Businesses in the United States: 1996, A Fact Sheet," NFWBO Washington, DC, 1997; U.S. Department of Labor, Bureau of Labor Statistics, Employment and Earnings, Washington, DC, 1996; "The Top 50 Women Business Owners," *Working Woman Magazine,* May 1994, May 1995, October 1997.

3. Teikoku DataBank Ltd., Tokyo, 1994.

4. The discrepancy may lie in the different criteria and measures used by the international group and the Japanese group.

5. Teikoku Ltd., Tokyo, 1994.

6. *Nikkei Woman,* 1995.

7. "All in the Family: Nepotism in the Japanese Company," *Tokyo Business Today,* November 1992, pp. 26–31.

8. Mariko Tamura, *Women Entrepreneurs,* Nikkei Business Publishing, Tokyo, 1997.

9. A mandala is a circle design symbolizing the universe, totality, and wholeness. The images in the mandala vary for Hinduism, Buddhism, Tibeten Buddhism, and American Indian rituals. The symbolism is also used for meditation, concentration, and healing in the West.

10. National Foundation for Women Business Owners, *Women-Owned Businesses,* Washington, DC, 1996, with sources from Internal Revenue Service, House Committee on Small Business and Small Business Administration data.

11. "Fact-finding Survey on Women Entrepreneurs," Nikkei Research Institute of Industry and Markets and *Nikkei Woman,* September–October, Tokyo, 1992.

Chapter 9

1. *The Life of a Japanese Painting,* Freer Gallery, Washington, DC, 1996.

2. Nikkei Business Journal, *Nikkei Woman,* annual ranking of best companies for women, November 1994.

3. Reported in the *San Diego Union,* June 24, 1996, by Heather Haveman, associate professor of organizational behavior, Cornell University.

4. "The TBT 300," *Tokyo Business Today,* July 1994.

5. Likert found that forced-choice psychological tests were more effective with five choices, allowing people middle and end choices. Thus the 5-point scale is referred to as a Likert Scale.

6. Chapter 4, "Organization Culture," defines levels of management.

7. David Stipp, "Biological Warfare: How the U.S. Triumphed and Japan Beat Itself," *Fortune,* April 1, 1996, 40.

8. Takeru Ishikawa, Chair, Keidanren Committee on Economic Research, *Keidanren Review,* August 1992.

9. Rieko Tanaka, "Woman Exec Chides Industry over Condescending Attitudes," *Japan Times,* November 4, 1992, 3.

10. Roundtable, "When Will the Individual Come First? Three Executives Discuss How Organizational Behavior Can Be Changed," *Japan Update,* February 1992.

Chapter 10

1. Congressman Cellar of Virginia, 1963.

2. Gunnar Myrdal, *The American Dilemma,* McGraw-Hill, New York, 1962.

3. Alice Lam, *Woman and Equal Employment Opportunities in Japan,* Nissan Occasional papers, Nissan Institute of Japanese Studies, Oxford, November 1990.

4. Adapted from Nancy J. Adler, and Dafna N. Israeli, "Assumptions About Women's Role in Management," in *Women in Management World Wide,* ed. Nancy J. Adler and Dafna N. Israeli, M. E. Sharpe, Armonk, NY, 1988.

5. Women manager, sogo-shoku, 25, corporate finance, Mitsubishi Corporation, quoted in Murakami, Asako, "Women's work limits studied," *Japan Times,* September 26, 1991.

6. Glen Fukushima, former U.S. trade representative, AT&T vice president *Business Tokyo,* Tokyo, 1994.

7. UNDP, *Human Development Report 1995,* Oxford University Press, New York, 1995.

8. Shidzue Kato, 100, feminist and birth control advocate, *Economist,* June 1, 1996.

Chapter 11

1. Prime Minister Lee Kuan Yew, speech to graduating class, Singapore National University, reported in *Asia Business,* 1994.

2. Takie Sugiyama Lebra, *Above The Clouds: Status Culture of the Modern Japanese Nobility,* University of California Press, Berkeley, 1993.

3. Anne Allison, *Nightwork: Sexuality, Pleasure and Corporate Masculinity,* University of Chicago Press, Chicago, 1994.

4. Yasuo Kurita, "A Sip of Success," *Asahi Evening News, Asahi Shimbun,* August 13, 1996.

5. Ministry of Education, Science and Culture, *Education in Japan: A Graphic Presentation 1994,* Research and Statistics Planning Division, Ministry of Education, Science and Culture, Gyosei Corporation Printers, Tokyo, 1994.

6. Personal communication, Ministry of Education, 1997.

7. Interview by Dr. Jackie Young on the Japanese naval training ship, Honolulu, 1996.

8. Prime Minister's Office, "Public Opinion Survey on Gender Equality 1995," Tokyo, 1996.

9. Carol E. Franz and David C. McClelland, "Lives of Woman and Men Active in the Social Protests of the 1960s: A Longitudinal Study," *Journal of Personality and Social Psychology,* 66, no. 1 (1994): 196–205.

10. Nicholas D. Kristol, "A Plain School Uniform as the Latest Aphrodisiac" *New York Times,* April 2, 1997.

11. Masao Miyamoto, M.D. *Straitjacket Society: An Insider's Irreverent View of Bureaucratic Japan,* Kodansha International, Tokyo, 1994.

12. "The Citadel Battles for Way of Life," *New York Times,* May 22, 1996.

13. William D. Montalban, "No Longer a Step Behind in Turkey" *LA Times,* November 13, 1993.

14. Prime Minister's Office, *New National Plan of Action Towards the Year 2000, The Creation of a Society of Joint Participation by Both Men and Women,* Headquarters for the Planning and Promoting of Policies Relating to Women, Prime Minister's Office, Tokyo, May 1987, 1992, 1995.

Chapter 12

1. Chizuko Uero in Sandra Buckley *Broken Silence: Voices of Japanese Feminism,* University of California Press, Berkeley, 1997, 293–301.

2. Council for Gender Equality, *Vision of Gender Equality—Creating New Values for the 21st Century,* Tokyo, 1996.

3. *United Nations Human Development Report 1993,* UNDP, Oxford University Press, New York, 1993.

4. Katherine Graham, "Women Journalists Provide New Perspectives on What's News," *Harvard Gazette,* June 17, 1994.

5. Judy B. Rosener, *America's Competitive Secret: Utilizing Women as a Management Strategy,* Oxford University Press, New York, 1995; Sally Helgesen, *The Female Advantage: Women's Ways of Leadership,* Doubleday Currency, New York, 1995.

6. Jon Entine and Martha Nichols, "Good Leadership: What's Its Gender?" *Executive Female,* January/February 1997, 50–51.

7. Rosener, *America's Competitive Secret;* Helgesen, *The Female Advantage.*

8. Takeru Ishikawa, Chair, Keidanren Economic Research Committee, *Keidanren Review,* August 1992.

9. Economic Planning Agency, *White Paper on the Life of the Nation Summary,* Tokyo, February 1994.

10. James Flanigan, "GM and IBM Face That Vision Thing," *Los Angeles Times,* October 25, 1992.

11. Quoted in Patrick Smith, "The Crown Prince's New Wife," *Emerging Markets IMF/World Bank Daily,* September 28 1993, 61.

12. Naoko Takeuchi, cartoonist, *Sailor Moon, Nakayoshi; manga* (comic book), television, CDs, with many accessories and a market of at least $500 million. In the story series, a fourteen-year-old high school girl becomes Sailor Moon when needed, and she rights the wrongs of the world. She is clearly in charge, although she calls in girlfriends or boyfriends when needed.

13. Shinichi Katsukata, "New Struggles Await Woman on Career Path," *Yomiuri Shimbun,* May 7, 1993.

14. Takashi Oka, "Japan's Culture-by-Consensus: Strength or Weakness?" *The Christian Science Monitor,* May 27, 1994.

15. *Working Woman,* Anita Roddick speaks out, President Body Shop International, June 1996.

16. Marija Gimbutas, *The Civilization of the Goddess: The World of Old Europe,* HarperCollins, San Francisco, 1991, preface; Marija Gimbutas, *The Language of the Goddess,* Harper and Row, San Francisco, 1989.

17. Raicho Hiratsuka's poem is often quoted as a women's manifesto. It was the introduction to the journal SEITO (*Blue Stockings*), published in Tokyo from 1911 to 1916.

Epilogue

1. Jean Renshaw, "A Future for Japanese Women Managers?" *Sankei Shimbun,* Seiron column, Tokyo, March 15, 16, 1996.

2. Ryoko Akamatsu, *Autobiography,* Tokyo, 1997.

3. Ryoko Dozono, *Köenki Kashira, Is this Menopause? Body Mind Living at The Turning Point,* Shufo Notomo, Tokyo, 1996.

4. Mariko Tamura, *Jösei Kigyökatachi, Women Entrepreneurs: New Power to Transform Business Society,* Nihon Keizai, Tokyo, 1996.

5. Kiyomi Saito. *Mohito Ganbari, Working Women: One More Effort,* NTT, Tokyo, 1995.

6. Health and Welfare Ministry, *White Paper on the Life of the Nation,* Tokyo, 1997.

7. Ichiro Ozawa, *Blueprint for a New Japan,* Kodansha Publishing Inc., Tokyo, 1994.

8. Pamela McCorduck and Nancy Ramsey, *The Futures of Women: Scenarios for the 21st Century,* Addison-Wesley, Menlo Park, CA, 1996, pp. xi, 15.

9. Zoher Abdoolcarim, quoting Harumi Sakamoto, "How women are winning at work, Asia's business culture as corporate women see it," *Asian Business,* November 1993.

References

Abegglen, James C. *Sea Change: Pacific Asia as the New World Industrial Center.* Free Press, New York, 1994.

Adams, Jane. *Women on Top: Success Patterns and Personal Growth.* Hawthorn Books, New York, 1979.

Adler, Nancy J., and Dafna N. Israeli, eds. *Competitive Frontiers: Women Managers in a Global Economy.* Blackwell Publishers, Oxford, 1994.

———. *Women in Management Worldwide.* M. E. Sharpe, Armonk, NY, 1988.

Akamatsu, Ryoko. *Japanese Women.* Japan Institute of Women's Employment, Tokyo, 1990.

Allgin, E. R., ed. *Changing Boundaries: Gender Roles and Sexual Behavior.* Mayfield Publishing, Palo Alto, CA, 1982.

Allison, Anne. *Nightwork: Sexuality, Pleasure and Corporate Masculinity.* University of Chicago Press, Chicago, 1994.

Aoki, Masahiko, and Ronald Dore. *The Japanese Firm: Sources of Competitive Strength.* Oxford University Press, Oxford, 1994.

Astin, Helen S., and Carole Leland. *Women of Influence, Women of Vision: A Cross-Generational Study of Leaders and Social Change.* Jossey Bass, San Francisco, 1991.

Bando, Mariko Sugahara. *Japanese Women Yesterday and Today.* Foreign Press Center, Toyko, Japan, 1996.

Bartu, Friedemann. *The Ugly Japanese: Nippon's Economic Empire in Asia.* Yenbooks, Tokyo, 1993.

Beard, Mary R. *The Force of Women in Japanese History.* Public Affairs Press, Washington, DC, 1953.

Beck, John C., and Martha N. Beck. *The Change of a Lifetime: Employment Patterns Among Japan's Managerial Elite.* University of Hawaii Press, Honolulu, 1994.

Ben-Ari, Eyal, Brian Moeran, and James Valentine, eds. *Unwrapping Japan: Society and Culture in Anthropological Perspective.* University of Hawaii Press, Honolulu, 1990.

Bennis, Warren. *An Invented Life: Reflections on Leadership and Change.* Addison-Wesley, Reading, MA, 1993.

———. *On Becoming a Leader.* Addison Wesley, Reading, MA, 1989.

Bernstein, Gail Lee, ed. *Recreating Japanese Women, 1600–1945.* University of California Press, Berkeley, 1991.

Block, Peter. *The Empowered Manager: Positive Political Skills at Work.* Jossey Bass, San Francisco, 1987.

Bloom, Floyd E., Arlyne Lazurus, and Laura Hofstader. *Brain Mind and Behavior.* Freeman, New York, 1985.

Bornoff, Nicholas. *Pink Samurai: An Erotic Exploration of Japanese Society.* Grafton Hammersmith, London, 1992.

Brinton Mary C. *Women and the Economic Miracle: Gender and Work in Postwar Japan.* University of California Press, Berkeley, 1993.

Buckley, Sandra. *Broken Silence: Voices of Japanese Feminism.* University of California Press, Berkeley, 1997.

Burstein, Daniel. *Turning the Tables: A Machiavellian Strategy for Dealing with Japan.* Simon and Schuster, New York, 1993.

Cannings, Kathleen, and William Lazonick. "Equal Employment Opportunity and the Managerial Women in Japan." *Industrial Relations* 33, 1 January 1994.

Cantor, Dorothy W., and Toni Bernay. *Women in Power: The Secrets of Leadership.* Houghton Mifflin, Boston, 1992.

Catalyst. *Census of Women Corporate Officers and Top Earners.* Part of a series on women in corporate leadership, Catalyst, New York, 1996.

———. *Women Board Directors of the Fortune 500.* 1996 Catalyst Census. New York, 1996.

———. *Women in Corporate Leadership: Progress and Prospects.* New York, 1996.

Condon, Jane. *A Half Step Behind: Japanese Women of the '80s.* Dodd, Mead, 1985; Tokyo, Tuttle, 1991.

Condon, John, and Mitsuko Saito, eds. *Intercultural Encounters with Japan: Communication-Contact and Conflict.* Simul Press, Tokyo, 1974.

Conn, Peter. *Pearl S. Buck: A Cultural Biography.* Cambridge University Press, Cambridge, 1996.

Cooper, Gary M. *Would You Care to Comment on That, Sir? A Look at 50 of Japan's Top Businessmen.* The Japan Economic Journal *Nihon Keizai Shimbun,* Toyko, 1976.

Costello, Cynthia, and Anne J. Stone for The Women's Research and Education Institute. *The American Woman, 1994–95: Where We Stand.* Norton, New York, 1994.

———. *The American Woman 1999–2000: A Century of Change—What's Next?* Norton, New York, 1998.

DECISIONLINE/Technology, *USA TODAY* Database, Special Gender Package, July 13, 1990.

DENTSU Inc., *Japan Marketing and Advertising Yearbook 1996,* Dentsu Inc., Tokyo, 1995.

Dobbs-Higginson, M. S. *Asia Pacific: A View on Its Role in the New World Order/ Disorder.* Longman Group, Hong Kong, 1993.

Doi, Takeo, MD. *The Anatomy of Dependence.* Kodansha International, Tokyo, 1971.

Doktor, Robert H. "Asian and American CEOs: A Comparative Study." *Organizational Dynamics* (Winter 1990): 46-56.

Dozono, Ryoko. *Kōnenki Kashira, Is this Menopause? Body Mind Living at The Turning Point.* Shufo Notomo, Tokyo, 1996.

Drucker, Peter F. *Managing for the Future.* Butterworth Heinemann, Oxford, 1992.

———. *The Practice of Management.* Harper and Row, New York, 1954.

English Discussion Society. *Japanese Women Now.* Women's Bookstore Shoukadoh, Kyoto, 1992.

Entine, Jon, and Martha Nichols. "Good Leadership: What's Its Gender?" *Executive Female,* January/February 1997, 50–51.

Fallows, James. *Looking at the Sun: The Rise of the New East Asian Economic and Political System.* Pantheon Books, New York, 1994.

Faludi, Susan. *Backlash: The Undeclared War Against American Women.* Crown Publishers, New York, 1991.

Farley, Jennie, ed. *Women Workers in Fifteen Countries: Essays in Honor of Alice Hanson Cook.* ILR Press, Cornell University, Ithaca, NY, 1985.

Felsenthal, Carol. *Power, Privilege and* The Post: *The Katharine Graham Story.* Putnam, New York, 1993.

Field, Norma. *In the Realm of a Dying Emperor: A Portrait of Japan at Century's End.* Pantheon Books, New York, 1991.

Fierman, Jaclyn. "Why Women Still Don't Hit the Top." *Fortune,* July 30, 1990, 40-62.

Franck, Irene M., and David M. Brownstone, *Women's World: A Timeline of Women in History,* HarperCollins, New York, 1995.

French, Marilyn. *Beyond Power: On Women, Men and Morals.* Summit Books, New York, 1985.

Fujimura-Fanselow, Kumiko, and Atsuko Kameda, eds. *Japanese Women: New Feminist Perspectives on the Past, Present, and Future.* Feminist Press, New York, 1995.

Fukuzawa, Yukichi on Education. Edited and translated by Eiichi Kiyoka. University of Tokyo Press, Tokyo, 1988.

Furuki, Yoshiko. *The White Plum: A Biography of Ume Tsuda, Pioneer in the Higher Education of Japanese Women.* Weatherhill, New York, 1991.

Geertz, Clifford. *Local Knowledge: Further Essays in Interpretive Anthropology.* Basic Books, New York, 1983.

Gilbreth, Frank B. *Primer of Scientific Management.* Van Nostrand, New York, 1914; Hive Publishing, Easton, PA, 1985.

Gilbreth, Lillian M. *The Psychology of Management.* Reprinted, Hive Publishing, Easton, PA, 1973.

Gilson, Edith, with Susan Kane. *Unnecessary Choices: The Hidden Life of the Executive Woman*. William Morrow, New York, 1987.

Gimbutas, Marija. *The Civilization of the Goddess: The World of Old Europe*. Harper-Collins, San Francisco, 1991.

Glaser, B. G., and A. L. Strauss. *The Discovery of Grounded Theory: Strategies for Qualitative Research*. Aldine, Chicago, 1967.

Gleick, James. *Chaos: Making a New Science*. Penguin Books, New York, 1988.

Godfrey, Joline. *Our Wildest Dreams: Women Entrepreneurs Making Money, Having Fun and Doing Good, A Whole New Definition of Success and an Entirely New Paradigm of Working Life*. HarperCollins, New York, 1992.

Gumperz, John J., ed. *Language and Social Identity,* Cambridge University Press, New York, 1982.

Hakuhodo Institute of Life and Living. *Japanese Women in Turmoil: Changing Lifestyles in Japan*. English editor, Mariko Fujiwara. HILL, Tokyo, 1984.

Halcomb, Ruth. *Women Making It: Patterns and Profiles of Success*. Ballantine Books, New York, 1979.

Hall, Edward T., and Mildred Reed. *Hidden Differences: Doing Business with the Japanese*. Anchor Press/Doubleday, Garden City, NY, 1987.

Hamabata, Matthews Masayuki. *Crested Kimono: Power and Love in the Japanese Business Family*. Cornell University Press, Ithaca, NY, 1990.

Hamada, Tomoko. "Absent Fathers, Feminized Sons, Selfish Mothers and Disobedient Daughters: Revisiting the Japanese Ie Household." *Japan Policy Research Institute Working Paper No. 33*, Japan Policy Research Institute, Cardiff, CA, May 1997.

Handy, Charles. *The Age of Paradox*. Harvard Business School Press, Boston, 1994.

Harvey, Kim. *Six Korean Women*. Westview Press, 1978.

Hearn, Lefcadio. *Japan: An Attempt at Interpretation,* Grosset and Dunlap, 1904.

Heinemann, Sue. *Timelines of American Women's History*. Berkeley Publishing Group, New York, 1996.

Helgesen, Sally. *The Female Advantage: Women's Ways of Leadership.* Doubleday/Currency, New York, 1990.

Hemphill, Elizabeth Anne. *The Least of These: Miki Sawada and Her Children*. John Weatherhill, New York, 1980.

Hendry, Joy. *Becoming Japanese: The World of the Pre-school Child*. University of Hawaii Press, Honolulu, 1986.

Hennig, Margaret, and Anne Jardim. *The Managerial Woman*. Pocket Books, New York, 1976.

Hesselbein, Frances, Marshall Goldsmith, and Richard Beckhard, eds. *The Leader of the Future: New Visions, Strategies, and Practices for the Next Era*. Jossey Bass, San Francisco, 1996.

Higuchi, Keiko. *Bringing Up Girls—Start Aiming at Love and Independence (Status of Women in Japan)*. Shoukadoh Booksellers, Kyoto, 1985.

Hofstede, Geert. *Culture's Consequences: International Differences in Work-Related Values*. Sage, Beverly Hills, CA, 1980.

Hofstede, Geert, and Michael Harris Bond. "The Confucius Connection: From Cultural Roots to Economic Growth." *Organizational Dynamics* 16 (Spring 1988): 4–18.

Holstein, William J. *The Japanese Power Game.* Penguin Books, New York, 1991.

Homma, Nagayo. "What Does It Mean to Understand America?—A Japanese View." *IHJ Bulletin* 14, no. 2 (Spring 1994): 1–7.

Hunter, Janet. *Japanese Women Working.* Routledge, London, 1993.

IGSW. *Empowerment of Women: Constructing a Global Humane Society.* Proceedings of '94 Tokyo Symposium on Women, The International Group for the Study of Women, Tokyo, 1994.

————. *Working Women and Their Impact on Society, Tokyo Symposium on Women and Work.* International Group for the Study of Women, Tokyo, Asian and Pacific Development Center, Kuala Lumpur, Malaysia 1983.

Imamura, Anne E. *Urban Japanese Housewives at Home and in the Community.* University of Hawaii Press, Honolulu, 1987.

————, ed. *Re-Imaging Japanese Women.* University of California Press, Berkeley, 1996.

Inohara, Hideo. *Human Resource Development in Japanese Companies.* Asian Productivity Organization, Tokyo, 1990.

Ishimoto, Baroness Shidzue (Kato). *Facing Two Ways: The Story of My Life.* Holt, Rinehart and Winston, New York, 1935; Stanford University Press, Stanford, CA, 1984.

Ishinomori, Shotaro. *JAPAN INC.: Introduction to Japanese Economics (The Comic Book).* University of California Press, Berkeley, 1988.

Itzen, C., and J. Newman, eds. *Gender, Culture and Organizational Change: Putting Theory into Practice.* Routledge, New York, 1995.

Iwao, Sumiko. *The Japanese Woman: Traditional Image and Changing Reality*, Free Press, New York, 1993.

Jamieson, Kathleen Hall. *Beyond the Double Bind: Women and Leadership.*, Oxford University Press, New York, 1995.

Japan 1998: An International Comparison. Keizai Koho Center, Japan Institute for Social and Economic Affairs, Tokyo, 1998.

Japan: A Pocket Guide. Foreign Press Center, Tokyo, 1996.

Japan Almanac 1997. Asahi Shimbun Publishing, Tokyo, 1997.

Japan Almanac 1998. Asahi Shimbun Publishing, Tokyo, 1998.

Japan Almanac 1999. Ashai Shinbun Publishing, Tokyo, 1999.

Japan Institute of Women's Employment. *Japan's Working Women Today.* Tokyo, 1991, 1992, 1993, 1994, 1995.

The Japan Institute of Labor. *Japanese Working Life Profile 1996–97 Labor Statistics.* Japan Institute of Labor, Tokyo, 1997.

Jelinek, Mariann, and Claudia Bird Schoonhoven. *The Innovation Marathon: Lessons from High Technology Firms.* Basil Blackwell, Cambridge, MA, 1990.

Jennings, C. Cox, and C. L. Cooper. *Business Elites: The Psychology of Entrepreneurs and Intrapreneurs.* Routledge, New York, 1994.

JETRO Business Information Series. *Japanese Corporate Decision Making.* Japan External Trade Organization, Tokyo, 1992.

Johnson, Chalmers. *Japan: Who Governs: The Rise of the Developmental State.* Norton, New York, 1995.

———. *MITI and the Japanese Miracle: The Growth of Industrial Policy, 1925–1975.* Stanford University Press, Stanford, CA, 1982.

Johnston, William B. *Workforce 2000.* Hudson Institute, and the U.S. Department of Labor, Indianapolis, IN, June 1987.

Kageyama, Reiko, and Yoshiro Kawakami, eds. *Empowerment of Women: Constructing a Global Humane Society.* Proceedings of '94 Tokyo Symposium on Women, International Group for the Study of Women, Tokyo, December 1994.

Kanowitz, Leo. *Equal Rights: The Male Stake.* University of New Mexico Press, Albuquerque, 1981.

Kantor, Rosabeth M. *Men and Women of the Corporation.* Basic Books, New York, 1977.

Kaplan, Robert E. *Beyond Ambition: How Driven Managers Can Lead Better and Live Better.* Jossey Bass, San Francisco, 1991.

Katz, Daniel, and Robert L. Kahn. *The Social Psychology of Organizations.* Wiley, New York, 1978.

Kendall, Laurel. *Shamans, Housewives, and Other Restless Spirits: Women in Korean Ritual Life.* University of Hawaii Press, Honolulu, 1985.

Kennedy, Paul. *Preparing for the Twenty First Century.* Vintage Books, New York, 1993.

Kerber, Linda K. "Men and Women: Boredom, Violence and Political Power: Prospects for the Twenty-First Century." *IHJ Bulletin* 14, no. 1 (Winter 1994): 1–5.

Kondo, Dorinne K. *Crafting Selves, Power, Gender and Discourses of Identity in a Japanese Workplace.* University of Chicago Press, Chicago, 1990.

Koren, Leonard. *Success Stories: How Eleven of Japan's Most Interesting Businesses Came to Be.* Chronicle Books, San Francisco, 1990.

Kundsin, Ruth B. *Women and Success: The Anatomy of Achievement.* William Morrow, New York, 1974.

Kuno, Akiko. *Unexpected Destinations: The Poignant Story of Japan's First Vassar Graduate, Sutematsu Oyama.* Kodansha International, Tokyo, 1993.

Lam, Alice. *Women and Japanese Management: Discrimination and Reform.* Routledge, Chapman and Hall, New York, 1992.

Laurie, Dennis. *Yankee Samurai: American Managers Speak Out About What It's Like to Work for Japanese Companies in the U.S.* HarperCollins, New York, 1992.

Lebra, Takie Sugiyama. *Above the Clouds: Status Culture of the Modern Japanese Nobility.* University of California Press, Berkeley, 1993.

———. "Gender and Culture in the Japanese Political Economy: Self-Portrayals of Prominent Businesswomen." In Shumpei Kuon and Henry Rosovsky, eds., *The Political Economy of Japan.* Vol. 3, *Cultural and Social Dynamics,* 364–419. Stanford University Press, California, 1992.

———. *Japanese Patterns of Behavior.* University of Hawaii Press, Honolulu, 1986.

———. *Japanese Women: Constraint and Fulfillment.* University of Hawaii Press, Honolulu, 1985.

———, ed. *Japanese Social Organization.* University of Hawaii Press, Honolulu, 1992.

Lerner, Gerda. *The Creation of Patriarchy.* Oxford University Press, New York, 1986.

Lo, Jeannie. *Office Ladies, Factory Women: Life and Work at a Japanese Company.* M. E. Sharpe, Armonk, NY, 1990.

Marami, Hiroshi, and Harumi Befu, eds. *The Challenge of Japan's Internationalization: Organization and Culture.* Kodansha International, Tokyo, 1983.

Marshall, Judi. *Women Managers Moving On: Exploring Careers and Life Choices.* Routledge, New York, 1995.

Masuda Foundation Research Project Team for Japanese Systems. *Japanese Systems: An Alternative Civilization?* SEKOTAC Ltd., Yokohama, 1992.

Maynard, Herman Bryant, Jr., and Susan E. Mehrtens. *The Fourth Wave: Business in the 21st Century.* Barrett-Koehler, San Francisco, 1993.

McCorduck, Pamela, and Nancy Ramsey. *The Futures of Women: Scenarios for the 21st Century.* Addison-Wesley, Menlo Park, CA, 1996.

Ministry of International Trade and Industry. *MITI Handbook 1992.* Japan Trade and Industry Publicity, Tokyo, 1992.

Ministry of Labour. *Year Book of Labour Statistics 1995.* Policy Planning and Research Department, Minister's Secretariat, Ministry of Labor, Toyko, 1996.

Mintzberg, Henry. *The Nature of Managerial Work.* Harper and Row, New York, 1971.

Miyamoto, Masao. *Straitjacket Society: An Insider's Irreverent View of Bureaucratic Japan.* Kodansha International, Tokyo, 1994.

Morita, Akio. *Made in Japan: Akio Morita and Sony.* Dutton, New York, 1986.

Morrison, Ann M. *The New Leaders: Guidelines on Leadership Diversity in America.* Jossey-Bass, San Francisco, 1992.

Morrison, Ann M., Randall P. White, Ellen Van Velsor, and the Center for Creative Leadership. *Breaking the Glass Ceiling: Can Women Reach the Top of America's Largest Corporations?* Addison-Wesley, Menlo Park, CA, 1987.

Mulhern, Chieko I. *Heroic with Grace: Legendary Women of Japan.* M. E. Sharpe, London, 1991.

Mumford, Karen. *Women Working.* Allen and Unwin, Sidney, Australia, 1989.

Murakami, Yasushuke, and Yutaka Kosai, eds. *Japan in the Global Community: Its Role and Contribution on the Eve of the 21st Century.* Round Table discussions on Japan in the Global Community, University of Tokyo Press, Tokyo, 1986.

Myrdal, Gunnar. *The American Dilemma.* McGraw-Hill, New York, 1962.

Naff, Clayton, "Beyond Beijing: The Course of the Women's Struggle for Equal Opportunity in Japan," IC2 Institute-JIMT Series Working Paper, University of Texas at Austin, February 1997.

Nakane, Chie. *Japanese Society.* Charles E. Tuttle, Rutland, VT, 1970.

Nakano, Ann. *Japanese Women: A Century of Living History.* Rigby Publishers, Adelaide, Australia, 1986.

Nester, William R. *The Foundation of Japanese Power: Continuities, Changes, Challenges.* MacMillan, London, 1990.

Nevins, Thomas J. *Taking Charge in Japan.* The Japan Times, Tokyo, 1990.

Nippon 1997: Business Facts and Figures. Japan External Trade Organization (JETRO), Tokyo, 1997.

Norbeck, Edward, and Margaret Lock, eds. *Health, Illness, and Medical Care in Japan: Cultural and Social Dimensions.* University of Hawaii Press, Honolulu, 1987.

Norinaga, Motoori, "The True Tradition of the Sun Goddess" from Motoori Norinaga, *Zenshu VI* 3–6 and *V* 59–62, in *Sources of Japanese Tradition Volume II* compiled by Ryasku Tsunoda, Wm. Theodore de Bary, and Donald Keene, Columbia University Press, New York, 1958.

Ohmae, Kenichi. *The Borderless World: Power and Strategy in the Interlinked Economy.* Harper Business, McKinsey & Co., New York, 1990.

Ohnuki-Tierney, Emiko. *Rice as Self.* Princeton University Press, Princeton, NJ, 1993

Okimoto, Daniel I., and Thomas P. Rohlen, eds. *Inside the Japanese System: Readings on Contemporary Society and Political Economy.* Stanford University Press, Stanford, CA, 1988.

Ozawa, Ichiro. *Blueprint for a New Japan.* Kodansha, Tokyo, 1994.

Peters, Thomas, and Robert Waterman, Jr. *In Search of Excellence: Lessons from America's Best-Run Companies.* Harper and Row, New York, 1982.

Pfeffer, Jeffrey. *Managing with Power: Politics and Influence in Organizations.* Harvard Business School Press, Boston, MA, 1993.

Pharr, Susan J. *Losing Face: Status Politics in Japan.* University of California Press, Berkeley, 1990.

———. *Political Women in Japan: The Search for a Place in Political Life.* University of California Press, Berkeley, 1981.

Philip, Leila. *Hidden Dialogue: A Discussion Between Women in Japan and the United States,* Japan Society, New York, 1992.

Porter, Michael E. *Competitive Advantage: Creating and Sustaining Superior Performance.* Free Press, New York, 1985.

Powell, Gary N. *Women and Men in Management.* Sage, Newbury Park, CA, 1988.

Prime Minister's Office, The Present Status of Gender Equality and Measures, Report on the Plan for Gender Equality 2000 (First Revision). The Prime Minister's Office, Tokyo, June 1997.

Quah, Stella R., ed. *The Family as an Asset.* Times Academic Press, Singapore, 1990.

Quinn, J. R., H. Mintzberg, and R. James, eds. *The Strategy Process: Concepts, Contexts, and Cases.* Prentice Hall, Englewood Cliffs, NJ, 1988.

Rauch, Jonathan. *The Outnation: a Search for the Soul of Japan.* Harvard Business School Press, Boston, 1992.

Reischauer, Edwin O. *The Japanese,* Harvard University Press, Cambridge, MA, 1980.

Reischauer, Haru Matsukata. *Samurai and Silk: A Japanese and American Heritage.* Harvard University Press, Cambridge, MA, 1986.

Renshaw, Jean R. "Culture Savvy—the Essential Factor." *Multinational Business, The Economist Intelligence Unit,* Summer 1987, No. 2, pp. 33–36.

———. "Exploring Pacific Stereotypes: Women in Management in the Pacific Islands." In *Women in Management Worldwide,* edited by Nancy Adler and Dafna N. Israeli. M. E. Sharpe, Armonk, NY, 1988.

Reskin, Barbara F., and Heidi I. Hartmann, eds. *Women's Work, Men's Work: Sex Segregation on the Job.* Committee on Women's Employment and Related Social Issues, National Research Council, National Academy Press, Washington, DC, 1986.

Restak, Richard M. *The Mind*. Bantam Books, New York, 1988.

Ries, P., and A. Stone, eds. *The American Woman 1992–93: A Status Report*. Norton, New York, 1992

Robins-Mowry, Dorothy. *The Hidden Sun: Women of Modern Japan*. Westview Press, Boulder, CO, 1983.

Roddick Anita, *Body and Soul*. Ebury Press, London, 1991.

Roh, Mihye. "Women's Employment." *Women's Studies Forum,* pp. 47-96, Korean Women's Development Institute, Seoul, 1988.

Rosaldo, Michelle Zimbalist, and Louise Lamphere, eds. *Woman, Culture and Society*. Stanford University Press, Stanford, CA, 1974.

Rosaldo, Renato. *Culture and Truth: The Remaking of Social Analysis*. Beacon Press, Boston, 1990.

Rosener, Judy B. *America's Competitive Secret: Women Managers*. Oxford University Press, Oxford, 1995.

——. "Ways Women Lead." *Harvard Business Review* 68, no. 6 (November–December 1990): 119–125.

Saisho, Yuriko. *Women Executives in Japan: How I Succeeded in Business in a Male-Dominated Society*. Yuri International, Tokyo, 1981.

Saito, Kiyomi. *Mohito Ganbari, Working Women: One More Effort*. NTT, Tokyo, 1995.

Sakaiya, Taichi. *The Knowledge-Value Revolution, or a History of the Future*. Translated by George Fields and William Marsh. Kodansha International, Tokyo, 1991.

Saso, Mary. *Women in the Japanese Workplace*. Hilary Shipman, London, 1990.

Schumer, Fran. *Most Likely to Succeed: Six Women from Harvard and What Became of Them*. Random House, New York, 1986.

Scott, Anne Firor. *Making the Invisible Woman Visible*. University of Illinois Press, Urbana, 1984.

Senge, Peter. *The Fifth Discipline: The Art and Practice of the Learning Organization*. Doubleday Currency, New York, 1990.

Schwarz Vanderroth, Barbara, and Audry Armstrong Young, *The Work and Family Revolution,* Facts on File. Princeton University Press, New York.

Shimizu, Ikkö. *The Dark Side of Japanese Business: Three "Industry Novels."* Translated by Tamae K. Prindle. M. E. Sharpe, Armonk, NY, 1996.

Shinya, Arai. *Shoshaman: A Tale of Corporate Japan*. Translated by Chieko Mulhem. University of California Press, Berkeley, 1991

Shlain, Leonard. *The Alphabet vs. the Goddess: The Conflict Between Word and Image,* Viking Penguin, New York, 1998.

Sievers, Sharon L. *Flowers in Salt: The Beginnings of Feminist Consciousness in Modern Japan*. Stanford University Press, Stanford, CA, 1983

Silver, A. David. *Enterprising Women: Lessons from 100 of the Greatest Entrepreneurs of Our Day*, American Management Association, New York, 1994.

Smith, Bruce L. *The Advisers: Scientists in the Policy Process,* Brookings Institution, Washington, DC, 1992.

Still, Leonie, *Enterprising Women: Australian Women Managers and Entrepreneurs*. Allen and Unwin, 1993.

Sulloway, Frank. *Born to Rebel*. Pantheon Books, New York, 1996.

Swiss, Deborah J. *Women Breaking Through: Overcoming the Final 10 Obstacles at Work.* Peterson's/Pacesetter Books, Princeton, NJ, 1996

Takemi, Momoko, and Chika Fujiwara et al., eds. *Women and Work: Annotated Bibliography, 1970-1980.* International Group for the Study of Women, Tokyo, 1988.

Tamura, Mariko. *Jōsei Kigyōkatachi, Women Entrepreneurs: New Power to Transform Business Society.* Nihon Keizai, Tokyo, 1996.

Tannen, Deborah. *Talking from 9 to 5: Women and Men in the Workplace: Language, Sex, and Power.* Avon Books, New York, 1994.

———. *You Just Don't Understand: Women and Men in Conversation.* Ballantine Books, New York, 1990.

Tatsuno, Sheridan M. *Created in Japan: From Imitators to World-Class Innovators.* Ballinger, New York, 1990.

Taylor, Frederick W. "Principles of Scientific Management." First published in *American Magazine,* March, April, May 1911. Reprinted, Hive Publishing, Easton, PA, 1985.

Taylor, Jared. *Shadows of the Rising Sun: A Critical View of the "Japanese Miracle."* Charles E. Tuttle, Tokyo, 1983.

Terasaki, Etsuko. "Is the Courtesan of Eguchi a Buddhist Metaphorical Woman? A Feminist Reading of a No Play in the Japanese Medieval Theater." *Women's Studies* 21 pp. 431-456, Gordon and Breach, United Kingdom. 1992.

Thompson, Arthur A., and A. J. Strickland. *Strategic Management Concepts and Cases.* Business Publications, Plano, TX, 1987.

Thurow, Lester. *Head to Head: The Coming Economic Battle Among Japan, Europe and America.* William Morrow, New York, 1992.

Tichy, Noel, and Mary A. Devanna. *The Transformational Leader.* Wiley, New York, 1986.

Toffler, Alvin. *Creating a New Civilization: The Politics of the Third Wave.* Atlanta Turner Publishing, 1995.

———. *Future Shock.* Bantam Books, New York, 1970.

———. *The Third Wave.* William Morrow, New York, 1980.

Tokyo Metropolitan Government. *Stride by Stride, Women's Issues in Tokyo: The Current Situation.* Tokyo Metropolitan Government, Tokyo, 1983.

Ueda, Makoto, ed. *The Mother of Dreams and Other Short Stories: Portrayals of Women in Modern Japanese Fiction.* Kodansha International, Tokyo, 1989.

UNDP. *Human Development Report 1993.* United Nations Development Programme, Oxford University Press, New York, 1993.

———. *Human Development Report 1995.* United Nations Development Programme, Oxford University Press, Oxford, 1995.

U.S. Department of Labor, Department of Education, *Building a Quality Workforce.* Washington DC, July 1988.

van Wolferen, Karel. *The Enigma of Japanese Power: People and Politics in a Stateless Nation.* Random House, New York, 1990.

Ward, Kathryn, ed. *Women Workers and Global Restructuring.* ILR Press, Cornell University, Ithaca, NY, 1990.

Waring, Marilyn. *If Women Counted: A New Feminist Economics*. HarperCollins, New York, 1990.

Weinstein, Martin E. *The Human Face of Japan's Leadership: Twelve Portraits*. Praeger Publishers, New York, 1989.

Wheatley, Margaret J. *Leadership and the New Science: Learning About Organization from an Orderly Universe*. Berrett-Koehler, San Francisco, 1994.

White, Jane. *A Few Good Women: Breaking the Barriers to Top Management*. Prentice Hall, Englewood Cliffs, NJ, 1992.

White, Merry I. *Challenging Tradition: Women in Japan*. Japan Society, New York, 1991.

White, Merry I., and Susan Pollak, eds. *The Cultural Transition: Human Experience and Social Transformation in the Third World and Japan*. Routledge and Kegan Paul, London, 1986.

Williams, Calvin. *How Brains Think: Evolving Intelligence Then and Now*. Basic Books, New York, 1996.

Wood, Christopher. *The End of Japan Inc. and How the New Japan Will Look*. Simon and Schuster, New York, 1994.

World Bank. *Toward Gender Equality: The Role of Public Policy*. International Bank for Reconstruction and Development, Washington, DC, 1995.

The World's Women 1970–1990 Trends and Statistics. United Nations, New York, 1991.

Wright, Susan, ed. *The Anthropology of Organizations*., Routledge, New York, 1995.

Yamamoto, Takuma. *Fujitsu: What Mankind Can Dream, Technology Can Achieve*. Translated by Dick Belcher. Toyo Keizai, Tokyo, 1992.

Index